I0123485

Litigation as Lobbying

Litigation as Lobbying

*Reproductive Hazards and
Interest Aggregation*

Julianna S. Gonen

The Ohio State University Press
Columbus

Copyright © 2003 by The Ohio State University.
All rights reserved.

Library of Congress Cataloging-in-Publication Data

Gonen, Julianna S.
Litigation as lobbying : reproductive hazards and interest aggregation
/ Julianna S. Gonen.
p. ; cm.
Includes bibliographical references and index.
ISBN 0-8142-0942-4 (hardcover : alk. paper) — ISBN 0-8142-9018-3 (CD-ROM)
1. Political questions and judicial power—United States. 2. Pressure groups—
United States. 3. Human reproduction—Law and legislation—United States.
4. Women—Legal status, laws, etc.—United States.
I. Title.
KF8775.G66 2003
342.73'05—dc21
                                                    2003012481
Paper (ISBN: 978-0-8142-5722-7)

Cover design by Dan O'Dair
Type set in Adobe Minion

I dedicate my first book to my mother and role model,

Susan Jane Duvé, M.D.

Contents

List of Cases   ix

List of Acronyms   xi

List of Tables   xiii

Acknowledgments   xv

1. Interest Groups, Litigation, and Public Policy   1
2. Women in the Workforce and the Labor Movement   14
3. Challenging Fetal Protection Policies in Court   43
4. Friends of the Court and Friends of the Plaintiffs   73
5. Friends of the Status Quo   109
6. Litigating for Political Change   142

Appendix: Interviews   163

Notes   167

Bibliography   173

Index   183

List of Cases

Adkins v. Children's Hospital, 261 U.S. 525 (1923)
Baker v. Carr, 369 U.S. 186 (1962)
Board of Regents of the University of California v. Bakke, 438 U.S. 265 (1978)
Bray v. Alexandria Women's Health Clinic, 506 U.S. 263 (1993)
Brown v. Board of Education, 347 U.S. 483 (1954)
Califano v. Goldfarb, 430 U.S. 199 (1977)
California Federal Savings & Loan v. Guerra, 479 U.S. 272 (1987)
Craig v. Boren, 429 U.S. 190 (1976)
Dothard v. Rawlinson, 433 U.S. 321 (1977)
Geduldig v. Aiello, 417 U.S. 484 (1974)
General Electric Co. v. Gilbert, 429 U.S. 125 (1976)
Goesart v. Cleary, 335 U.S. 464 (1948)
Grant v. General Motors, 908 F2d 1303 (6th Cir. 1990)
Green v. Biddle, 21 U.S. (8 Wheat.) 1 (1823)
Griggs v. Duke Power, 401 U.S. 424 (1971)
Harris v. Forklift Systems, 510 U.S. 17 (1993)
Hayes v. Shelby Memorial Hospital, 726 F2d 1543 (1984)
In re A.C., 573 A.2d 1235 (D.C. 1990)
International Union, United Auto Workers v. Johnson Controls, 680 F. Supp. 309
    (E.D. Wis. 1988); 886 F2d 871 (7th Cir. 1989); 499 U.S. 187 (1991)
Johnson Controls v. California Fair Employment and Housing Commission, 267 Cal
    Rptr. 158 (1990)
Lochner v. New York, 198 U.S. 45 (1905)
Muller v. Oregon, 208 U.S. 412 (1908)
NAACP v. Button, 371 U.S. 415 (1963)
Newport News Shipbuilding & Dry Dock v. EEOC, 462 U.S. 669 (1983)
Ohio v. Akron Center for Reproductive Health, 497 U.S. 502 (1990)
Oil, Chemical, and Atomic Workers Union v. American Cyanamid, 741 F2d 444
    (D.C. Cir. 1984)

Phillips v. Martin Marietta, 400 U.S. 542 (1971)
Planned Parenthood v. Casey, 505 U.S. 833 (1992)
Price Waterhouse v. Hopkins, 490 U.S. 228 (1989)
Radice v. New York, 264 U.S. 292 (1924)
Reed v. Reed, 404 U.S. 71 (1971)
Roe v. Wade, 410 U.S. 113 (1973)
Rosenfeld v. Southern Pacific Co., 444 F2d 1219 (1971)
Rust v. Sullivan, 500 U.S. 173 (1991)
Silkwood v. Kerr McGee, 476 U.S. 1104 (1986)
United States v. Virginia, 518 U.S. 515 (1996)
United Steelworkers v. Marshall, 647 F2d 1189 (1980)
Wards Cove Packing Co. v. Atonio, 490 U.S. 642 (1989)
Webster v. Reproductive Health Services, 492 U.S. 490 (1989)
Weeks v. Southern Bell, 408 F2d 228 (5th Cir. 1969)
West Coast Hotel v. Parrish, 300 U.S. 379 (1937)
Wright v. Olin, 697 F2d 1172 (4th Cir. 1982)
Zuniga v. Kleberg County Hospital, 692 F2d 986 (1982)

List of Acronyms

AAUW	American Association of University Women
ACLU	American Civil Liberties Union
AFL-CIO	American Federation of Labor–Congress of Industrial Organizations
AFSCME	American Federation of State, County, and Municipal Employees
ANA	American Nurses Association
APHA	American Public Health Association
BFOQ	bona fide occupational qualification
CEDAPW	Coalition to End Discrimination Against Pregnant Workers
CLUW	Coalition of Labor Union Women
CRROW	Coalition for the Reproductive Rights of Workers
CWA	Communications Workers of America
	Concerned Women for America
EEAC	Equal Employment Advisory Council
EEOC	Equal Employment Opportunity Commission
ELC	Employment Law Center
ERA	Equal Rights Advocates
	Equal Rights Amendment
GE	General Electric
HIAA	Health Insurance Association of America
IHLP	Industrial Hygiene Law Project
ILGWU	International Ladies Garment Workers Union
IUE	International Union of Electrical, Radio, and Machine Workers
LDEF	Legal Defence Education Fund
LIA	Lead Industries Association
MALDEF	Mexican-American Legal Defense and Education Fund
NAM	National Association of Manufacturers
NAACP	National Association for the Advancement of Colored People
NARAL	National Abortion Rights Action League

NCLC	National Chamber Litigation Center
NELF	New England Legal Foundation
NIOSH	National Institute for Occupational Safety and Health
NOW	National Organization for Women
NRDC	Natural Resources Defense Council
NSWI	National Safe Workplace Institute
NWLC	National Women's Law Center
NWPC	National Women's Political Caucus
NWTUL	National Women's Trade Union League
OCAW	Oil, Chemical, and Atomic Workers Union
OSHA	Occupational Safety and Health Administration
OSHRC	Occupational Safety and Health Review Commission
PDA	Pregnancy Discrimination Act
PLF	Pacific Legal Foundation
TLPJ	Trial Lawyers for Public Justice
UAW	United Auto Workers
WEAL	Women's Equity Action League
WLDF	Women's Legal Defense Fund
WLF	Washington Legal Foundation

List of Tables

1.	UAW Counsel	50
2.	Summary of Amici for UAW	60
3.	Amicus Curiae Briefs in *UAW v. Johnson Controls*	65
4.	Amici Supporting the UAW	74
5.	Alignment of Amici Supporting Petitioner UAW	75
6.	Parties to Brief Supporting Certiorari Filed by ACLU	81
7.	Amici Supporting Johnson Controls	110
8.	Johnson Controls Amici with Prior Activity on Pregnancy Discrimination and/or Fetal Protection Policies	111

Acknowledgments

A book like this is the end product of a long and iterative process, which means that there are many people who helped along the way and deserve thanks.

This began as my doctoral dissertation, and many members of the faculty, as well as fellow graduate students, in the School of Public Affairs at American University made a contribution at one point or another. Tricia Patterson first suggested to me that a pending Supreme Court case on fetal protection policies might present an interesting public policy dilemma to study. My faculty advisor, Patricia Sykes, provided further encouragement, as did Neil Kerwin, Jerome Hanus, and David Rosenbloom. I am, of course, particularly indebted to the members of my dissertation committee: Gregg Ivers, Ron Shaiko, and Karen O'Connor. I could not have assembled a more ideal and complementary set of minds to advise a work on interest group litigation.

By the time the dissertation was completed, I was working full time at the Jacobs Institute of Women's Health in Washington, D.C., and its Executive Director, Martha Romans, provided the support and flexibility to allow me to bring the endeavor to fruition. As an adjunct faculty member at American University I had the opportunity to continue to develop some of the themes contained herein with the students in my Politics of Reproduction classes. While they are too numerous to name individually, I extend my thanks to them as well. The project evolved from a dissertation into a book manuscript during my tenure at the Washington Business Group on Health. Both Dr. Mary Jane England, immediate past president of WBGH, and Helen Darling, the current president, not only tolerated but supported my chronic distractions of teaching, writing, and attending law school. For this I am grateful.

Naturally before I had the privilege of meeting and working with these professional colleagues, I enjoyed the love, support, and encouragement of my family. My parents instilled in me from an early age the essential value of education and pushed me to go as far as I possibly could. My mother, Dr. Susan J. Duvé, remains my original and most enduring role model. Her self-motivation and determination carried her through medical school at a time when she had few women as classmates or mentors. Her premature passing was a loss that cannot be measured. My father, Dr. Jay Gonen, provided a further model of a working professional with intellectual and academic pursuits, and he continues to encourage me to this day. My brother, David, now also pursuing a law degree, has grown into a worthy intellectual sparring partner and a great friend, and I thank him for his support as well.

My deepest thanks of all go to Becky Bonzano, whose love and encouragement as a partner and best friend sustained me through the simultaneous pursuit of a law degree and this book. She shared in the sacrifice, tolerating late nights and weekends devoid of recreation, and I will be forever grateful.

1

Interest Groups, Litigation, and Public Policy

*T*he toxic substance is not identified but referred to only as "blue." We do not know what the behemoth factory produces, only that it is located in rural Texas and is the only nearby employer offering a decent wage. Laura Sangiacomo—of Hollywood hit movies *Sex, Lies, and Videotape* and *Pretty Woman*, as well as the sitcom *Just Shoot Me*—is a tough-talking ACLU attorney imported from New York to wage a quixotic battle against the company on behalf of a handful of working-class women who have been sterilized to comply with a company "fetal protection policy." Elizabeth Perkins and C. C. H. Pounder play victimized female factory workers. Charles Haid, the lovable Officer Renko from television's *Hill Street Blues* has been transformed into a sexist and surly foreman. This is the ABC Monday Night Movie of April 5, 1993, entitled "For Their Own Good," which has taken the unglamorous subject of corporate fetal protection policies and the litigation that they inspired and turned it into television drama.

Why would a handful of federal court cases that focused on an arguably narrow and fairly technical set of legal conflicts become the stuff of a made-for-TV movie? If one thinks of blood lead levels, OSHA rulemaking, and the pathology of teratogenesis, it seems a difficult leap. But what was really at issue was indeed much larger, much more fundamental. The real world legal battles over fetal protection policies were but the next stage in a long-standing conflict over women's roles in the paid work force and the way in which women's reproductive capacity has hindered opportunities beyond the domestic sphere. At issue were gender discrimination claims, the notion of fetal rights, the specter of employer liability for catastrophic fetal injury, and the lives and livelihoods of many very real people, some of whom sacrificed their reproductive abilities to retain desperately needed wages. So the conflicts were at once societal, pivotal, and also intensely personal.

The TV movie was based on the case of *Oil, Chemical, and Atomic Workers v. American Cyanamid,*[1] a precursor to the landmark case *UAW v. Johnson Controls,*[2] and it thus foregoes following the latter case all the way to the United States Supreme Court, where the real life plaintiffs would be the eventual victors. For it is not the legal maneuvering that truly matters for those most affected. Rather, the film ends with a dubious and hollow settlement, focusing instead on the irreversible nature of the sterilization undergone by several of the women. This again underscores why this topic and these cases would prove compelling, for they invoke fundamental issues of fairness, families, childbearing, and economic survival. This is precisely why fetal protection policies, litigated to the nation's highest tribunal in *Johnson Controls,* elicited the level of interest group pressure that was brought to bear on this case.

Organized groups are one of the primary means by which interests are expressed in American politics. While our electoral processes remain structured around political parties, interest groups have in many ways eclipsed some of the functions political parties once served. Groups educate the public on issues, provide a forum in which to associate with others sharing similar concerns, and pressure institutions of government to enact policy reflecting their interests. Groups are such an integral part of the political process that it seems they have always played this role, but it was really in the twentieth century that organized interests came to rival parties as a means of mobilizing individuals and articulating policy choices (Clemens 1997).

To fully understand policy formation, one must apprehend the role played by interest groups. And it is not only in the explicitly policy-making institutions that group activity must be understood. The judiciary in the United States now stands equal to the other branches as at least an expositor if not an actual formulator of policy and law, and groups operate regularly in the courts as well as the more traditional forums.

Scholars study and disagree over the extent to which courts can actually effect major policy or social change. Cases such as *Brown v. Board of Education*[3] or *Roe v. Wade,*[4] it must be acknowledged, are atypical. Nevertheless, courts operate regularly not only to settle discrete disputes but to clarify, affirm, or sometimes reject the law as set forth by legislatures or regulatory bodies. Courts continually shape law, and even if most cases lack the society-altering effect of a *Brown* or a *Roe,* they do affect the application of the law in virtually all areas. Interest groups are well aware of this and participate extensively in policy-oriented litigation. It is thus essential to consider how groups do—or do not—affect public law litigation.

This book seeks to demonstrate that interest groups in the United States mobilize and act in the courts much as they do in other policy arenas, subject to the unique institutional requirements of the judiciary. Courts are no longer, or perhaps never have been, outside of the policy process but more typically now constitute just another (often inevitable) stage in the highly iterative process of policy formation. But the unique nature of the judicial forum and its associated institutional constraints affect not only the process of law formation but the types of issues that can be addressed as well as who can champion them. Public law litigation can be at once a very open and also very limiting mechanism through which to seek policy change, and it is critical to understand how groups operate in and through the courts in the course of mobilizing and representing diverse interests. If the courts are an integral part of policy formation, yet present significant constraints to full interest representation, this has significant implications for the democratic process.

INTEREST GROUPS AND LITIGATION

The role of groups in American politics has always been of interest to political observers, from James Madison's dire warnings of the "mischiefs of faction" in *Federalist #10* and Alexis de Tocqueville's observations about Americans' affinity for associations to contemporary studies of interest groups and their lobbying activities. Groups represent an essential element in the functioning of a pluralist political system, providing an additional or alternative way in which citizens involve themselves in politics beyond voting for elected representatives. This activity in turn engenders questions regarding participation and representation. Does the extant collection of private interests approximate some sort of "public interest?" Do the groups themselves even faithfully represent their own members and, if so, how?

Groups have been thought to lobby primarily through grassroots and legislative efforts; their behavior in the judiciary has received less attention, largely because it has traditionally not been the venue of choice for groups (Epstein and Rowland 1991; Scheppele and Walker 1991). But interest group participation in litigation has been increasing (O'Connor and Epstein 1981–1982; Koshner 1998), as has scholarly attention to it.

The advent of groups engaging in political litigation necessitates brief consideration of what they are seeking and whether it occurs. That is, do courts actually produce significant social or political change? The evidence is somewhat mixed, but scholars tend to think the answer is no, at least as far as truly fundamental change (Bickel 1962; Neier 1982; Rosenberg 1991). But even if this is so, it does not make inquiring into the nature of litigation by organized interests any less important. For it is not only Supreme Court decisions on the magnitude of *Brown v. Board of Education* or *Roe v. Wade* that matter. Litigation now constitutes a nearly inevitable stage of public policy formation, as courts are called upon to clarify statutory provisions and determine the validity of implementing regulations. Not every case is a *Brown* or a *Roe*, but a significant number of decisions have a very real impact on the application of numerous laws. Groups understand this and seek to influence these judicially created policy outcomes in ever-increasing numbers. "Legal scholars and political scientists have argued that the importance organized interests have come to place on law and litigation reflects their more sophisticated awareness of the power residual in the judicial process to effect substantive change on matters that involve the definition and application of public law" (Ivers 1995).

As early as 1908, it was becoming clear that pluralism extended into the arena of litigation just as it characterized legislative politics (Bentley 1908). Years later, the focus on this extension returned, as Truman (1951) documented how groups used the courts to solidify their gains in other venues. But it soon became evident that litigation was not solely the province of interests seeking to preserve the status quo. Recourse to the courts came to be seen as a natural move for interests disadvantaged in majoritarian legislative politics (Vose 1958, 1959; Manwaring 1962; Barker 1967; Cortner 1968; Sorauf 1976; Wasby 1984), although some question this thesis (Olson 1981; Scheppele and Walker 1991). Broadening litigation campaigns to include supportive amici signaled the further natural progression of policy-oriented litigation, as it serves to expand the scope of conflict, a tactic that benefits those currently on the losing end (Schattschneider 1960). Now, competing groups on both sides of the issue are the norm in litigation before the Supreme Court, solidifying pluralism's movement into the judiciary (O'Neill 1985; Ivers and O'Connor 1987; Epstein 1993).

While scholars debate the efficacy of litigation (Hakman 1966; Caldeira and Wright 1988; Kearney and Merrill 2000), groups clearly believe there are gains to be had from bringing suits and filing briefs, as they have done so with increasing frequency over the years (O'Connor and Epstein 1981–1982; Epstein 1993; Koshner 1998). Amicus filings have in fact increased more than 800 percent since the middle of the twentieth century (Kearney and Merrill 2000). Explanations offered for the increase include the formation of more groups committed to litigation (Schlozman and Tierney 1986; O'Connor and Epstein 1989), groups coming to see litigation as a viable tactic (Schlozman and Tierney 1986; Scheppele and Walker 1991), and encouragement by the Supreme Court itself (Orren 1976; O'Connor and Epstein 1983d).

Does the vast increase in group litigation mean that it is something in which all organized interests engage? Not necessarily. As noted above, initially it was primarily a tactic employed by those who could not realize their goals through legislation (Cortner 1968). The NAACP's steady erosion and eventual defeat of state-sponsored segregation stands as the model of a politically disfavored group using litigation to achieve what it could not accomplish through other means (Wasby 1984, 1995). Other "liberal" groups—the women's movement, those seeking to maintain church-state separation, environmental groups—followed suit (Berger 1980; O'Connor 1980; O'Connor and Epstein 1983a; Ivers 1995). But then business and conservative interests began to mobilize their own litigating arms as well (Epstein 1985; Kobylka 1991). Many organizations have litigated at least once (Scholzman and Tierney 1986), but their intensity of use of litigation varies considerably (Scheppele and Walker 1991; Epstein 1993). Now participation in political litigation is not solely the province of the left. "The sorts of participants engaged in judicial, executive, and even legislative lobbying are monolithic. That is, contrary to conventional beliefs, the same sorts of interest groups that dominate other branches of government also dominate in the Supreme Court" (Epstein 1993).

Groups that litigate do so for a variety of reasons, not only to "win" the case (Vose 1959). An organization might have a long-range strategy to increase its visibility and credibility by participating in key lawsuits without a realistic expectation of winning each one (Galanter 1974). Others might litigate to demonstrate vigilance to members, gain leverage in other venues, or generally raise their public profiles (Epstein 1993). Thus, while winning a case is certainly a goal, it might not be the only one for many organized interests.

Once an organization deems itself a viable litigant, there are various internal (group type, intensity of commitment, nature of goals, dynamics between leaders and members) and external (growth in rights consciousness, expanded judicial access, changes in the law, existence of other political threats) factors that influence when a group decides to bring a suit or file an amicus brief (Olson 1981; O'Neil 1985; Tushnet 1987; Kobylka 1987; Ivers 1995). These include the existence of favorable statutory or case law on which to base a challenge or response and available resources, including legal expertise (Vose 1958; Cortner 1968).

Groups must also decide whether to sponsor a case directly or to allow someone else to assume that role and instead file an amicus brief in support

(Krislov 1963; Barker 1967). There are some indications that direct sponsorship is preferred (Vose 1959; Tushnet 1987), and more effective in achieving the goal of influencing the courts (Cortner 1968; Hakman 1969), but the amicus role is a viable option for those unable for various reasons to sponsor a case directly (Krislov 1963). Each role has advantages and   disadvantages, including expense, degree of control, and accountability to a client/plaintiff. Sometimes such a decision is not made alone but in concert with other like-minded groups. Liberal groups in particular, more so than conservative ones, have been shown to coordinate litigation activity, assembling amici to support litigants in well-orchestrated campaigns (Baker and Asperger 1982; O'Connor and McFall 1992; Epstein 1993).

Does policy-oriented litigation work? Because groups might have several goals in participating in litigation, it is tricky to define what constitutes "success" (O'Connor 1980; Epstein and Rowland 1986, 1991). One might in fact assess success at different stages of litigation: gaining access to the courts, decisions on the merits, and the broader impact on society (Epstein 1993). Certainly, if a group brings suit seeking a particular interpretation of law, especially if it would be a significant departure from the status quo, and the court renders such an opinion, that would count as a success. But even if this is not the result, a group might still consider the endeavor successful if it generates additional members, raises its profile, prompts legislative or regulatory change, or provides a platform for an appeal to an even more influential tribunal.

At the core of why political science must consider litigation by organized interests is the implication for interest representation. The highly circumscribed, adversarial litigation process differs in several ways from other policy forums, even if the very presence of interest groups at times does render litigation similar to legislative politics (Olson 1981). Indeed, while the literature at times notes certain similarities between "lobbying" through litigation and other forms of pressing an agenda before policymaking bodies, the question of just how similar or different litigation is from other types of lobbying has not been extensively addressed. Because of the nature of litigation, issues must be contested through individual (or sometimes classes of) plaintiffs. This prompts questions regarding how aligned the interests of those plaintiffs and the organizations litigating on their behalf are (Birkby and Murphy 1964; Tushnet 1987). While Hakman (1969) asserted that cases "are carried to the Supreme Court primarily to resolve the immediate disputes among private adversaries," Epstein (1993) observes that "to be sure, the converse is true today; if anything, today's cases represent the struggle of interest groups to etch their broader policy views into law." Are those being "represented" central or peripheral to the case? Does this matter?

The literature on interest group litigation to date has thus revealed a great deal about this important but still under-studied aspect of American pluralism. Yet, as with most fields, there is more to learn. This book seeks to extend our understanding by linking interest group litigation more closely with groups' activities in other policy venues. This study will illustrate how when an issue moves from the legislative to the regulatory and into the judicial arena, the interests that initially mobilized in the first venue will often follow the issue into court. It is quite clearly the extension of pluralism into the judicial forum. Closely examining one major litigation campaign reveals the importance of linking legal with political expertise once the issue does cross into the judiciary. The broader inquiry concerns the implications for interest representation of moving policy issues into the adversarial litigation forum. If the courts often have the last word on many policy issues, it is important to understand how the forum might affect not only the process but the outcome. "The arguments groups present to the Court can shape the way the Court resolves issues and can set the context in which the Court interprets the law" (Epstein 1993).

The specific research questions and expected findings will be set forth in greater detail below. First, however, the following section will set the stage for the alignments and cleavages that both preceded and manifested in the civil case that ultimately reached the Supreme Court, illustrating how the same interests follow an issue through various policy stages and how they alter their strategies when entering the unique environs of litigation.

THE *JOHNSON CONTROLS* LITIGATION

Judge Frank Easterbrook of the Seventh Circuit Court of Appeals called *Johnson Controls*, which went from the Seventh Circuit to the Supreme Court in October 1990, "the most important sex discrimination case in any court since 1964."[5] The case concerned fetal protection policies, just like the one implicated in our prime time drama, which many industrial firms including Johnson Controls had instituted to exclude women of childbearing age (defined as anywhere from 15 to 65) from working in certain jobs in which they might be exposed to substances harmful to a developing fetus. Typically, all women of childbearing years who could not prove sterility were banned from working with hazardous substances under such policies, regardless of their family circumstances or future intentions concerning having children. Companies with such policies stated that their goal was to protect the offspring of their employees; critics countered that they were illegally discriminating against women and merely protecting themselves from the remote possibility of devastating liability claims.

The liability that companies implementing fetal protection policies encountered, however, was not of the sort they anticipated. They were indeed sued, but not over wrongful birth, wrongful death, or any other such tort claims arising out of a poor birth outcome resulting from toxic exposure. Rather, the fetal protection policies *themselves* gave rise to several causes of action under Title VII's sex discrimination provision. They became a new battleground in a preexisting conflict over women's roles and rights in the workplace. Several cases were decided in federal and state court, with the *Johnson Controls* case ultimately reaching the Supreme Court. While the first cases over fetal protection decided in the early 1980s consistently ruled that such practices were permissible, the Supreme Court's 1991 decision came down the other way.

The United Auto Workers union initiated its suit in federal court in the Eastern District of Wisconsin, home to Johnson Controls' headquarters. Losing on summary judgment there, the union appealed to the Seventh Circuit, only to lose again following an en banc hearing. The stage was set, however, for a Supreme Court challenge, with several amici already on board in support of the union and several noteworthy dissents from Judges Easterbrook and Richard Posner in the Seventh Circuit. When the High Court granted certiorari, additional amici signed on in droves, this time on both sides; the scope of the conflict had widened considerably. No longer was this suit about eliminating gender barriers at this one company. According to the various interests that filed briefs, at stake was the very nature of gender equality before the law, the rights of the unborn to health, the rights of employers to enact programs to forestall potentially ruinous tort liability, and how regulatory agencies and businesses should use science to guide their decisions. The case was therefore a vehicle for myriad agendas. The Court's 9–0 decision declared that sex-based employment decisions such as this were in direct violation of Title VII and the Pregnancy Discrimination Act (PDA) and thus could not stand.

The Supreme Court's attention, combined with the wide range of interest groups that joined in contesting the issue, attests to the high public policy significance of workplace reproductive hazards and related employment practices. More fundamentally, the issue also holds value for illustrating how complex policy questions often make their way to the federal judiciary for resolution, and how interest groups increasingly recognize this and attempt to participate in the process and influence judicial outcomes.

The study of fetal protection policies as industrial America's response to women entering the toxic workplace is at once a look into the limitations of OSHA standards and EEOC guidelines, a labor relations struggle, the maturing of the women's rights movement, and the dovetailing of the interests of organized labor and women's rights advocates around a common challenge. As would be expected, an issue with these complex dimensions did not emerge unexpectedly without considerable prior history, including interest group involvement. The basic alignments that manifested in the Johnson Controls litigation—women's rights activists and organized labor on one side, business and other conservative (including pro–fetal rights) interests on the other—predated this case by many years.

The dilemma of the reproductive hazards issue has engaged all three branches of the federal government, but the lack of clear policymaking by legislative and regulatory bodies has meant that it has been left to the judiciary to formulate most of the existing policy in this area. Samuels (1995) reviews the behavior of all three branches on this issue in the context of equality doctrine and gender discrimination, and argues that uncertainty over gender roles, combined with the symbolic connection to the abortion debate, stymied policymakers attempting to respond to the challenges of fetal protection policies. Samuels as well as Kenney (1992) have undertaken the most comprehensive works on the fetal protection policy issue and litigation, but like most of the literature do not go beyond government policy to include the large and critical role played by interest groups.

In the view of many, particularly activists devoted to advancing women's rights, corporate fetal protection policies represented simply another form of unwarranted and illegal employment discrimination based on sex (Bayer 1982a). Many focused on how the policies had the tendency to reinforce traditional and outmoded notions of gender roles (man as breadwinner, woman as homemaker) (Petchesky 1979; Kenney 1992) and to define women—but not men—by their reproductive potential (Chavkin 1979; Stellman and Henifin 1982; Rothstein 1983–1984; Maschke 1991). Those holding this view maintained that these assumptions—and employer actions based upon them—forced upon women the dubious choice between childbearing or essential income (Bayer 1982a; Kirp 1991). They also note that exclusionary policies did not emerge in low-wage industries dominated by women (Chavkin 1979; Stellman and Henifin 1982; Wilson and Sapiro 1985; Kirp 1991; Blank 1991a), and that little if any concern for adverse reproductive consequences for men was advanced by employers, suggesting that discrimination rather than true concern over reproductive hazards underlies these policies (Bell 1979; Rothstein 1983–1984). The lack of research on reproductive toxicity in general, and of reproductive effects on men in particular, represents not only a bias in medical research but a misuse of what available evidence does exist (Chavkin 1979; Stillman 1980; Walsh 1980; Scott 1984; Hatch 1984; Williams 1988; Kirp 1991 Kenen 1993; Schroedel and Peretz 1994).

This antifetal protection policy perspective was not limited to feminists but also came to represent the position of organized labor on this issue, despite labor's historical support for policies limiting women's occupational opportunities (Bell 1979; Chavkin 1979; Petchesky 1979; Wright 1979; Scott 1984; Graham 1993). When unions began to side with women in challenging employers' exclusionary policies, they did so by urging a narrow reading of Title VII's bona fide occupational qualification (BFOQ) defense. If an employer's practice is found to be facially discriminatory (a case of disparate treatment), it can only be justified on the grounds that the classification used is fundamentally related to ability to perform the job. (This defense was not to be allowed in cases of racial discrimination.) Subsequently, the courts developed an additional framework for instances in which an employer's practice is facially neutral but has a disproportionate impact on one race or sex. The defense for these disparate impact cases is that of a "valid business necessity," a defense that grants an employer a greater degree of latitude in justifying the questioned practice.[6] Courts, however, were initially rather unclear on the appropriate legal framework to apply to fetal protection policies (Samuelson 1977; Furnish 1980; Howard 1981; Becker 1986; Katz 1989).

Others advocated the view that fetal protection policies constituted justifiable conduct by employers (Clyne 1980; Bernacki 1990). Those siding with employers would do so for distinct but related reasons. Key to this side of the argument is a belief that fetuses (or potential fetuses) are entities deserving of protection (Rosen 1989), and that businesses were justified in attempting to do so by minimizing the risk of prenatal exposure to toxins at the workplace. The increasing attention to the notion of "fetal personhood" provides an important backdrop to this line of argument (Johnsen 1986; Benshoof 1989). Movement in the law to hold women civilly and criminally liable for behavior during pregnancy that might be harmful to a fetus demonstrates that this is more than an academic argument (Blank 1991a; Roth 1993; Gonen 2001).

Business supporters favored a more flexible reading of Title VII and the Pregnancy Discrimination Act that would allow for fetal protection policies to come within the business necessity defense; some went even further to advocate changing the Constitution to confer fetal citizenship so as to allow for consideration of fetal welfare in situations such as this (Finneran 1980; Mattson 1981).

There are thus several core issues at play in the policy debates over these corporate programs. As would be expected in a pluralist political system, groups emerged to present these various perspectives to Congress, regulatory agencies, and eventually the courts as the legitimacy of determining women's employment options according to reproductive capacity was repeatedly contested.

METHODS AND AIMS OF THIS STUDY

As noted earlier, literature on interest group litigation tends not to emphasize the link between groups' litigation activity and their advocacy around similar issues in other venues. The thesis presented here is that groups mobilize around issues and, especially now, follow those issues as they move through various policy-making forums, including the judiciary. While there are discrete litigating organizations that specialize in bringing court cases, they are often linked either directly or indirectly to organizations that engage in broader forms of activity. There is not one set of interests that seeks change through legislation and a distinctly different set of interests that chooses to litigate. Those who organize to effect policy change increasingly seek to apply pressure in whichever venue is most conducive to its agenda at a given time. Much of this book, in fact, addresses just how groups determine when litigation is the appropriate strategy, as it tracks the players on both sides who worked on issues of equal employment opportunity for women (and then pregnant women), occupational safety and health, and eventually fetal protection policies.

"Lobbying" through litigation is quite similar to doing so in other venues, although in certain critical ways it is very different. For one thing, advocates must of necessity involve the expertise of lawyers (if they were not already part of a group's efforts on a particular issue). Interviews with the actors in the fetal protection story reveal some interesting aspects of how this plays out. Litigation requires that issues be framed as cognizable claims, which is an inherent limitation on what can be sought from a court. Thus the second part of the thesis of this book is that the unique institutional features of litigation do have significant implications for how policy can be framed for judicial action and that this affects policy outcomes. Because litigation is an inherently adversarial process that is limited to claims that are cognizable under existing law, moving an issue into the judicial forum may serve to substantially narrow the range of options available in terms of real policy change.

Many would argue that courts were in fact never designed to be the institutions promulgating policy. Reality, however, has moved far from this ideal, and now it is commonplace for not only the most contentious but also many more routine issues to wind up in litigation. Thus it matters that the nature of the institution might affect the way interests are represented in litigation as well as the available outcomes. Litigation adds a particular twist to the otherwise broad notion of interest representation, as it involves actual plaintiffs and defendants. As courts are charged with deciding genuine controversies between discrete adversaries, it cannot only be the broad policy agenda of the litigating organization that takes priority, as attorneys are obligated to act in the best interest of clients. Thus an aspect for exploration is the extent to which the interests of individual parties (usually plaintiffs) align with those of the sponsoring interest group.

A number of findings might be anticipated in a study such as this. One is that the resort to litigation would serve as a narrowing or moderating influence on the issue and those seeking the articulation of a particular legal doctrine. As noted above, seeking change via lawsuits requires appealing to a narrower set of potential justifications for the policy outcome sought, requiring the issue to be framed to fit within the confines of existing law. This might preclude presenting more far-reaching challenges to how the workplace is structured and to notions of gender roles in childbearing. The process also has the potential to narrow participation in a policy debate such as this, because with the exception of cases dealing with potential retrenchment over abortion or affirmative action, litigation efforts are not often widely publicized. Thus only those with the requisite expertise will be aware of significant pending litigation and be able to participate in it. With a narrow range of participants comes the likelihood that not all pertinent information will necessarily be presented to the deciding tribunal, unlike legislative campaigns that are often conducted within a far more open process.

The primary data for this book were derived from participant interviews. I spoke either in person or via telephone with at least one individual involved with each litigating party or amicus brief, and often with more than one individual when the party was a significant player in the case. For the petitioner United Auto Workers, numerous attorneys were interviewed, as the lead litigator changed with each stage of the lawsuit. For each amicus brief, typically the individual interviewed was the lead attorney or counsel of record. A total of thirty-three interviews were conducted from November 1995 through October 1996. (See Appendix for a complete list of interviews.) Interview subjects were asked about their organization's prior involvement in the fetal protection issue (and in litigation generally) and about their strategies in this particular case. The other primary data sources were the briefs filed in the case, the Supreme Court oral argument transcript, the decisions in the Supreme Court case, and relevant lower court decisions. These primary data were supplemented by secondary accounts of the history of the movements for women's equality and for federal occupational safety and health legislation.

Chapter 2 provides a brief historical account of the development of the policy cleavages that manifested in the *Johnson Controls* litigation but were far from new. The issue is placed within the context of protective employment policies that limited women's occupational choices, vestiges of which were to be found in the fetal protection policies being challenged in this case. The interests that lined up through the decades of the twentieth century to either remove limits on women's employment or defend them were largely the same as the issue transformed from overtly gender discriminatory laws and practices to those linked to reproduction and risks of fetal harm. This therefore provides a rich example through which to observe how policy advocates adjust to the confines of the judicial forum, and what this means for the broader agenda for which they work.

Chapters 3 through 5 explore each side of the *UAW v. Johnson Controls* litigation, both the litigating parties themselves and their respective amici. Chapter 3 describes how the United Auto Workers came to be involved in Title VII litigation over fetal protection policies, and tracks the case through its various levels. Chapter 4 explores how the union effectively marshaled the resources of a cadre of amicus organizations, many with prior involvement in this and related issues, to wage its fight in federal court. Chapter 5 examines the respondent company's efforts to defend its policy, and how various and disparate interests joined in as the case moved to the Supreme Court. Finally, chapter 6 sets forth some general observations from the insights gained by looking at this complex litigation effort. The resulting conclusions should contribute to our understanding of how groups mobilize around interests and how the process of interest mobilization changes when activity moves away from the grass roots, through legislation, and into litigation.

2

Women in the Workforce and the Labor Movement

*T*his book employs a case study approach to illustrate the dynamics of interest group litigation, using the 1991 U.S. Supreme Court case of *UAW v. Johnson Controls* as the illustrative case to show how interests mobilize through the various available policy arenas and carry their agendas (and adversaries) into litigation. The goal is to illuminate not only the complexities of that particular litigation effort but also to highlight important issues of group dynamics and interest representation that such efforts implicate.

In order to paint a sufficiently detailed picture of this case that culminated in the early 1990s, however, it is necessary to reach back into the nineteenth century to trace the emergence of the precursor issues and actors that would come to bear on this modern litigation. Only then can one fully appreciate how modern group litigation has evolved into a complex alternative form of lobbying. While the *Johnson Controls* case represents a high-profile civil lawsuit over a particular late-twentieth-century form of employer personnel practices, it had its roots in the battles over women's protective labor laws of the nineteenth and early twentieth centuries, the emergence and eventual convergence of the labor and women's movements, the growth of the federal regulatory apparatus, and the rise in "litigation as a form of pressure group activity" (Vose 1958). This chapter describes the involvement of the key organized interests in the legislative, regulatory, and litigation battles that have accompanied women's entry into the paid labor force, and how these various precursor issues set the stage for the *Johnson Controls* case.

THE EARLY YEARS

Nineteenth Century through World War I

Employer policies and public laws restricting employment capacities for women have a long history in the United States, dating from the nineteenth century and continuing in various forms through the present. Also, women's experiences with and within organized labor reach back into the 1800s.[1] The two have in fact been closely interrelated, for the established U.S. trade and industrial unions historically supported special "protective legislation" for women, even though it contradicted labor's philosophical and practical opposition to government regulation of terms of employment. It was not until relatively recently that unions' stance toward protective measures that restricted employment opportunities for women changed.

Fetal protection policies are only the most recent manifestation of exclusionary policies aimed at women in employment. Since their entry into the labor force in the United States, women have been subject to ostensibly protective measures that have limited their employment opportunities (Baer 1978; Hill 1979; Lehrer 1987). While ostensibly adopted for benevolent purposes such as protecting women themselves and their offspring, the effects of such policies and laws generally have been more restrictive than protective. They have limited the number of hours women could work and the types of jobs that they could hold. Modern fetal protection policies, instituted by industrial firms and designed to bar women of childbearing age from jobs involving toxic exposure, have had the same effect. The common theme of restrictive labor laws and policies for women has been society's interest in protecting the health of future generations; thus the health of women, as bearers of children, was seen as a legitimate interest of the state, and of the employer who is regulated by the state. As described by feminist scholar Joan Hoff-Wilson, "history has shown that favorable treatment can have unfavorable results when it is rationalized in the name of 'women's special procreational capacity.' If history repeats itself, pregnant workers of the 1980s and 1990s might find themselves right back where their ancestors were in the era of protective legislation following *Muller v. Oregon* in 1908" (Hoff-Wilson 1987).

In 1836 the Committee on Female Labor of the National Trades' Union reported that "the physical organization, the natural responsibilities, and the moral sensibilities of woman prove conclusively that her labors should be only of a domestic nature" (quoted in Kenneally 1978). In the late 1800s, women were beginning to gain some representation in and recognition by

the American Federation of Labor (AFL), which was becoming the dominant national union organization (eclipsing the Knights of Labor). But in
the 1890s, the AFL was urging special legislation for women, advocating
limits on hours and types of machinery that women could operate. In
1898 the organization introduced a resolution at its national convention
that would "remove all women from government employment, and
thereby encourage their removal from the everyday walks of life and rele-
gate them to the home" (quoted in Berch 1982). Samuel Gompers, president of the AFL, published in 1906 a position paper on working women,
in which he stated that "the wife or mother, attending to the duties of the
home, makes the greatest contribution to the support of the family . . .
there is no necessity for the wife contributing to the support of the family
by working—that is . . . by wage labor . . . the wife as a wage-earner is a dis-
advantage economically considered, and socially is unnecessary" (also
quoted in Berch 1982). Women thus had to struggle on two fronts, bat-
tling "management exploitation and recurring union sexism" (Kenneally
1978). "Historically, the record of the organized labor movement in representing working women has been poor. It has included the exclusion of
women from male unions and male occupations, and a lack of support for
organizing those employed in female occupations. Such tactics have reinforced the sex segregation of the work force and the marginalization of
women workers" (Blum 1991). Further hindering women's progress was a
reticence toward unionization displayed by many working women themselves, which may have prevented them from influencing union policy
from within.

When protective labor laws for women first emerged in the late 1800s,
trade unions and many women's movement activists actually agreed that
they were needed. They shared a common view that women possessed special qualities and virtues related to the domestic sphere, and that these
qualities must be protected when women had to enter the harsh, male
world of paid labor. This conception of women's roles provided justification for state regulation of the health of women workers. The unions supported such regulation both because of their beliefs about the social role of
women and in order to limit competition for jobs (Kessler-Harris 1984).
Because working conditions for women during this era were extremely dis-
mal, many women saw these protective measures as a benefit, notwith-
standing their exclusive application to women. For these women at this
time, relief from brutal working conditions was a greater imperative than
formal gender equality.

Thus, even in the laissez-faire era of the turn of the century, when the
Supreme Court in *Lochner v. New York*[2] struck down a maximum hours

law for (male) bakers on the grounds that it interfered with freedom of contract, the same Court three years later in *Muller v. Oregon*[3] upheld a maximum hours law for women based on the belief that women were inherently the weaker sex. *Muller* explicitly did not overrule *Lochner*—it did not need to, because women were regarded as a special class of workers due to their capacity to bear children. The language of the *Muller* decision is instructive, for it articulates how women were viewed at the time—as childbearers first and only secondarily, if at all, as wage earners.

> That woman's physical structure and the performance of maternal functions place her at a disadvantage in the struggle for subsistence is obvious. This is especially true when the burdens of motherhood are upon her. Even when they are not, by abundant testimony of the medical fraternity continuance for a long time on her feet at work, repeating this from day to day, tends to injurious effects upon the body, and, as healthy mothers are essential to vigorous offspring, the physical well-being of women becomes an object of public interest and care in order to preserve the strength and vigor of the race.

Muller v. Oregon provided the legal (and social) justification for restricting women's employment for years to come. The Supreme Court went on to uphold prohibitions on women holding night jobs[4] and serving as bartenders,[5] and validated a state minimum wage law for women only.[6] Restating the *Muller* rationale, the Court again asserted that women's health was a matter of public interest warranting special protection. The overall effect of all of these "protective" measures was that they eliminated some competition for men and perpetuated sex segregation in the workforce (Hill 1979).

As protective laws and court cases upholding them became more frequent, however, some women became wary of the authority that the state was asserting over an ever-widening range of employment opportunities. While trade unions in general opposed state regulation of male workers (as protection from the government could obviate the need for workers to organize), they favored such regulation of women. Organized labor was able to justify this apparent inconsistency by adhering to the notion of women as a "special class" of more vulnerable workers. When some trade union men asserted that they too might enjoy some of the protections being afforded women, the AFL's Gompers objected on the grounds that "an 8-hour day established by law is enforced by government agents. The workers' welfare is taken from under their immediate control . . ." (quoted in Berch 1982).

At the same time, many women workers favored protective legislation precisely because they were having considerable difficulty gaining support for their needs from organized labor. Thus unions fostered the proliferation of protective labor laws for women directly and indirectly, by forcing women to turn to such laws themselves as a result of union indifference. Even the National Women's Trade Union League (NWTUL), which formed as a result of this very indifference, favored protective legislation. But the result was that women workers were relegated to marginal status in the labor movement, in spite of the fact that their earnings were not luxuries but often vitally necessary. "The ideology of protection seems only to have reinforced the difficulties working women faced. It left women isolated from the trade union movement" (Berch 1982, 50).

During World War I, many women in the United States entered defense industries to replace men who had been called into military service.[7] As a result, male workers became alarmed, as they feared that women would lower wages, impede unionization, and displace men in these occupations (Brito 1987). During this era, the notion still prevailed that female workers needed special protection for themselves and for future generations. Male-dominated unions found this a convenient rationale to continue to support state regulation of women's employment, despite their ideological opposition to government intervention in regulating labor. The unions' practical concerns with limiting competition thus superseded their aversion to state intervention in labor regulation.

Suffrage through the Early Post–World War II Period

The cleavages over protective labor legislation were not simply between unionized male workers and women seeking their place within labor's ranks. The issue of protective labor laws for women was in fact one of the major issues that divided the women's movement itself in the early twentieth century. Advocates of pure equality of the sexes opposed such measures as restrictive of women's individual rights and opportunities. Many trade union women, however, favored these laws and the benefits they derived from them. When the Equal Rights Amendment (ERA) was first proposed in 1923, many women opposed it precisely because it would nullify the protective labor laws that they favored. When the Supreme Court struck down a women's minimum wage law in 1923 in *Adkins v. Children's Hospital*,[8] reasoning that women's attainment of suffrage three years earlier invalidated the "unique status of women" argument used in *Muller v. Oregon*, the NWTUL and the AFL responded with a renewed call for the unionization of women and for collective bargaining (Kenneally 1978).

Women's fortunes in the labor movement began to shift slowly in the interwar years. The industrial unions that broke with the AFL in 1937 to

form the Congress of Industrial Organizations (CIO) were more conducive to women's advancement, as several of them, including the Amalgamated Clothing Workers Union and the International Ladies Garment
Workers Union (ILGWU), had a large proportion of female members.
John L. Lewis, the CIO's first president, had long been supportive of
women in the labor force. Throughout the 1940s, CIO conventions were
more sympathetic to the concerns of women than were those of the AFL.

Women's experiences in the formation and development of the United
Auto Workers (UAW), a CIO member union, are especially pertinent.
Their involvement began through auxiliaries of wives, daughters, and
female employees, but by the mid-1940s a woman had become the vice
president and then president of a UAW local.

> Responding to the needs of their female members, unions began to bargain
> collectively to eliminate wage differentials. . . . Albeit motivated chiefly by a
> desire to protect men's wages, the UAW was usually solicitous of its women,
> studying and responding to their needs, and in 1945 warning locals that
> women's seniority rights must have the same backing and protection as
> men's. As early as 1941 the UAW began advocating the inclusion of sex and
> age provisions in the nondiscriminatory clause of Executive Orders dealing
> with fair employment, and a few years later at its fourteenth convention,
> pledged that pay, hiring, promotions, and seniority rights would be equal.
> (Kenneally 1978, 175)

Despite the progressivism of the UAW, unions' overall resistance to the
elimination of protective treatment for women workers persisted through
the middle of the twentieth century. For example, in 1944 the Democratic
Party included support for the ERA in its platform even though organized
labor was still opposed to it. The division persisted within the women's
movement concerning pure equality versus special treatment. The side of
the debate led by Alice Paul and the National Woman's Party, proponents
of the ERA, favored the eradication of protective labor laws aimed at
women, believing that they limited women's opportunities in the labor
market.

Following World War II, women began to enter and remain in the
workforce full time in increasing numbers, largely due to economic necessity. As their financial security was increasingly linked to their own work
outside the home, women began to put greater pressure on unions to
secure equal opportunities and benefits; this included removing the barriers created by outmoded protective laws. At first the unions resisted, in part
due to lingering notions of women's "proper" role as being in the home
rather than in the factory. But the tremendous influx of women into the

labor force during this war did not reverse itself upon cessation of hostilities—this time women were entering the world of paid work to stay.

Another related issue that signaled both the emergence of women's voices within organized labor and unions' evolution toward working for women's interests has been the movement for pay equity, or comparable worth. The notion was first advanced by women trade unionists during World War II, but it was not until the late 1970s and early 1980s that the issue reemerged with any true momentum (Blum 1991). By this time organized labor had undergone a significant shift in its stance toward employed women, and like gender- or pregnancy-based job limitations, pay equity represented an issue on which women's and labor activists united.

While the specific goals of the movements for comparable worth and the elimination of sex-based exclusionary policies are technically different, the two issues clearly are substantially related. One important common element is a recognition of the high degree of gender segregation in the labor force. The push for comparable worth is premised on this recognition and seeks to value "women's work" as highly as work traditionally performed by men. As was noted in chapter 1, many observers have noted the conspicuous absence of fetal protection policies in occupations dominated by women. This has been interpreted as an indication that these policies were largely adopted in order to perpetuate gender segregation in industry. Thus it is perhaps no surprise that these two issues represent areas in which feminists and labor unions have joined forces to advocate and litigate.

THE MODERN ERA

Breakthrough Legislation and Early Implementation

Slowly, organized labor began to come to terms with the reality of women's permanent presence in the paid labor force. In 1961 Esther Peterson, head of the Labor Department's Women's Bureau, persuaded President Kennedy to establish the President's Commission on the Status of Women. At the Commission's first meeting, the President called achieving equal pay for women "essential" (Kenneally 1978). Legislation was introduced and, during the hearings in 1962, one finds early foreshadowing of the lines of cleavage that would persist in subsequent policy skirmishes over women and employment: the Chamber of Commerce opposed the measure, while the AFL-CIO and the ACLU voiced their support. When it passed, the Equal Pay Act of 1963 amended the Fair Labor Standards Act of 1938; it was extended in 1972 and 1974 to cover most of the U.S. workforce.

The 1964 Civil Rights Act was the next major federal step taken to eliminate employment discrimination against women. The primary intent of the act was to alleviate racial discrimination in public accommodations, employment, education, and housing. The amendment to add sex in addition to race, color, religion, and national origin as prohibited classifications in employment was offered on the House floor by Representative Howard Smith of Virginia, Chair of the House Rules Committee, as a ploy to make the legislation seem absurd and thus ensure its defeat. Title VII of the act, the portion concerning discrimination in employment, had been controversial anyway. Many lawmakers, although in favor of granting additional rights to African Americans, were unsure about legislating in the area of employment decisions made by private employers. They were also wary of creating a new federal agency (the EEOC) to enforce such a provision (Bird 1968, 1–2).

The addition of the sex amendment did not receive a great deal of attention, however. The *New York Times* dismissed it as one of several "unexpected amendments" (Bird 1968, 11). It was in fact expected to be dropped when the bill was considered by the Senate, but by then women were actively defending it. President Johnson favored the amendment's retention, and he symbolically bolstered its fortunes by officially celebrating the effective date of the 1963 Equal Pay Act (Bird 1968, 11–12). The Civil Rights bill, including Title VII *with* the sex discrimination provision, passed in its entirety on July 2, 1964. Because of the unexpected nature of the sex discrimination provision, there was no discernible interest group mobilization around that issue; it would be in Title VII's implementation that group cleavages would again emerge.

In the first years following passage of Title VII, the EEOC devoted its full attention to what it saw as its legitimate mandate—removing employment barriers based on race. The sex discrimination provision was not a priority. The agency's first executive director, Herman Edelsberg, referring to the circumstances under which "sex" was added to Title VII, publicly stated in 1966 that the provision was a "fluke" that was "conceived out of wedlock."[9] A cadre of employees emerged within the EEOC, however, who sought to see its mandate against sex discrimination taken seriously. They believed that a sort of women's equivalent of the NAACP was needed to pressure the agency to fulfill its mission. The idea came to fruition when Betty Friedan and others attending the Third National Conference of Commissions on the Status of Women became frustrated that the conference would not resolve to pressure the EEOC for action on sex discrimination. On June 30, 1966, the National Organization for Women (NOW) was formed by Friedan, several former EEOC commissioners, a United Auto

Workers (UAW) Women's Committee representative, and several present and past members of State Commissions on the Status of Women (Freeman 1975, 54–55). And so again, as the contours of the policy debate around women's changing roles in the workforce took shape, one finds the UAW, already progressive on women's roles in the labor force for many years,[10] playing a direct role in founding one of the premier national-level women's rights organizations. When the UAW would challenge discriminatory workplace practices known as fetal protection policies into the 1990s, NOW would be there providing support as amicus curiae. Currently known for its advocacy of abortion rights, one of NOW's primary goals at is inception was in fact the eradication of sex discrimination in employment (McGlen and O'Connor 1983).

Not all of the EEOC's reticence in dealing with gender discrimination emanated from lack of conviction, as there was no consensus yet on the impact of Title VII on existing protective laws for women. For the EEOC, this meant determining how to interpret the bona fide occupational qualification (BFOQ) exception to Title VII. According to this statutory provision, employers may take sex into account in hiring if sex is a BFOQ for a particular position—a bona fide occupational qualification was defined as one "reasonably necessary to the normal operation of the business." Interpretation of this exception generated conflict among women's groups because of its potential impact on protective labor laws for women. A broad interpretation would allow most such laws to remain in effect, while a strict reading would do away with most of them.

Several groups, among them eventual supporters of the UAW's antifetal protection policy suit, appealed to the EEOC director for a broad interpretation, to allow "differential legislation" for females to stand. Among these eventual changeovers were the ACLU, AFL-CIO, the American Association of University Women (AAUW), the American Nurses Association (ANA), and some individual unions, including the ILGWU and the International Union of Electrical, Radio, and Machine Workers (IUE). On the other side were groups such as NOW and the National Woman's Party (NWP), as well as the UAW, which instead argued for a narrow reading in order to strike down so-called protective laws that served to exclude women from a number of jobs. Initial EEOC policy was equivocal. "The EEOC responded to the conflict between protective legislation and the BFOQ defense by firmly straddling the middle of the road" (Mezey 1992, 43). The Commission first tried to make intent (true protection versus invidious discrimination) the litmus test without addressing the practical difficulty in making this distinction. In its first guidelines on sex discrimination, issued on December 2, 1965, the EEOC stated:

the Commission does not believe that Congress intended to disturb such laws and regulations which are intended to, and have the effect of, protecting women against exploitation and hazard. . . . The Commission will not find an unlawful employment practice where an employer's refusal to hire women for certain work is based on a State law which precludes the employment of women for such work: Provided, That the employer is acting in good faith and that the effect of the law in question is to protect women rather than subject them to discrimination.[11]

This position of the EEOC essentially left the status quo unchanged with regard to exclusionary employment practices. The following year, on August 19, 1966, the Commission stated in a press release that where there was a direct conflict between a state law and Title VII, the EEOC would not make any decision, in part because the EEOC lacked any enforcement power and could not insulate employers against such state laws.

Throughout 1966 NOW and other women's groups pressured the EEOC to hold hearings on establishing regulations to implement the sex discrimination prohibition of Title VII; these hearings eventually occurred in May 1967. In December of that year the groups picketed EEOC offices around the country to protest the agency's reticence around the issue of gender discrimination. NOW also filed suit against the EEOC for its failure to adequately enforce Title VII (McGlen and O'Connor 1983).

In February 1968 the EEOC rescinded its 1966 statement, in which it had declined to intervene in cases regarding state protective laws, and reaffirmed its 1965 policy of allowing such laws considerable latitude. Reiterating the rationale used in the 1965 guidelines, the Commission stated that "where state law limits the employment of women in certain jobs, employers refusing to employ women in such jobs will not be found in violation of the act provided that . . . they act in good faith . . . and the effect of the legislation itself is protective rather than discriminatory."[12]

On August 19, 1969, the Commission, largely in response to pressure from the "equal treatment" women's rights advocates, who were gaining voice, issued a new regulation that signaled a major reversal in EEOC policy. This new rule stated that no prohibitory law could qualify as a BFOQ exception, removing the justification of protection for exclusionary practices. "Such laws and regulations conflict with Title VII of the Civil Rights Act of 1964 and will not be considered a defense to an otherwise established unlawful employment practice . . ."[13] But by now litigation had commenced.

The first federal appellate court decision to address the BFOQ and state protective laws was *Weeks v. Southern Bell*,[14] decided by the Fifth Circuit in 1969. At that point, Georgia's State Labor Commission Rule 59 prohibited women from lifting over 30 pounds on the job, and it was upon this rule that the company relied in defending its restrictive policy under the BFOQ exception. The district court agreed with the company, but the Fifth Circuit did not, stating that "an employer has the burden of proving that he had reasonable cause to believe, that is, a factual basis for believing, that all or substantially all women would be unable to perform safely and efficiently the duties of the job involved."

Because Georgia's Rule 59 had actually been repealed at the time of the *Weeks* decision, the Fifth Circuit was not able to rule on the validity of protective laws under Title VII, merely that Southern Bell's policy did not meet the federal BFOQ test. The case that would deliver the definitive blow to state protective laws was *Rosenfeld v. Southern Pacific Co.*,[15] a 1971 Ninth Circuit case involving California laws restricting weight lifting and overtime by women.[16] By now the EEOC was more aggressively pursuing sex discrimination claims, for the *Rosenfeld* litigation effort was orchestrated in part by the EEOC itself and its general counsel filed an amicus brief in favor of overturning the laws. The court was clearly aware that it was in the business of creating new policy with this case, stating that "while the resulting litigation is private in form, it is intended to effectuate the policies of the legislation" (at 1222). In a dissenting opinion, Judge Chambers pointed out that counsel for the EEOC "selected" the Rosenfeld case to bring forward, and that while "the plaintiff's counsel makes a frontal attack . . . the EEOC comes in with a flank attack by way of an amicus brief" (1,228). Both judges thus forthrightly acknowledged that this was litigation intended to have an effect on the state of the law, although each differed in his assessment of its propriety.

When the court struck down the California laws, it effectively ended the era of legally sanctioned labor policies that restricted women's employment opportunities; prior to 1969, every state had some sort of protective legislation for women on the books (Baer 1978). "[*Rosenfeld*] is widely regarded as having established that 'protective' labor laws similar to those that survived constitutional challenges from *Muller v. Oregon* onward violate Title VII . . ." (Lindgren and Taub 1988).

But, while the law may have been moving in women's favor, unions were progressing at varying rates. The Women's Equity Action League (WEAL), formed in 1968, reported in 1970 that a third of the complaints it had heard to that point dealt with the failure of unions to act on behalf of their women members (Kenneally 1978). Union WAGE was formed in California by disgruntled female unionists in California. But again, some unions were ahead of the curve, with the UAW continuing to be at the forefront of progressivism in matters of gender. When the Coalition of Labor Union

Women (CLUW) was formed in 1974, Olga Madar of the UAW became its first president. The UAW also supported passage of the Equal Rights Amendment in 1970, while the AFL-CIO changed its position from opposition to support only in the mid-1970s.

Phillips v. Martin Marietta[17] was the first gender discrimination case under Title VII to reach the U.S. Supreme Court. The Court ruled in 1971 that the company's policy of not hiring women with young children violated Title VII, as the same rule did not apply to men. The ACLU filed an amicus brief in the case, which was largely written by, although not credited to, Susan Deller Ross, then a law student. Ross would go on to the EEOC and then to the ACLU's Women's Rights Project as Clinical Director, leading the coalition that worked for passage of the Pregnancy Discrimination Act (see below) and playing an instrumental role in the development of U.S. sex discrimination law.

The Court's decision in *Phillips,* while a moderate victory for working women, left open the possibility of gender stereotypes qualifying under the BFOQ. It was in *Dothard v. Rawlinson*[18] in 1977 that the Supreme Court took a decidedly expansive view of the BFOQ defense and ruled that concern for women's safety was sufficient to bar them from prison guard positions. It would be fetal protection policies that would again bring the BFOQ to court, forcing the federal courts and the EEOC to grapple with its application within the context of reproductive hazards through the 1980s and into the 1990s.

In addition to pressuring the EEOC in the late 1960s, NOW and other women's rights groups began lobbying Congress to pass the Equal Employment Opportunity Act.[19] Prior to 1972, all that the EEOC could do upon finding instances of sex discrimination was to seek voluntary compliance. The EEO Act, which finally passed in 1972 as an amendment to the 1964 Civil Rights Act, granted the EEOC power to bring suit when it found violations. It also broadened the types of employers covered under the Civil Rights Act to include employers and unions of eight or more workers, employees of both the state and federal governments, and employees of educational institutions (McGlen and O'Connor 1983; Mezey 1992, 39–40).

Not all exclusionary employment practices of this era were broadly aimed at "protecting" women at all times; some focused only on pregnancy. As a combination of litigation and EEOC action slowly removed the legal underpinnings of straightforward sex discrimination, the use of pregnancy rather than gender as the basis for employment restrictions increased. Accordingly, the EEOC issued additional guidance, on April 5, 1972, to address pregnancy discrimination. This guidance was drafted by Susan

Deller Ross, who was then at the EEOC. The reasoning employed in the guidance was essentially the same as that eventually adopted in the Pregnancy Discrimination Act (PDA) of 1978 (also drafted in part by Ross): that pregnancy is a disability and should be treated the same as other disabilities for employment purposes.[20] The fact that the PDA would eventually become necessary is evidence that this EEOC rule had little impact on preventing discrimination based on pregnancy, despite the agency's enhanced enforcement capability following the 1972 Equal Employment Opportunity Act.

In the early 1970s, a cast of women's rights litigation groups emerged to take advantage of the new developments in the law that held promise for improving women's opportunities, not only in employment but in a number of other spheres as well. The National Organization for Women (NOW) created a Legal Defense and Education Fund (LDEF) in 1970. The ACLU formed its Women's Rights Project (WRP) in 1971, and the Women's Legal Defense Fund (WLDF) began operation that same year. The following year, the Center for Law and Social Policy created its own Women's Rights Project, which would become independent as the National Women's Law Center (NWLC). The Women's Rights Litigation Clinic at Rutgers University was also created in 1972, as were the Women's Law Fund and the Women's Equity Action League (WEAL) litigation fund. The Women's Law Project (1973) and Equal Rights Advocates (1974) followed. All of these groups would play alternating lead roles in significant cases that would define and develop women's status under the U.S. Constitution and Title VII; many would also work in the legislative and regulatory arenas. (Their roles and their work will emerge in greater detail below.) Thus, once a degree of legislative success had been won, in the form of the Equal Pay Act, Title VII, and the EEO Act, the stage was set for the emergence of the litigating arm of the movement for expanding women's rights. These organizations would work within the next stages of the policy process, pushing for clarification and enforcement through executive agencies and the courts to reinforce these initial gains.

The Pregnancy Discrimination Act

Cases such as *Reed v. Reed* (the first equal protection challenge to a gender-based policy) and *Phillips v. Martin Marietta* in the early 1970s took aim at the most overt forms of sex discrimination in employment, and served to remove state-sanctioned sex-based exclusions from the books throughout the United States. But the focus of women's rights advocates quickly expanded to pregnancy discrimination, which in its various forms (including forced leave, loss of seniority, lack of medical coverage, and outright dismissal) became targets of challenge by many women's rights groups. In 1972 the EEOC, in response to recommendations from the Citizens Advisory Council on the Status of Women and several women's groups, adopted regulations that specifically rejected the notion that "pregnancy is unique" and warranted differential treatment of women (McGlen and O'Connor 1983). However, in subsequent decisions, the Supreme Court declined to adopt the same view, signaling both how difficult it would be to overcome some traditional notions of women's roles and how ineffective the EEOC would be in furthering this effort.

The first major case was *Geduldig v. Aiello*,[21] an equal protection challenge to the state of California's exclusion of pregnancy from disability benefits. Once again, the familiar lines of cleavage emerged, as did some of the consistent participants. The ACLU filed an amicus brief urging that the state's policy be overturned, as did the AFL-CIO, the EEOC, the International Union of Electrical, Radio, and Machine Workers (IUE), the Physicians' Forum, and the Women's Equity Action League (WEAL). Amici defending the status quo were the Chamber of Commerce, the National Association of Manufacturers (NAM), and the Pacific Legal Foundation, all of which appeared in similar roles in the *Johnson Controls* case at the Supreme Court in 1990, as well as General Electric, the Merchant and Manufacturers Association, and AT&T. Two of these opposing amici, General Electric and the IUE, would clash as litigants over this same issue shortly after *Geduldig* in the *Gilbert* case (see below). The Court in *Geduldig* upheld the constitutionality of the state's policy, explaining that the policy was reasonable because not every risk or disability was covered, and therefore not covering pregnancy did not necessarily discriminate against women. The Supreme Court held that the state's plan did not differentiate between men and women, but rather between "pregnant and non-pregnant persons." Following this setback, women then turned to Title VII rather than equal protection doctrine as a means to combat pregnancy discrimination in employment.

The first test of this approach of using Title VII came in *General Electric Co. v. Gilbert*,[22] sponsored by the IUE. This case involved the disability plan of a private employer that was similar to that of California in the *Geduldig* case. The IUE lawyers argued that a penalty on childbirth was inherently discriminatory. They were supported by amici AFL-CIO, Communications Workers of America (CWA) and Women's Law Project, as well as the United States and the state of Ohio. GE had the backing of Alaska Airlines, the American Life Insurance Association, the American Society for Personnel Administration, repeat amicus AT&T, Celanese Corporation, the

Chamber of Commerce, NAM, Owens Illinois, and Westinghouse Electric. The employer and its allies prevailed again as the justices, citing their decision in *Geduldig*, disregarded the EEOC guidelines that found policies excluding pregnancy as discriminatory, and found no Title VII violation. Writing for the Court, Justice William Rehnquist stated that pregnancy need not be treated as other disabilities since it "is not a disease at all and is often a voluntarily undertaken and desired condition." He reasoned that because pregnancy is a special problem unique to women, excluding it from coverage was not discriminatory; by contrast, including it could be construed as discriminating against men since they would not benefit by such coverage. As long as women were compensated for everything that men were, no discrimination occurred, for the sexes were being treated equally. This reasoning ignored that fact that GE's plan covered several male-specific voluntary "disabilities" such as hair transplants and vasectomies.

The *Gilbert* decision created an uproar among women's rights groups. Within a day of the decision, announcement was made of a meeting of women's, labor, civil rights, and church organizations, and a coalition was formed—the Campaign to End Discrimination Against Pregnant Workers (CEDAPW). The campaign set its sights on a legislative reversal of *Gilbert*. It was co-chaired by Susan Deller Ross, at that point with the ACLU's Women's Rights Project, and Ruth Weyand of the IUE. This marked one of the first occasions in which women labor lobbyists worked with other non-labor women's groups to develop policy in which they had common interests (Spalter-Roth 1990).[23] This coalition contained over 300 groups and included the AFL-CIO, the ACLU, the IUE, NOW and the NOW LDEF, the Religious Coalition for Abortion Rights, the Women's Equity Action League (WEAL), the National Women's Political Caucus, and the UAW.

With the support of allies in the Carter administration, the coalition began lobbying Congress for legislation to explicitly outlaw discrimination based on pregnancy. Employers resisted having to absorb the costs of covering pregnancy disability, and groups such as the U.S. Chamber of Commerce, the National Association of Manufacturers, the National Retail Merchants Association, the American Retail Federation, and the Health Insurance Association of America lobbied vigorously against the proposed bill. But the feminist-labor coalition was victorious, and their efforts resulted in the passage of the Pregnancy Discrimination Act (PDA) in 1978. Because the legislation took a seemingly pro-motherhood stance, even antiabortion groups such as American Citizens Concerned for Life favored it because they saw it as encouraging women to have children rather than opt for abortions. In a striking illustration of the "strange bedfellows" adage, the ACCL was allied with the National Abortion Rights Action League (NARAL) in this legislative effort.

The Pregnancy Discrimination Act amended Title VII of the 1964 Civil Rights Act to include discrimination based on pregnancy, childbirth, or related medical conditions. While the impetus for enactment of the PDA was the *Gilbert* decision concerning an employer disability plan, the Act more broadly bans disparate treatment of pregnant women for all employment purposes. Now Title VII, the accidental law that had come to play a vital role in dismantling gender-based employment barriers, was broadened to include in its purview forms of exclusion based on women's childbearing capacity.

Ironically, the first Supreme Court case to involve the PDA found a company policy to be in violation of the statute because it discriminated against men. The case was *Newport News Shipbuilding & Dry Dock v. EEOC*[24] in 1983, and involved differential pregnancy benefits for female employees and the wives of male employees. A male employee brought suit, and then the United Steelworkers followed with a similar charge on behalf of other men at the company. Amici supporting the company included the Chamber of Commerce, Emerson Electric, the National Railway Labor Conference, and the Equal Employment Advisory Council (EEAC). The Chamber and the EEAC would turn up again on the side of Johnson Controls in the case study below. Supporting the union and the EEOC were the United Teachers–Los Angeles, the American Association of University Women, and the AFL-CIO. The AFL was represented by, among others, Marsha Berzon, who would later serve as lead counsel at the Supreme Court level for the UAW in the *Johnson Controls* case (and now serves on the Ninth Circuit Court of Appeals).

The PDA stated that pregnancy could not be treated less favorably than other disabilities, but left open the question of whether it could be treated *more* favorably. This debate would be addressed by the Supreme Court nearly ten years after the act's passage in *California Federal Savings & Loan v. Guerra*,[25] which concerned mandatory reinstatement of female employees returning from childbearing leave when such reinstatement was not guaranteed to employees returning from other disabilities. In its decision, the Court essentially held that pregnancy may be treated different from other conditions if "different" equals better, but not if it equals worse.

Perhaps even more significant than the actual decision was the rift that this case created in the women's rights community, characterized by many as the "East Coast–West Coast" split. The classic disagreement between "equal treatment" and "special treatment" feminists resurfaced, as these legal activists were bitterly divided over how pregnancy should be treated.

The East Coast, or equal treatment wing, urged that pregnancy be treated no better and no worse than other conditions, as they were afraid of the potential implications of revisiting "special" or "protective" measures for women that had historically proved to be quite restrictive. Proponents of this view that filed briefs in the *California Federal Savings & Loan* case were the ACLU WRP, the NOW LDEF, the Women's Law Project, the National Women's Law Center, and the Women's Legal Defense Fund (WLDF). The West Coast faction held that this approach ignored the very real differences between men and women associated with pregnancy and that it was more harmful to women to ignore their pregnancy-related needs. Groups on this side of the issue included Equal Rights Advocates, the California Teachers Association, the Mexican-American Legal Defense and Education Fund (MALDEF), the Northwest Women's Law Center, and the San Francisco Women Lawyers Alliance. Virtually all of these groups would be reunited in opposition to a different manifestation of pregnancy discrimination— fetal protection policies.

PROTECTION FOR ALL: THE EMERGENCE OF OCCUPATIONAL SAFETY AND HEALTH POLICY

Before turning to the advent of fetal protection policies, which really marked the next iteration of employer practices designed to restrict women's employment, a brief digression is in order to set the development of federal occupational health and safety policy alongside this account of policy developments over women's rights in employment. As the preceding discussion illustrated, the tension between women's roles as the bearers of children and as participants in the paid labor force has a long history, as does the evolving relationship between women and organized labor. When the conflict reemerged in the context of corporate fetal protection policies in the late 1970s and early 1980s, it did so in an era with a new federal regulatory dimension.

Occupational Safety and Health as a Federal Concern

Until 1967 occupational safety and health policy was primarily within the purview of the states, with little federal involvement. Moreover, enforcement of state regulations was weak, in part due to fears of driving away businesses (Mendeloff 1979). There was a Bureau of Occupational Safety and Health within the Department of Health, Education, and Welfare (HEW), but it was a small research office and had no regulatory authority. By the close of the 1960s, however, this would all change. "Occupational safety and health became a political issue in the 1960s as a result of the intersection of a complex set of social forces, including rank-and-file discontent over work, union efforts to reform existing state programs, middle-class movements for environmentalism and consumer product safety, and White House interest in the development of a new policy agenda" (Noble 1986).

In 1967 the Department of Labor included a proposal for a federal occupational safety and health bill in a package of legislative proposals submitted to the White House, commencing the process that would eventually result in the 1970 Occupational Health and Safety Act. President Johnson's 1968 State of the Union Message signaled that occupational safety and health was to become part of his program that year (Kelman 1980). Following the presidential message, the administration's occupational safety and health bill was introduced into Congress. Hearings were held in committees in both houses, beginning on February 1, 1968, in the House in a subcommittee of the Education and Labor Committee.

It was at this point that interest group involvement began, which took the expected form of unions versus business groups. Representatives from many international unions, as well as George Meany for the AFL-CIO, testified in favor of the bill; Chamber of Commerce and National Association of Manufacturers representatives argued against it. The Chamber claimed that unions were attempting to create a labor "czar" with potentially lethal power over U.S. business, and in its magazine *Nation's Business* warned that unemployed welfare clients would become OSHA inspectors to seek revenge on American capitalism.[26] Despite this initial interest on the part of the administration, Congress, and interested political groups, the occupational safety and health issue became overshadowed by the turbulent events of 1968 (including Johnson's withdrawal from the presidential race) and the bill was not reported out by either chamber.

The legislation was reintroduced in Congress in 1969 by Democrats who had initiated it the year before. By now, however, there was a Republican administration in office, which countered with its own version of an occupational safety and health bill. The administration version differed from the Democratic one in several ways, including the organizational form of the regulating authority and the process of setting penalties for violations. The Republican measure was designed in part to lure blue-collar workers over to their party from the Democratic Party, which was increasingly being identified with the radical left. With the introduction of a parallel Republican measure, the impetus was present for legislation to be enacted in some form. Business groups that had opposed the legislation the previous year came out in favor of the administration's bill, while unions increased their commitment to the original Democratic version.

Occupational safety and health became a divisive partisan issue in Congress, where Republicans boycotted House Education and Labor Subcommittee sessions in an attempt to keep the Democratic bill from being reported out. Floor fights ensued in both houses over the major controversial differences between the two proposed bills, including where to locate the regulating authority, how centralized that authority would be, who would set standards and who would enforce them. Votes on amendments were highly partisan. However, the final bill that was voted on after the amendment process—a bill that resembled the Democratic more than the Republican version—was approved 384–5 in the House and 83–3 in the Senate in mid-December of 1970. Having publicly committed itself to the issue of occupational safety and health, the administration did not want to oppose passage of federal legislation; President Nixon signed the Occupational Safety and Health Act on December 29, 1970. The Occupational Safety and Health Administration (OSHA) became an agency within the Department of Labor, headed by an Assistant Secretary of Labor for Occupational Safety and Health, one of seven presidentially appointed assistant secretaries for Labor.

While the major push for occupational safety and health legislation came from unions, whose membership was most directly affected, other forces allied themselves with this agenda as well, both directly and indirectly, by pushing other related social policy changes.

> As they did in the movements for consumer product safety and environmental regulation, middle-class reformers and radicals played a role in the demand for workplace regulation. . . . By calling attention to noneconomic issues and the indifference of many industrial corporations to the environmental effects of their market activities, [writers and reformers] prepared public opinion for workplace reform. . . . [I]n coalition with labor groups, environmental and public-interest lobbyists intervened at key junctures in the legislative battle over the OSH Act and helped mobilize wavering senators and representatives. The public health professionals and medical doctors who worked with unions and rank-and-file workers were particularly influential because they were able to counter the antistatist views of the industry-oriented private professional organizations. (Noble 1986, 77)

The combined efforts of progressive social forces[27] and technical experts (public health and medical professionals) that bolstered the unions' efforts toward attaining health and safety protections through legislation provide a telling backdrop for the later litigation over workplace reproductive hazards, which also involved organized labor and the support of many of these same forces and professionals (see chapter 4).

The OSHA Lead Standard

OSHA is generally charged with two functions: promulgating standards regarding workplace conditions and conducting inspections to monitor compliance with these standards. The OSH Act states that for toxic substances or other harmful physical agents, OSHA "shall set the standard which most adequately ensures, to the extent feasible, on the basis of the best available evidence, that no employee will suffer material impairment of health or functional capacity even if such employee has regular exposure to the hazard dealt with by such standard for the period of his working life."[28] This language, particularly the phrase "to the extent feasible," both grants OSHA a considerable degree of discretion and virtually ensures a legal challenge when standards are proposed, as employers and unions have continually disagreed on how to define feasibility.

At its inception, the agency adopted wholesale a number of existing federal and industry consensus standards. Because the process of developing a standard is so complex and time-consuming, very few new ones have been adopted by OSHA. Between 1971 and 1984, fifteen standards were implemented, and not all of them actually set exposure levels.[29] The effect has been that only a handful of toxins are regulated, while there are approximately 2,000 known or suspected carcinogens at use in the workplace (Noble 1986, 177–80).

Until the late 1970s, OSHA could find no friends among either labor or business groups. Employers have always opposed the imposition of health and safety standards, which are costly to implement and whose effectiveness they question. Prior to 1977, labor groups criticized the agency for not being stringent enough in passing and enforcing regulations. However, in 1977 President Carter appointed Dr. Eula Bingham, a cancer researcher with close ties to the trade union movement, as head of OSHA. This, combined with increasing political hostility to government regulation, served to bring organized labor into the role of defender of the beleaguered agency. During this time, unions had suffered political setbacks in labor law reform and on other issues, and subsequently defense of OSHA came to assume a prominent place in union political activity as labor refocused its efforts (Kelman 1980).

While the OSHA standard-setting process has been less than expeditious, one standard that was implemented, with a significant amount of accompanying controversy, was for exposure to lead. Originally proposed in 1974, the standard was not adopted in its final form until four years later. The original proposed regulation contained a provision for requiring periodic pregnancy tests for female workers, a provision that caused concern among many women's groups (Bell 1979).

Much of the debate over the proposed lead standard centered around a "rate retention" provision. Such provisions in health regulations prevent workers affected by symptoms of occupational disease from being transferred to lower-paying jobs or laid off. Not surprisingly, the Steelworkers Union and the Naderite Health Research Group supported inclusion of the rate retention provision in the 1977 hearings on the lead standard. The Lead Industries Association (LIA), the American Iron and Steel Institute, and other business groups opposed the provision. In early 1978 the LIA softened its position to favoring a modified version of the proposed standard. However, the Battery Council International, representing employers like Johnson Controls, continued to oppose the proposed rule, claiming that it "would put out of business the majority of firms in the battery industry" (McCaffrey 1982).

After a delay by the Council on Wage and Price Stability and the Council of Economic Advisors, the final standard was prepared for release on November 13, 1978. It included the controversial rate retention provision, to be phased in over five years. At the request of organized labor, it included provisions for outside review of blood lead levels (by noncompany doctors). The Health Research Group and the UAW voiced their approval of the rule, while industry groups lamented that it would be economically destructive (McCaffrey 1982). So the business and labor adversaries that had been accustomed to meeting in the legislative arena were facing one another in the rulemaking process as well, contesting industry's obligation to protect its workers from hazards. The judicial arena would be just around the corner, as the clashes over gender discrimination and health and safety policy manifested themselves in the struggle over reproductive hazards in the workplace.

After the release of the lead standard, the Labor Department (in which OSHA is located) was sued by the United Steelworkers, the Oil, Chemical, and Atomic Workers (OCAW),[30] and the Lead Industries Association (LIA).[31] The two unions claimed that the standard was inadequate, falling short on several key provisions, while the LIA, representing all industries affected by the standard, charged the opposite. The LIA challenged OSHA's rulemaking procedures, the standard's substantive provisions, and the evidence used to develop and support the standard. It argued that OSHA had exceeded its statutory authority in including the medical removal provision and had issued a standard that was too stringent (Maschke 1991, 10). The case was argued in late 1979, and in August 1980 the D.C. Circuit Court upheld the regulation as it was issued.[32] However, the ruling, and the gender-neutrality of the rule, did not prevent many companies from adopting policies excluding women from occupational exposure to lead.

FETAL PROTECTION POLICIES

During the 1970s, while the Pregnancy Discrimination Act eventually codified how childbearing was supposed to be treated in the employment context, a modified form of "protective" employment discrimination began to appear on the industrial scene, one that signaled "the emergence of a major new civil rights and civil liberties issue that poses medical, legal, economic and moral dilemmas" (Shabecoff 1979). Fetal protection policies, ostensibly designed to protect the potential or actual fetuses of female production workers, proliferated and often excluded virtually all women from a number of industrial jobs. National publicity and legal challenges to such policies at prominent companies served to bring these policies into public view.

Early Litigation

One of the first fetal protection cases to receive public attention involved the Bunker Hill Company, an Idaho mining firm. In 1975 the company adopted a policy barring women who could not prove that they were sterile from working in areas exposed to lead. The EEOC conducted an administrative investigation, upon which it asked the women concerned to recognize that lead exposure had potentially harmful effects and to agree to the company's exclusionary policy. After the Occupational Safety and Health Review Commission (OSHRC) ruled that OSHA did not have the statutory authority to investigate exclusionary policies, the agency dropped a citation against Bunker Hill (Maschke 1991, 8–9).

In 1978 American Cyanamid Company instituted a policy in its plant in Willow Island, West Virginia, that restricted jobs at the plant involving lead exposure to men or to women not capable of bearing children. Five female employees subsequently had themselves sterilized in order to retain their jobs with American Cyanamid.[33] As a result, the union representing the women at American Cyanamid, the Oil, Chemical and Atomic Workers Union (OCAW), filed suit against the company charging it with sex discrimination in employment at Willow Island.

Unlike the other cases that were brought concerning fetal protection policies, the case of *OCAW v. American Cyanamid Company* was not brought as a Title VII suit but rather as a violation of the OSH Act itself (although thirteen individual women filed a separate civil rights suit as well). After the company instituted its exclusionary policy, OSHA issued the company a citation in October 1979 for violation of the general duty clause of the OSH Act.[34] Following extensive administrative litigation,

OSHRC dismissed the citation on April 28, 1981. The Commission ruled that the hazard alleged by OSHA was not intended by Congress to be covered by OSHA, and that the choice of sterilization was due to external economic factors and not the fault of the company. The case was then appealed to federal court, where Joan Bertin of the ACLU's Women's Rights Project represented the women plaintiffs. By this time the Coalition for the Reproductive Rights of Workers (CRROW) had been formed and joined as amicus curiae supporting the union and the women; the Washington Legal Foundation filed in support of Cyanamid, as it would for Johnson Controls several years later.

During the litigation, industry asserted that engineering controls sufficient to protect fetuses were too expensive and therefore not feasible. Dow Chemical Company's director of health and environmental services, Perry Gehring, stated: "The difficulty and cost of implementing good industrial hygiene shouldn't be used as a blanket excuse to exclude women. But if the cost is going to rise exponentially to reach a certain low level for uniquely fetal toxins, then it's justified to take women out of the workplace" (Bronson 1979). Dr. Robert Clyne, Cyanamid's medical director, stated simply that "there's no practical, feasible level to protect the fetus primarily. We'd bankrupt American industry" (Bronson 1979). The D.C. Circuit ruled against OSHA and upheld the company's exclusionary policy.

As a result of interest in the issue generated by the *American Cyanamid* case, pressure grew for federal policy to counter the trend of excluding women from jobs based on their childbearing capacity (Singer 1980). The new sense of unity that had been forged between feminist activists and trade union women in the fight for the PDA continued between these two constituencies that had traditionally often found themselves at odds (Petchesky 1979). This growing activism and resistance to company exclusionary practices, and in particular the *American Cyanamid* case, was embodied in CRROW, which formed in the spring of 1979. It comprised representatives from: unions (including OCAW, which initiated the coalition, the United Steelworkers, the United Rubber Workers, the Amalgamated Clothing and Textile Workers Union, the International Chemical Workers, the Coalition of Labor Union Women, and the UAW); the women's health and reproductive rights movement (the Alan Guttmacher Institute, the Reproductive Rights National Network, Planned Parenthood, the Association for Voluntary Sterilization); and civil rights groups (NOW, the National Employment Law Project, Equal Rights Advocates, the Women's Legal Defense Fund, the Center for Law and Social Policy, and the ACLU). The coalition's purpose was to resist sex-based exclusionary policies, pressure companies to eliminate reproductive hazards affecting all workers, and devise alternative solutions (such as temporary leaves and transfers) when hazards to reproduction are encountered (Petchesky 1979, 241).

A Failed Attempt at a Regulatory Answer

This public pressure led the EEOC and the Labor Department's Office of Federal Contract Compliance Programs (OFCCP) to propose guidelines on reproductive hazards and fetal protection policies in 1980, at the tail end of the Carter administration. The guidelines were intended to prevent employers from excluding women from jobs based on reproductive risks unless the substance in question posed no similar reproductive risks to men, and would have allowed for exclusionary policies for pregnant women as a last resort only. Although it is up to OSHA to ensure that workers have safe and healthy workplaces, the EEOC is charged with preventing employers from adopting discriminatory employment practices. In this case, OSHA helped to develop the proposed EEOC guidelines on reproductive hazards and would have provided technical assistance in enforcement.

The proposed guidelines generated a tremendous amount of controversy, drawing criticism from both sides of the issue. Labor and women's rights advocates contended that they were insufficient, as they still allowed employers considerable leeway in adopting exclusionary policies. CRROW was concerned that the temporary emergency exclusion provision in the guidelines would not adequately protect women workers, as it did not provide for retention of earnings and seniority. Unions, such as the United Steelworkers, criticized the companies' insistence on trying to achieve a liability-free workplace at the expense of women (Bayer 1982b). Other supporters of the goal of the guidelines, if not the form in which they were proposed, included the American Nurses Association and the state of Massachusetts.

Industry also weighed in on the proposed rules; among those responding were the U.S. Chamber of Commerce, the Chemical Manufacturers Association, the Pharmaceutical Manufacturers Association, the Lead Industries Association, the Battery Council, AT&T, General Motors, DuPont, Dow Chemical, Exxon, Shell Oil, and Union Carbide. Business interests almost uniformly opposed the proposed guidelines, asserting that the EEOC and OFCCP were exceeding their authority and expertise, that fetal health was always more important than women's economic opportunity, that companies would be subjected to an unacceptable risk of tort liability, and that male exposure to toxins was not as much a danger as maternal exposure. Other outright opponents of the guidelines were the American Industrial Hygiene Association, the American Petroleum Institute, Air Products and Chemicals Inc., Borg & Warner Chemicals, the EEAC, Ethyl Corporation, the Mechanical Contractors Association of America, Monsanto, NALCO Chemical, Pennzoil, and the Synthetic Organic Chemical Manufacturers Association.

Because of strong opposition from business, as well as complaints from women's rights activists and labor that they were not strong enough, the guidelines were politically vulnerable. Eleanor Holmes Norton, then head of the EEOC, was reluctant to push for further action. Eventually, fearing that officials of the new Reagan administration would alter the proposed guidelines for the worse if left in pending form, advocates urged their withdrawal instead.[35] The guidelines were withdrawn as the new administration took office. Between the members of CRROW and the multitude of industry interests that weighed in on the proposed EEOC guidelines, this thwarted policy measure ranks close behind *UAW v. Johnson Controls* in the amount of interest group activity generated. Many of these groups would square off again when the failure to enact EEOC policy ensured that the issue would resurface in court.

The same year (1978) that American Cyanamid adopted its exclusionary policy, Olin Corporation implemented its own "fetal vulnerability" rule. This policy excluded all women of childbearing age, which it defined as between five and sixty-five, from jobs involving exposure to known or suspected abortifacient or teratogenic agents. When employees brought suit against the company over the policy, the Fourth Circuit Court became the first appellate court since passage of the PDA to review a Title VII sex discrimination claim based on a pregnancy exclusion. Amici for Theresa Wright (and other similarly situated workers) included: AFSCME, the ACLU, the Committee for Abortion Rights and Against Sterilization Abuse (CARASA), the Coal Employment Project, the Coalition for the Medical Rights of Women, CRROW, the Employment Law Center, Equal Rights Advocates, the International Chemical Workers Union, OCAW, Planned Parenthood, the Reproductive Rights National Network, the UAW, the United Rubber Workers, Women Employed, and the Women's Legal Defense Fund. Many of these groups were part of CRROW (which joined as an amicus party), but chose to also sign on separately. Olin was supported by the EEAC, American Cyanamid Company, the Chemical Manufacturers Association, and the Lead Industries Association.

In deciding *Wright v. Olin,* the appellate court applied the disparate impact standard in assessing Olin's exclusionary fetal protection policy, rather than considering the policy facially discriminatory, an instance of disparate treatment invoking the narrow BFOQ defense. Judged under the more lenient disparate impact standard, where the employer need only show a "valid business necessity" for the practice in question, Olin Corporation prevailed in the suit, decided in 1982.[36] The court ruled that fetuses were in the same legal class as business licensees and invitees, whose safety is a legitimate concern of the employer; the policy could therefore be considered a valid business necessity. The court also held that the Pregnancy Discrimination Act did not transform all pregnancy-based distinctions into instances of disparate treatment. The court in its decision did not mention OSHA's gender-neutral lead standard.

Johnson Controls, a manufacturer of car batteries, had instituted its own exclusionary fetal protection policy in 1982, the year that *Wright v. Olin* was decided in favor of Olin Corporation. Johnson Controls' policy prohibited women from working in jobs involving exposure to lead unless they could prove that they were unable to bear children. The company adopted the policy after several women employed there became pregnant with blood levels above 30 micrograms/dcl. This was within the limits of OSHA's lead standard, which called for a maximum level of 35, although the agency recommended that workers considering having children should maintain levels below 30. In April 1984 the United Auto Workers filed a class action Title VII suit against the company on behalf of several female workers (one of whom was sterilized in order to retain her job) and one male who attempted to obtain a temporary transfer when he wished to become a father. The U.S. District Court for the Eastern District of Wisconsin granted summary judgment for the company on January 21, 1988, employing the reasoning of the *Olin* decision.[37]

On October 3, 1988, the EEOC published its first "Policy Guidance on Reproductive and Fetal Hazards," consistent with the Commission's pattern of following the lead of the courts in fashioning its own policy. The guidelines declared that any exclusionary practice based on a reproductive hazard that is limited to one sex is unlawful under Title VII. They addressed the applicability of the more lenient "business necessity" defense in challenges to fetal protection policies, stating that in order to meet this defense employers must demonstrate that a substantial risk to the fetus exists and that it occurs only through maternal exposure, and that there are no less restrictive alternatives to exclusion of women from the workplace.

The *Johnson Controls* decision from Wisconsin was appealed by the UAW to the Seventh Circuit. At this point, interest group involvement began, with the American Public Health Association, the ACLU, and the Employment Law Center supporting the UAW as amici. Sitting en banc, the court on September 26, 1989, affirmed the Wisconsin District Court's summary judgment for Johnson Controls and ruled 7–4 in favor of the company.[38] The decision stated that the fetal protection policy was "reasonably necessary to the industrial safety-based concern of protecting the unborn child from lead exposure." The Seventh Circuit employed the reasoning adopted by the Supreme Court in the recently decided case of *Wards Cove Packing Co. v. Atonio*[39] and placed the burden of proving discrimination on the employees challenging the fetal protection policy. It stated, in effect, that while the company must indicate a valid business necessity for the questioned policy, it is up to the employee to disprove the company's claim.[40]

The decision was accompanied by strong dissents from two of the most conservative members of the court, Judges Easterbrook and Posner. Judge Easterbrook called the case "likely the most important sex-discrimination case in any court since 1964, when Congress enacted Title VII." The dissenters argued that "fetal protection" policies are facially discriminatory and should be held to the narrow BFOQ standard.

In January 1990 the EEOC issued additional policy guidance on reproductive hazards in response to the Seventh Circuit's decision in *Johnson Controls*. The guidelines, which essentially instructed EEOC compliance officers outside of Seventh Circuit jurisdiction to disregard the court's ruling, were issued just before the *Johnson Controls* case was appealed to the Supreme Court. Supplementing those issued in 1988, the new EEOC guidelines were critical of the Seventh Circuit's ruling and rejected the court's finding that the burden of proof should be on the employee. The EEOC stated that fetal protection policies were facially discriminatory and that the employer should be held to a narrower BFOQ defense, rather than that of business necessity. The agency's guidelines indicated that in cases that it handles, employers will be required to show that such policies are reasonably necessary to the normal operation of their business, based on objective evidence (a supposed good faith intention of protecting employees' offspring or attempting to avoid liability would be an insufficient defense). In March the Supreme Court granted certiorari in *Johnson Controls*.

Before the High Court was to consider the case, however, two other cases on the issue of fetal protection policies were decided. The first, decided at the end of February 1990, came in the California Court of Appeal and also involved Johnson Controls.[41] The second was a Sixth Circuit case, *Grant v. General Motors Corporation*, decided in July,[42] a ruling that prompted the litigants in the pending *Johnson Controls* case to file additional briefs to the Supreme Court. In both of these cases, the respective courts applied the more stringent disparate treatment standard in reviewing the companies' fetal protection policies, and found that they failed to meet the narrow BFOQ defense.[43] Like *Johnson Controls* and the earlier *American Cyanamid* and *Olin* cases, these two cases also involved exposure of employees to lead.

On October 10, 1990, the Supreme Court heard oral arguments in *International Union, UAW v. Johnson Controls.* The court issued its unanimous 9–0 decision the following March, attracting considerable media attention. The ruling held that the company's policy was facially discriminatory and classified employees on the basis of potential for pregnancy, which constitutes explicit discrimination under Title VII as amended by the Pregnancy Discrimination Act (PDA). Justice Harry Blackmun's opinion for the court stated that even a benevolent motive such as protecting employees' offspring does not negate the discriminatory effect of the policy, and that the BFOQ standard must apply. He stated that Title VII's BFOQ provision, the PDA, legislative history and case law all prohibit employer discrimination based on the capacity to become pregnant, and that unconceived fetuses are neither customers nor third parties whose safety is essential to the operation of the business. The decision went on to assert that the company's professed concerns for the next generation do not establish sterility as a bona fide occupational qualification, and that therefore the fetal protection policy could not meet the BFOQ defense. The opinion also noted that the employer's possible tort liability for damage to a fetus and the associated costs do not figure into the decision, that the incremental costs of hiring members of one sex do not justify discrimination.

Although the decision was 9–0, the justices were not entirely unified in their reasoning. Four justices wrote two concurring opinions, in which they stated that not all such fetal protection policies would necessarily fail Title VII scrutiny. Justices Byron White, Anthony Kennedy, and William Rehnquist asserted that some such policies could meet the BFOQ defense, and that employers could cite potential tort liability as a valid reason for exclusion of female employees. In his own concurrence, Justice Antonin Scalia also stated that costs may be taken into consideration when ruling on a BFOQ defense.

Women's rights groups and unions hailed the decision as a victory. UAW President Owen Bieber declared that "this important decision by the nation's highest court is a major victory for working women and women's rights." The AFL-CIO press release similarly stated that the ruling was "a major victory for working women" and indicated that "women workers cannot be relegated to second-class status in the workforce." Business groups, on the other hand, were predictably disappointed. A National Association of Manufacturers press release stated that the "Supreme Court decision leaves employers with a difficult choice—continue operations

knowing of unavoidable risk to the unborn, or cease doing business altogether." A statement from the U.S. Catholic Conference said that it was
"disappointed that the Court did not include the safety of unborn children—our future—as a legitimate consideration in deciding Title VII
cases." Following its historical pattern of reacting to judicial policy directions, the EEOC issued a new policy guidance to reflect the Supreme
Court's ruling in *Johnson Controls.* Issued in June 1991, the new policy,
which superseded previous EEOC documents pertaining to fetal protection policies, stated that policies that exclude members of only one sex
from the workplace for the purpose of protecting fetuses could not be justified under Title VII.

CONCLUSION

The foregoing account reveals that the social and political debate around
how to address reproductive hazards in the workplace has deep roots in the
history of labor unions and women's roles in both society and the work
force. The notion of protecting women on the job, either for their own
well-being or that of their offspring, is not at all new, and has figured
prominently in the struggle of both business and organized labor to accept
women among their ranks. Once the laws changed, beginning the modern
era of sex discrimination law, other interest groups began to appear on the
policy landscape as well, joining the fray as the interpretation and implementation of these new laws went forward. Thus the cast of groups that
have appeared in the numerous examples of legislation, rulemaking, and
litigation around this issue has fluctuated but contains a number of consistent participants. The ACLU, the AFL-CIO, the UAW, and the array of
women's rights legal groups have continued to push the law to expand
women's opportunities. The Chamber of Commerce and several major
corporations, who saw their economic well being threatened, pushed back
at every turn. Through shifting venues, the underlying issue of how to
accommodate women who bear children in the male-dominated world of
paid employment has been contested by a core cast of interest groups with
varying sets of allies. These players will emerge in fuller detail in the ensu-
ing chapters. The history reviewed above will place the *UAW v. Johnson
Controls* litigation and its myriad group participants into a perspective that
will help to illustrate how group litigation fits into the overall policy
process that is highly permeated by organized interests.

3

Challenging Fetal Protection
Policies in Court

*T*he UAW and its class of plaintiffs were not the first to challenge company policies that barred fertile women from working around reproductive hazards. The Oil, Chemical, and Atomic Workers (OCAW) union had challenged American Cyanamid's similar policy in the early 1980s under the OSH Act, and the plaintiffs represented by Theresa Wright had taken on Olin Corporation under Title VII during that same era. As outlined in the previous chapter, however, neither of these groups of plaintiffs prevailed. On the heels of those defeats, the UAW initiated its own Title VII complaint against Johnson Controls, an automobile battery maker based in Milwaukee. It took six years for *UAW v. Johnson Controls* to reach the U.S. Supreme Court from its initiation in Wisconsin. Despite adverse decisions at the district and appellate levels, the UAW continued and ultimately prevailed in its quest against fetal protection policies.

This chapter will begin by exploring how the United Auto Workers came to be part of the cadre of interests working to eradicate sex-based employment barriers, primarily through accounts of the *Johnson Controls* litigation by UAW attorneys. The previous chapter provided some initial indications that the UAW was perhaps not a typical labor union with regard to women, and the discussion in this chapter further develops this theme. This will begin to demonstrate the first of the two premises of this study, that interests increasingly follow their issues through various policy venues, and often with a recurring set of strategic allies. The latter part of the chapter will examine the particular arguments that the UAW put forth in its litigation effort against Johnson Controls, to illustrate the second study premise—that issues must often be recast in the litigation arena due to the unique nature of the judiciary.

SEX DISCRIMINATION AND THE UAW AGENDA

The UAW as Atypical Labor Union

Given the historical pattern of organized labor as a whole with regard to the roles of women, it is not necessarily to a union that one would look for leadership in a campaign against discriminatory employer practices. Why then did the fetal protection policy issue come to assume a place of priority on the agenda of the UAW and of organized labor generally? One possible reason for the focus on this issue is that unions were acting pragmatically by responding to an issue that was of concern to female industrial workers, a growing and potentially vital constituency for labor as traditional membership flagged. Indeed, from 1977 to 1992, the period in which fetal protection policies proliferated and were challenged, women climbed from 28 to 38 percent of total union membership in the U.S.[1] Since World War II, women have been the fastest growing segment of both the wage-work force and the labor movement, and by the mid-1980s the percentage of women currently unionizing was greater than men, at a time when overall union membership was declining precipitously (Balser 1987; Gelb 1989). It would indeed seem logical for union leaders cognizant of these developments to begin to focus on the needs of women workers in order to render unions salient to women.

But the gender composition of organized labor, or even of the UAW itself, does not tell the whole story. Within the UAW, women's post–World War II high in terms of proportion of total membership, reached in 1975, was only 21 percent. When Title VII was passed in 1964 and the UAW began to advocate for the repeal of state protective laws, women constituted only 12.5 percent of the union's membership. And at the time that the suit against Johnson Controls was filed, the UAW itself noted in its initial complaint that women comprised no more than 10 percent of the workers in any of the involved bargaining units.

It is important to establish the distinction between the UAW and other unions and the AFL-CIO, for in the latter half of the twentieth century, union dynamics with regard to women became more complex. It would no longer be possible to make statements about "labor's" position or behavior toward women, as the policies of the various unions differed more than they had in the past. For one thing, the auto workers' union, being relatively young compared to the mainstays of the AFL, lacked a longstanding tradition of gender-based exclusion. At the time of the UAW's formation in 1937, the *West Coast Hotel v. Parrish* case had just reaffirmed the viability of gender-based state protective measures, so gender stereotypes and segregation in the labor market were by no means historical artifacts. The UAW has always seemed ahead of the curve within organized labor on gender issues.

As noted in chapter 2, the UAW had a woman president of a local in the 1940s and had been quite responsive to its female constituents when compared with other unions; in 1944 it was the first to establish a Women's Department, which attained full department status in 1955 (Gabin 1990). This is especially significant given the UAW's prominence within the labor movement and the Democratic Party (Boyle 1995). In other words, this was not a relatively marginal or radical organization supporting women's advancement in the labor force, but a dominant and fairly mainstream labor union (albeit one located within labor's more militant wing under the CIO). So, while the UAW was mainstream in one sense, it had a progressive posture on many issues in addition to women's rights. UAW president Walter Reuther co-founded Americans for Democratic Action and the Leadership Conference on Civil Rights, and was an NAACP supporter.

Despite the UAW's reputation as one of the most liberal and egalitarian labor organizations in the United States, it still would not seem an ideal setting for women's activism, as it has always been as male-dominated as any other union. The UAW's record on women has indeed been mixed. Women were marginalized in the union hall and on the shop floor and were denied equal access to leadership positions, and gender equality never became a central demand of the collective bargaining agenda.

And yet women's activism and union efforts on behalf of women have long been hallmarks of the history of women and the UAW (Gabin 1990). The UAW did acknowledge the problem of gender discrimination and put an advocate for women into its structure early on, and had already made some important collective bargaining gains in the interest of gender equity when the civil rights and feminist movements began to legitimize the principle. Despite limitations inherent in the male-dominated union structure and culture, union membership nevertheless served as a resource for female collective action (Balser 1987; Gabin 1990). The women in the UAW took advantage of the democratic principles of industrial unionism and its implicit challenge to sex discrimination and were able to convince the union to at least acknowledge the legitimacy of their goals (Gabin 1990). Some argue that students of the revival of feminism have overlooked the presence of feminist values, attitudes, and actions in a place and time in which they were assumed not to exist—a trade union in the period from the mid-1930s through the mid-1970s (Gabin 1990).

Setting the Stage: Taking on Protective Legislation

In the early twentieth century, protective legislation for women had in many ways symbolized a fundamental division within the women's movement, a disagreement over seeking pure equality versus recognizing and accommodating sexual differences. During the Depression and World War II this debate quieted somewhat, but was revived following passage of Title VII and renewed efforts behind the ERA in the 1960s. In the conflict over the benefits versus adverse effects of state protective laws during the late 1960s, many reformers and some labor unions sought to preserve them, while feminist activists and other unions sought to have them either invalidated by Title VII or extended to men (Babcock et al. 1975). The challenge to protective legislation applying only to women was indeed the UAW's principal strategy in the 1960s for securing equal opportunity for women (Gabin 1990).

The tangible focus of these debates was the bona fide occupational qualification (BFOQ) exception to Title VII. After several years of public pressure and several equivocal attempts at crafting an administrative policy, the EEOC decided to hold public hearings in May 1967. Among those urging preservation of gender-specific state protective laws were the AFL-CIO and many individual unions, including the IUE, the Amalgamated Meat Cutters, the Amalgamated Clothing Workers, and the ILGWU. A portion of the AFL-CIO statement follows.

> We have a major concern that benefits available to women under state labor laws be retained and that they be extended to men to the maximum extent possible. . . . Where an existing law serves a valid protective purpose but is in a form not readily appropriate for direct extension to men, our position is that such a law, benefiting significant portions of the female work force, should not be invalidated because of adverse effects on particular individuals or groups bringing charges of denial of "equal employment opportunity."

In contrast, the UAW at the same hearings testified in favor of declaring the laws in violation of Title VII. Its statement before the EEOC is telling in its variance from the AFL-CIO position and its strong language.

> Because employers have used these laws to circumvent our collective bargaining contracts and to discriminate against the women who are members of our union, the UAW has taken the position that so-called "protective" state laws—that is, those based on stereotypes as to sex rather than true biological factors—are undesirable relics of the past. . . . Now what has happened since Title VII became law? More and more employers have been able to discriminate against women because of anachronistic, so-called "protective" state

laws regulating the employment of women. . . . We are unhappy with the EEOC's performance in this area of law. Its lack of courage here has brought long neglected laws and regulations out of the woodwork. This commission's interpretation of BFOQ is too broad. The states are even worse. . . . It is a plain fact of life that the discrimination against women in the employment market is class discrimination almost as gross and as evil as race discrimination. It cannot be rectified through a faint-hearted approach. We urge the Commission to take a more positive approach to the problems presented here by state "protective" legislation and to cause Title VII to have real meaning for the women of America.

This debate over the fate of longstanding state protective laws that limited women's employment prospects does much to illuminate how even at this point the UAW was in a very different place from much of the rest of organized labor on women's roles in the work force. In addition to objecting to the continuation of protective legislation, the UAW was also directly involved in the formation of the National Organization for Women (NOW), which quickly became the premier women's rights advocacy organization; two UAW leaders were among NOW's founders. One of NOW's original goals was the elimination of discriminatory employment practices, a goal also being pursued by the UAW. The UAW was also the first large union to endorse the ERA in 1970; the AFL-CIO did not follow suit for another three years, eventually reversing its previous public opposition.

Fostering the Labor-Feminist Alliance

Another telling illustration of the UAW's relatively feminist orientation comes from its role in the founding of the Coalition of Labor Union Women (CLUW) in the mid-1970s. The concept for CLUW grew out of a meeting of trade union women in Chicago in 1973; among those in attendance were Olga Madar and Edith Van Horn of the UAW (the former was a UAW Vice President). Other unions represented included the Amalgamated Meat Cutters and Butcher Workmen, the United Steelworkers, the American Federation of Teachers (AFT), the Amalgamated Clothing Workers, and the Communications Workers (CWA). The attendees agreed to a follow-up conference, where formal plans were made to launch a national coalition of union women the following year.

At the CLUW founding convention in March 1974, Madar of the UAW was chosen as the Coalition's first president, and the UAW had the largest contingent at the convention.[2] The important relationship between labor union women and feminism was a prominent theme at the convention, where Madar emphasized the importance of feminism and working women's debt to the women's movement. She had specific kudos for NOW, WEAL, and the National Women's Political Caucus, which would all become future allies in the fetal protection policy litigation years later. The feminist movement outside the UAW helped to legitimize the quest for equality of the women inside the UAW, and provided fresh ideas and insights. However, the internal quest had been present virtually since the UAW's inception and was not a new development resulting entirely from the broader women's movement (Gabin 1990).

It is significant that CLUW strategy consistently remained committed to working within the established labor movement. By the end of the 1970s, the rest of labor was beginning to come around, as greater cooperation and links could be seen between CLUW and the AFL-CIO. Numerous unions played instrumental roles in the Coalition for the Reproductive Rights of Workers (CRROW), and there was significant collaboration between women's rights advocates and unions on OSHA and EEOC policy. By the late 1970s, the women's rights and labor communities had become allies;[3] joint efforts on reproductive health-based exclusions and comparable worth provide some of the most illustrative examples.

The Advent of Fetal Protection Policies

The UAW first confronted the reproductive hazards issue in 1976, when one employer with which it contracted adopted a fetal protection policy. The issue was debated at the International Executive Board, as it was anticipated that the issue would resurface and affect many more workers. The board was surprised to learn how little was known about the risks of low-level lead exposure. What they did find was that the clearest evidence available at that time concerned effects on male fertility. The union requested a National Institute for Occupational Safety and Health (NIOSH) study on reproductive hazards to men from lead in battery plants, which turned out to be inconclusive and was not published. Lacking evidence that there were *not* reproductive dangers to male workers, the UAW concluded that the risks present applied to both sexes, and that fetal protection policies that singled out women were discriminatory. These determinations were communicated to all of the union's locals, and the UAW took the position that the solution was not to bar women but to clean up the workplace (Graham et al. 1993). Industry, meanwhile, including Johnson Controls, was waging a strong battle against OSHA's lead standard. Thus the UAW was perhaps the first union to directly confront the issue of employer exclusions based on reproductive risk, and, recognizing the gender inequity inherent in the company policy in question, initially sought a regulatory solution.

By the late 1970s, health and safety were also firmly on the agenda of CLUW, as the national executive board made a major commitment to the issue in March 1979 (Balser 1987). A major aspect of this commitment was the fight against reproductive hazards in the workplace. When CLUW added a column on health and safety issues to its newspaper, the first column was authored by Sylvia Krekel of the Oil, Chemical, and Atomic Workers (OCAW) and devoted to reproductive damage. OCAW was the union that first challenged the fetal protection policy at American Cyanamid, doing so under the OSH Act, in a forerunner case to the UAW's Title VII challenge.

The foregoing review of how the UAW has positioned itself on women's equality in employment provides a backdrop to its eventual involvement in litigation over fetal protection policies. Contrasting its unique history to the somewhat less progressive stance taken by other sectors of organized labor renders somewhat less surprising its decision to initiate a test case for women's employment rights. Still more revealing are the views shared by individuals internal to the UAW.

Views from the Inside

Over the course of the seven years that elapsed from the initiation of the UAW's Title VII suit to the U.S. Supreme Court's decision in *UAW v. Johnson Controls,* numerous attorneys were involved in the case for the union (see Table 1). I asked each attorney for the union, as well as some affiliated with amicus organizations that worked particularly closely with the UAW, how this particular litigation effort fit within the UAW's agenda of working on behalf of its women members.

Each interview subject had a unique perspective on the role of the UAW in challenging fetal protection policies, yet several common themes emerged. The factor cited most commonly as contributing to the union's taking on the litigation was the existence of a cadre of committed, progressive attorneys among the UAW's legal staff. It was observed by nearly every UAW attorney and one outside the union that this was a critical element. Miriam Horwitz, local counsel for the UAW in Milwaukee, surmised that the presence of Jordan Rossen as legal counsel for the UAW in Detroit probably had a significant impact on the union's decision to pursue the case to higher levels of the judiciary, as he is, in her view, "very committed to women's rights" despite the fact that the union itself continues to be very male dominated.[4] Beverly Tucker, the UAW attorney in Detroit who worked on the case at the district court level, described the existence within the UAW headquarters of a number of committed attorneys with a keen

TABLE 1.

UAW Counsel

EEOC Complaint	Marley Weiss (UAW Detroit)
E. D. Wisconsin	Miriam Horwitz (Milwaukee) Beverly Tucker (UAW Detroit) Ralph O. Jones (UAW Detroit)
Seventh Circuit	Miriam Horwitz (Milwaukee) Ralph O. Jones Jordan Rossen (UAW Detroit) Carin A. Clauss (U. Wisconsin) Kenneth Loebel (Milwaukee)
Supreme Court	Marsha Berzon (AFL-CIO/San Francisco) Ralph O. Jones (UAW Detroit) Jordan Rossen (UAW Detroit) Laurence Gold (AFL-CIO/Washington) Carin A. Clauss (U. Wisconsin)

interest in discrimination policy that seized upon the case and took it forward. Tucker offered that the legal department tended to employ "people on a mission" to effect changes in labor law and working conditions, among other issues. So, while it may not have been the grand design of the UAW to pursue sex discrimination aggressively, it *was* the design of Jordan Rossen and others on the legal staff, who viewed these policies as "last vestiges of paternalism that could have begun a very slippery slope of curtailing women's behavior."[5] Ralph Jones, from the Detroit legal staff, also cited the interest of a small number of key union officials as a key factor.

When the case was appealed to the Seventh Circuit, the UAW enlisted outside counsel Carin Clauss, former Solicitor of Labor in the Carter administration and self-described "academic brought in from the outside."[6] While this was her only involvement in litigation on behalf of the UAW, she had been involved as a government official in both the OSHA lead standard and the aborted EEOC guidelines, as well as in CRROW, and so had extensive familiarity with the issues involved. Clauss believed that the presence of an exceptional internal legal staff in Detroit, including "strong women attorneys interested in Title VII," probably had a significant impact on the union's decision to litigate. Marsha Berzon, the Supreme Court litigator in this case, noted the presence of several very good lawyers at the UAW at that time who "thought this particular policy was an abomination" (interview with Marsha Berzon). Those outside the union but who nonetheless worked closely with UAW attorneys, such as Joan Bertin of the ACLU, also maintained that the decision to pursue this case was largely a leadership-driven move.

Interestingly, given the emphasis that these actors placed on progressive attorney leadership within the UAW's top leadership in Detroit, several of those involved in the case also asserted that the UAW pursued this case in large part as a response to employee grievances. Marley Weiss, who filed the initial EEOC complaint against Johnson Controls, opined that the litigation effort was initiated and pursued due to a combination of factors, including rank-and-file pressure. It was Horwitz's opinion that the union took on the case because women were complaining of not making the same wages as their male counterparts, and also because fetal protection policies were no longer viewed as acceptable in the modern era of reproductive choice. In Beverly Tucker's opinion, this was not a case of public interest lawyers with an agenda locating appropriate plaintiffs through which to further that agenda; this case arose out of bona fide employee grievances. The AFL-CIO's Berzon offered that the "original genesis of the case was that there were a lot of upset people in this particular plant." Thus it appears that it was not that the UAW legal leadership decided on its own to initiate this litigation, but rather that upon becoming cognizant of complaints within the membership about these policies, they decided to pursue it with considerable conviction.

One of the other common reasons cited for the UAW's involvement in this litigation was that it fit logically within the union's longstanding commitment to health and safety issues. It was noted by Weiss as one of a number of factors. Ralph Jones also observed that concern for the health and safety of all workers had been on the union's agenda for some time, and it had evidence of reproductive harm to male workers as well. Carin Clauss also pointed to the UAW's strong track record in the area of health and safety.

Those interviewed about the case differed in their opinions regarding the extent to which the UAW might have taken on this litigation in order to prove itself responsive to women, a key and growing membership constituency. Weiss allowed that an attempt at responsiveness to a potentially growing segment of the membership might have provided some of the UAW's reason for pursuing the case, but that it was "a minority share of the causality" (interview). She observed that the UAW is the "quintessentially internally political organization," even likening it to a municipality or political party, and that internal politics are what determines how an issue reaches the union's agenda and which issues are litigated. At the same time, she said, the UAW is actually more democratic (albeit in a "machine-dominated sort of way") than many public interest groups (such as the ACLU) in which there is little connection between the membership and the leadership and staff who are making decisions about organizational policy. Within the broader UAW agenda (outside the legal department) it was likely viewed more as a member servicing issue.

Beverly Tucker noted that the broader context at this time was a declining core industrial membership, of which the UAW was quite aware, and so it undertook a big push to organize women and focus more on their needs. The legal staff viewed their work in the area of sex discrimination as consistent with this larger-scale increase in emphasis on women's needs by the UAW. And so, like Weiss, Tucker also viewed the litigation as somewhat a response to member needs, but also as the result of an internal dynamic at UAW headquarters. Jones said that while he did not doubt that the case was litigated to some extent as a pragmatic attempt to respond to women's concerns, it was not done "just to impress women."

Of particular significance for purposes of this study, several participants in the *Johnson Controls* litigation for the UAW referred to prior work with coalitions of other organizations as another important factor in the union's decision to pursue this case. Marley Weiss cited the Coalition for the Reproductive Rights of Workers (CRROW), in which the UAW was active, as one starting point for this litigation, terming it a "conspiracy place" where the union/feminist coalition could develop strategy. CRROW was formed following passage of the Pregnancy Discrimination Act in 1978 to press for the PDA's enforcement, and its initial focus became drafting guidelines for the EEOC, the guidelines discussed in the previous chapter that were proposed and ultimately withdrawn. Weiss herself, who was with the UAW at the time; Carin Clauss, Solicitor of Labor under President Carter; and Donna Lenhoff of the Women's Legal Defense Fund were the principal drafters of those guidelines. When the issue of fetal protection policies was beginning to emerge in the late 1970s, the labor and feminist activists opposing them, fresh from their legislative victory in seeing the PDA enacted, thus turned to regulation first to seek application of the PDA's principles to the fetal protection issue. Litigation was not the initial avenue chosen. But when the EEOC failed to meaningfully deliver on its enforcement mandate with regard to women and workplace reproductive hazards, the UAW sought a federal court holding that would interpret Title VII and the PDA as proscribing fetal protection policies.

Weiss explained that during this phase there was a parallel effort among several unions, including the UAW, the Steelworkers, and OCAW, to develop bargaining positions consistent with the draft EEOC guidelines. This integration of feminist legal activists and women within these unions further exemplifies the strengthening ties between the two sectors. Weiss stated that there was a conscious effort on behalf of labor to take a positive stance in CRROW based on what had been learned through working with feminist activists for the PDA.

The roles of Marley Weiss and Carin Clauss in the case point to a key factor that likely affected not only the UAW's internal decision making regarding whether to litigate but also how it chose to litigate the case. Both are illustrative of the strong linkages in existence at that time between labor attorneys, particularly those within the UAW, and feminist attorneys outside the unions, all of whom were pursuing similar goals. Even while at the Department of Labor, Clauss had been involved with the ACLU's Women's Rights Project (WRP), and was even more so upon leaving government. She worked with Joan Bertin of the ACLU on *Wright v. Olin,* the first fetal protection policy case, and was then plaintiff's counsel in *Grant v. General Motors,* a subsequent case on the same issue.

Clauss stated that it was actually through her work with Bertin and the ACLU that she became involved with the UAW in its case, as the two became "alarmed" when summary judgment was granted to Johnson Controls by the federal district court in Wisconsin. Bertin had been of counsel to the UAW on the case, but then withdrew to coordinate the amicus activity, while Clauss became the lead attorney on the appeal to the Seventh Circuit. Clauss observed that while Weiss was a union lawyer, she was one with a strong interest in Title VII who had ties to CRROW and other women's legal groups. She was in fact "part of the network of public interest groups who were active on the issue," an involvement that "probably influenced her thinking."[7] And so, rather than considering the UAW's legal team and the active feminist attorney network as distinct and working in separate spheres, in reality there was a significant degree of connection between them through which the philosophies and strategies of each affected the other. This bears noting in particular when considering the role of the various amici, which will be explored further below.

More instrumental even than Weiss and Clauss, Joan Bertin of the ACLU's WRP was the "mastermind" behind the overall campaign against fetal protection policies who "tracked all the developments."[8] Clauss even likened the effort of Bertin and the WRP to that of the NAACP against racial segregation in education, noting that Bertin had a long-range incremental plan, one that included regulation and legislation as well, to eventually overturn these employer practices. (Bertin's role is discussed at length in the following chapter on the amici that sided with the UAW.) Bertin and the ACLU had "spent ten years programmatically investing in the issue," developing legal arguments and laying the groundwork, for it was their long-range strategic plan that *some* case would reach the Supreme Court. The case might be theirs or someone else's, but a case would go forward.[9] As it turned out, it was indeed "someone else's case" that went to the Supreme Court, but Bertin played an integral role in *Johnson Controls* nonetheless, as will become evident below and further in chapter 4. Bertin in fact allowed that part of the ACLU's strategy was to encourage greater union involvement in this litigation, as they had found their involvement in the *Cyanamid* case quite costly.

Earlier in this chapter, it was asserted that the UAW has traditionally been more progressive than organized labor as a whole, both in general and with regard to women. When discussing the case, Ralph Jones was insistent that the UAW not be lumped into an overly broad category of "labor" but rather be considered as an organization in its own right, as not all unions have the same concerns. Although at one time "everyone favored such laws," he said, he would not want the UAW to "take a presumptive hit on behalf of labor."[10] He asserted that not only is the UAW a progressive union but it is a progressive *organization* in terms of its broader social goals. Because of this, he stated, it may have been easier for the UAW to pursue this case than it would have been for other unions.

Susan Deller Ross, who had been active on these issues at the ACLU and the EEOC, echoed Jones's depiction of the UAW as somewhat unique within the family of organized labor. In her view, the UAW has indeed been one of the most progressive unions in terms of gender issues, lacking some of the paternalistic impulses manifested by other male-dominated unions and the AFL-CIO in the 1960s and 1970s. Her assessment of why organized labor in general came to support the dismantling of the protectionist policy framework that excluded women from many opportunities was that it was essentially a recognition of change that was occurring outside of their purview, making resistance increasingly futile. Ross observed that once Title VII and the EEOC were in place, women themselves recognized that there was finally a mechanism through which they could thwart the barriers that had heretofore prevented their progress in the workplace. Once women throughout the United States began to bring suits and win them, labor unions no longer had any means with which to justify their own desire to keep women confined to traditional roles and occupations. In essence, the federal courts "took it away from them as an issue," according to Ross.[11]

There were clearly a number of factors at play that brought the UAW to an active litigation posture with regard to exclusionary fetal protection policies. First, the presence of a cadre of attorneys within the UAW committed to eliminating gender discrimination, who were closely linked with public interest women's legal advocates outside the union, contributed significantly to the union's decision to pursue this litigation. Second, there were genuine grievances being articulated by affected workers, grievances that these attorneys took seriously. Third, the UAW was also proactive in the area of workplace health and safety. To the extent that the fetal protection policy issue combines elements of gender discrimination and workplace health hazards, it in fact seems natural for the UAW to involve itself in this controversy. Fourth, the union had prior experience working with women's rights activists in various coalitions working to end gender discrimination in employment. Finally, the UAW had historically been better than most unions in its treatment of women and in its stances on gender-based work practices and policies. The UAW had fought for comparable worth and for the elimination of state protective laws in the 1960s, had joined in the forming of NOW in 1966, and had endorsed the ERA in 1970. There was therefore precedent within the union to intervene on behalf of women experiencing discrimination.

THE LITIGATION STRATEGY

The reasons that the UAW trained its sights upon fetal protection policies were therefore myriad. But having deemed such policies as contrary to the interests of its female members, why did the union choose litigation in particular as the means to oppose them? The answers should yield important insights into when, why, and how groups pursue policy-oriented litigation. The group litigation literature has identified several motivations for groups to go to court, including: actually influencing a judicial outcome; gaining publicity or at least having its view presented (Vose 1972); effecting an increase in collective rights consciousness (Olson 1981); and compensating for lack of success in other arenas (Barker 1967; Cortner 1968; O'Connor 1980). In addition, there are several other possible reasons that the UAW might have believed that the courts would be a viable policy forum, including: the increasing propensity of judges to take on perceived regulatory lapses or conflicts; prior judicial actions on similar matters (O'Connor 1980; O'Connor and Epstein 1983c); and a notion that framing the conflict as an issue of economic choice would prevail in an institution committed to individual rights. It may also have had in mind a strategy to utilize extant legislation and precedent instead of pursuing new law; in fact, it had a previous model in the implementation pattern of Title VII that would encourage this view.

Johnson Controls implemented its fetal protection policy on August 9, 1982, at all of its Globe Battery divisions, the same year that the first judicial decisions upholding such exclusionary policies were handed down.[12]

While *UAW v. Johnson Controls* would eventually prove to be the definitive case on the issue, being the only one to reach the Supreme Court, several of the key players from this case were involved in other fetal protection cases in the early 1980s as well. The UAW was an amicus party in *Wright v. Olin,* the first fetal protection policy case decided, as was the ACLU, whose counsel included Joan Bertin and Carin Clauss, both of whom played critical roles in the *Johnson Controls* litigation. Bertin and the ACLU also filed an amicus brief in *Zuniga v. Kleberg County Hospital* (another fetal protection case). Marsha Berzon and Laurence Gold were among the counsel on the amicus brief of the AFL-CIO in *Newport News,* which was not a fetal protection case but the first Supreme Court case to address the Pregnancy Discrimination Act. In *Hayes v. Shelby Memorial Hospital,*[13] another fetal protection case decided in 1984, the EEOC itself filed an amicus brief, as did the ACLU and Joan Bertin again. Bertin directly represented the plaintiffs in the case of *OCAW v. American Cyanamid,*[14] decided in 1984, in which the Coalition for the Reproductive Rights of Workers (CRROW) filed an amicus brief, and she also worked with the plaintiffs in the parallel case that was decided in California under state law (see chapter 4). Finally, in *Grant v. GM,*[15] which began in 1984 with EEOC charges and was decided in 1990 while the *Johnson Controls* case was pending before the Supreme Court, Carin Clauss was the plaintiffs' attorney. The issue had clearly moved into the litigation phase by the early 1980s, and many of the actors involved in the ultimately pivotal *Johnson Controls* case thus had prior experience in these early cases.

The Case Begins

The first step taken by the workers affected by Johnson Controls' new fetal protection policy was to file grievances through their collective bargaining agreements; the first of these grievances seems to have been filed at the Owosso, Michigan, plant.[16] When this avenue proved fruitless, charges were filed by the union and several individual employees with the EEOC; they received right-to-sue notices from the EEOC in early 1984. The principal attorney on the case was Marley Weiss, UAW Assistant General Counsel, who filed the EEOC charges and was the "fact gatherer with the local union membership."[17] Weiss was quick to take ownership of the case at its outset, noting that this was "a seven or eight plant case" involving an employer policy that was at odds with the UAW's collective bargaining agreement and affected all UAW units.[18]

The UAW filed its suit on behalf of the international and nine local unions located in Ohio, Texas (2), California, Michigan, Kentucky,

Vermont, Delaware, and Georgia. The individual plaintiffs named in the suit were all members of the Bennington, Vermont; Middletown, Delaware; and Atlanta, Georgia, locals. All were female except one, a male worker who had requested and was denied a temporary transfer away from lead exposure in order to lower his blood lead level while attempting to father a child.[19]

When Weiss subsequently left the UAW, just prior to the District Court filing, Beverly Tucker, who had recently joined the UAW legal staff and had a background in employment discrimination law, continued the effort. The UAW filed its formal complaint in the U.S. District Court for the Eastern District of Wisconsin, on May 31, 1984. According to Weiss, there was some discussion as to where to file the suit, as the union had affected workers throughout the United States, but Wisconsin was chosen both because it was the location of the Johnson Controls corporate headquarters and because of the perceived suitability of that court.

In its complaint, the UAW carefully notes that each named plaintiff is represented by the UAW, and that the union and Johnson Controls have had a collective bargaining agreement in place at all times material to the suit—an agreement it contends is violated with regard to seniority, promotion, and transfer by fetal protection policies. The complaint asserts that the suit is being brought individually and on behalf of a class of employees similarly situated, and specifies subclasses for male and female employees, each of which it contends is harmed in different ways by the policies in question. The complaint also asserts that these policies violate both the OSHA General Duty clause and the OSHA lead standard, despite the fact that these regulations do not form the legal basis for the suit.

The UAW also observes that Johnson Controls "until recently . . . has discriminated on the basis of sex in hiring. Consequently, the percentage of women workers is under 10 percent in each of its production and maintenance bargaining units." The complaint also draws attention to the "embarrassment and humiliation" to which women were subjected, as "their private reproductive functions were made public without their consent," and to the fact that "female employees felt harassed and intimidated by the company's explicit declaration that women workers were not wanted at production facilities." Thus it was not only economic deprivation cited in the union's challenge but also the nonfinancial impact experienced by its women members.

Tucker stated that the plaintiffs themselves were "adamant" about pursuing the case, even when she herself expressed some initial reservations due to newly released research findings on harm from lead at lower exposure levels than previously thought. The workers, she said, understood the medical research and the potential risk; in their view, however, they weighed risk all the time and felt themselves competent to do so. None of the female plaintiffs expected to conceive a child while working at the battery plant. The male plaintiff in the case had requested a temporary transfer to lower his own blood lead levels so that he could father a child, and the company refused, which further convinced the employees that the fetal protection policy was merely a subterfuge for excluding women from jobs. Tucker said that the UAW's legal staff "knew that this case would go to the Supreme Court" because it was complex and difficult. Weiss and Tucker in particular were quite excited about it because of their interest in discrimination issues, for here was an instance of blatant sex discrimination that was having a "tremendous real impact" on workers. Nonetheless, the UAW felt that it had a greater chance of success by challenging these policies at a smaller company like Globe/Johnson Controls than at a larger company like General Motors, which also employed these rules. The core issue, Tucker noted, was paternalism in its last vestiges. For if the case had been decided the other way, the Court would have started down a very "slippery slope" of curtailing women's behavior in the name of fetal protection.[20]

Miriam Horwitz, a lawyer with a private firm in Milwaukee, performed the research and filed the class certification motion and directed the discovery process. Horwitz served as counsel of record at the District Court level, and Joan Bertin of the ACLU Women's Rights Project was of counsel as well. Horwitz conceded that she never did actually meet the local workers in the class that were party to the suit. As she termed it, "I was on the team" that brought the case forward, and she assisted Marsha Berzon with the Supreme Court certiorari petition. Weiss asserted that the case "was always meant to be run from Detroit, was always meant to be a test case, a policy case" and that using Horwitz and the local firm was routine, as they served as the UAW's local counsel. The UAW was awarded class certification for the suit in February 1985.

Appealing to the Seventh Circuit and the U.S. Supreme Court

When Tucker also left the union, Ralph Jones took over the case internally for the UAW, and it was he who performed the summary judgment briefing to Judge Warren in the U.S. District Court for the Eastern District of Wisconsin (there were no oral arguments at this stage—all was decided on briefs). When summary judgment for the company was granted in January 1988, Weiss encouraged Jones and the UAW to retain Carin Clauss of the University of Wisconsin–Madison to handle the union's appeal to the Seventh Circuit. (Horwitz and Jones remained involved counsel; Jordan

Rossen, General Counsel at the UAW in Detroit, and another private attorney in Milwaukee, were also added to the legal team.) Clauss had served as Solicitor of Labor during the Carter administration when the OSHA lead standard was promulgated, and with Weiss and others had drafted the aborted 1980 EEOC guidelines on fetal protection policies. She was also part of the team that drafted the PDA, and in addition, was at that time litigating a parallel challenge to fetal protection policies at General Motors in the Sixth Circuit. This longstanding interest in the issue, Berzon later speculated, was why Clauss and Bertin "pounced on" this case at the outset.[21] Bertin in particular represented what Berzon termed "an institutional women's movement interest" in the issue; here was now a case that could serve as the vehicle to alter policy in the direction that these longtime advocates had sought.

The UAW filed notice of its appeal to the Seventh Circuit on February 18, 1988. At this point, several outside interests that had been involved in earlier related efforts over similar employment policies joined in and began the process of widening the array of actors and the scope of conflict. There were several amici supporting the UAW that became involved at this stage and remained as the case moved to the Supreme Court: the ACLU, Queen Elizabeth Foster/Employment Law Center (the plaintiffs in a similar ongoing suit against Johnson Controls in California), and the American Public Health Association (APHA) each filed separate briefs. Joan Bertin, who was at the ACLU and had been of counsel for the plaintiffs in this case at the outset of the litigation, had withdrawn from participating directly in the case in order to coordinate the amicus activity. Because summary judgment had been granted at the District Court level, there was no trial record on which to rely on appeal, and Bertin set out to assemble a cast of amici that would bring forth the necessary information to make the union's case to the Seventh Circuit. The ACLU later filed the lone amicus brief supporting the UAW's certiorari petition to the Supreme Court, which the other parties above joined, along with a host of other groups. When certiorari was granted and the ACLU filed an amicus brief on the merits, the APHA split off again to file its own brief for reasons explained in the following chapter. (See Table 2 for a summary of the amici for the UAW throughout the litigation.)

When the case was again decided for Johnson Controls by the Seventh Circuit in September 1989 and moved to the Supreme Court level, Miriam Horwitz was no longer officially part of the litigating team (as the case had moved well beyond Milwaukee), while two AFL-CIO attorneys were added: Laurence Gold from the Washington office, and Marsha Berzon, Associate General Counsel in San Francisco, the latter of whom argued the

TABLE 2.

Summary of Amici for UAW

Level of litigation	Amicus briefs	Counsel of record
E. D. Wisconsin	None	N/A
Seventh Circuit	APHA Queen Foster/ELC ACLU	Nadine Taub Pat Shiu Joan Bertin
Petition for Certiorari	ACLU* APHA* Equal Rights Advocates* Massachusetts* NAACP LDF* NRDC New York City Bar Association* State of California TLPJ The United States/EEOC	Joan Bertin Nadine Taub Susan Deller Ross Majorie Heins Ronald Ellis Thomas McGarity Arthur Leonard Manuel Medeiros Arthur Bryant Kenneth Starr

case before the Court. As the case progressed, therefore, legal assistance was garnered from a wider geographic and organizational range.

While the attention given the case and the expertise retained to pursue it indicate the significance the union gave to the effort, Berzon herself acknowledged that when she was brought in, late in the game, there was some initial mistrust and resentment from those who had been involved earlier on.[22] Interestingly, though, such apprehension apparently was mutual. Earlier participants such as Bertin were skeptical about bringing in new counsel, while Berzon initially questioned the commitment of the UAW attorneys to some of the important gender issues at stake and, more pragmatically, their ability to litigate at the Supreme Court level, where she herself had considerable experience.[23] In addition to having Supreme Court experience, Berzon was hardly an interloper with regard to the issues at stake; she had been one of the principal drafters of the Pregnancy Discrimination Act, which amended Title VII and upon which the legal challenge in *Johnson Controls* rested. She was also counsel in the *Newport News* case in 1983, the first Supreme Court case to address the PDA. She in fact asserted that the language of the PDA was drafted specifically with just such exclusionary fetal protection policies in mind. Berzon, though, termed herself "sort of a technician in this case" who was brought in essentially for her Supreme Court experience, and she acknowledged that she was able to draw on the invaluable expertise of the earlier litigators. She also did not meet the actual plaintiffs until late in the process, but said that once she had the chance to hear their personal perspectives, on aspects like the violation of privacy that they felt, it helped her to focus her arguments.

Berzon offered an opinion as to why their petition for certiorari to the Supreme Court was successful. While she believed that the petition was good on its merits, and that this undoubtedly had an impact on the decision, she also conceded that there were likely political factors at play. For example, there was speculation that Judge Easterbrook of the Seventh Circuit, who wrote one of the dissents when Johnson Controls' policy was upheld by that court, crafted his dissent in order to ensure that the Supreme Court would take the case up, perhaps to further his own ambitions to the High Court. In addition, Berzon thought it unlikely that it was coincidental that the EEOC released its revised policy guidance on fetal protection policies, in which the commission "finally got its act together and said such policies were disparate treatment," two days prior to the deadline for filing the certiorari petition. In her view this serendipitous timing served to effectively substitute for the commission filing an amicus brief, which is rare for the government to do at the certiorari stage.

When this litigation campaign began, a relatively short period of time had elapsed since women's rights and labor advocates (and others) had successfully battled for the 1978 Pregnancy Discrimination Act. According to Berzon, the legislation was intended to encompass employer practices like fetal protection policies, but clearly did not deter companies from adopting them. The PDA itself had amended Title VII, which had eventually proved to be an effective tool against sex discrimination once the EEOC and the courts together came to interpret the BFOQ in a way that would not render the statute useless. In other words, once Title VII was in place and subsequent regulatory enforcement proved tepid and ineffective, favorable court decisions (such as *Rosenfeld*) helped to render the legislation useful to women. A similar pattern was emerging with this new iteration of discriminatory policies. Once enacted, the PDA was not immediately effective at eradicating discrimination based on childbearing capacity, and the EEOC proved unable to help (much as it had been both unwilling and unable in the 1960s to take on basic gender discrimination). Rather than pursue still more legislation (which would have in effect amended an amendment), the feminist-union coalition sought a favorable reading of law already in place.

There are also features unique to the UAW as a labor union that influenced the path of this issue into court. In their 1985 survey of interest groups regarding their litigation activities, Scheppele and Walker (1991) found that while only 55 percent of responding groups said they used the courts for some reason, 100 percent of responding unions said that they did. "Trade unions . . . have strong reasons to use the courts. Because unions are governed by an elaborate regulatory apparatus that relies heavily on court interpretation and because the relationship between unions and management is largely contractual, leading any breach into at least arbitration and often litigation, we would expect to see unions using the courts extensively to achieve their policy goals" (Scheppele and Walker 1991, 169). Indeed, the early stages of what became the Supreme Court case of *UAW v. Johnson Controls* were union grievances filed under collective bargaining agreements. The same authors also identified several other explanatory factors associated with the importance of litigation to groups that apply to the UAW, including: having resources to wage a litigation campaign; the degree to which a group's fortunes were affected by the shift to a Republican presidency in 1980; the degree to which a group is generally active in seeking political influence; and the intensity of policy conflict. As will become strikingly evident at the Supreme Court level, this issue indeed invoked an intense policy conflict, drawing in myriad groups with an interest in the outcome.

Judith Kurtz of Equal Rights Advocates, one of the amici on the side of the UAW, offered that the strategic decision to pursue litigation is often closely tied to the present constitution of the relevant legislative body. She observed that, at the time of this case, the UAW was having difficulty moving any socially progressive legislation in Congress, which may have made the judiciary seem a more promising venue. Also, she said, groups recognize that sometimes a loss in court is a necessary prerequisite to getting the attention and sympathy of legislators. A clear example of this was the *Gilbert* decision that mobilized the coalition of forces that got the PDA enacted within two years. Joan Bertin added that whether or not to adopt a litigation strategy depends upon the issue itself and the receptivity of various institutions (see Scheppele and Walker 1991), which for courts includes whether it is the state or federal court system and the existence of relevant prior decisions. For individual organizations, resources and a relationship with potential plaintiffs are also relevant practical considerations; in this case, the UAW indeed had both.

Part of litigation strategy, after deciding to undertake it, is deciding how to pursue it, including whether or not to actively solicit amici. Ralph Jones of the UAW offered that, depending on the issue, the UAW will at times recruit amici when it is involved in litigation, as they might "get more attention with more groups." Such solicitation did occur in the *Johnson Controls* case, as Jones, Berzon, Clauss, and Bertin strategized together and divided up the work of retaining sympathetic interest groups. Berzon also stated that the AFL-CIO will often actively solicit amici in litigation efforts. Bertin explained how a litigating party, like the AFL in this case, will line up an array of supportive amici among whom to parcel out key arguments that need to be made to the Court, but that the main party does not have room to address in its own briefs.

In discussing the differences between various political forums, particularly between the legislative and judicial processes, Bertin stated that they are not necessarily as different as one might think. All political battles are adversarial, she said, and involve advocates for each side building a case—the format in which that case is presented is what varies. She observed that while theoretically the regulatory arena is the preferred forum for public health issues, in reality this may not always be true, as all policy forums have become adversarial in recent times. Regulatory policy, once crafted, frequently winds up in litigation anyway. Even if the legislature has attempted to weigh completely all of the competing interests in a policy issue and devise a solution, it is likely that those whose interests did not carry the day will turn to another venue to seek relief. Frequently, Congress avoids making clear statements in the first place, virtually ensuring that the conflict will move to the regulatory or judicial arena.

Thus, for the UAW, there were many reasons for pursuing policy change around fetal protection policies through litigation. There was an experienced group of attorneys, both within the union and outside, who were committed to eradicating discrimination and possessed prior experience litigating the same issue. This case was viewed as a policy or test case from the outset. There were also many genuinely aggrieved plaintiffs who had experienced directly the impact of this company policy and were eager to pursue a remedy. The existence of an established course of action for the union to follow for alleged contract violations (in this case seniority, promotion, and transfer requirements in the collective bargaining agreement) also led to the courts. In addition, the controversy over fetal protection policies came on the heels of enactment of the Pregnancy Discrimination Act, which was thus available as a statutory basis for a legal challenge. The EEOC was providing weak enforcement and Congress was not receptive to new legislative policy, and so enforcement through the judiciary became the avenue of choice.

REPRESENTATION, RELATIONSHIPS, AND COALITION POLITICS

A central goal of this study is to explore the relationship between litigating organizations, be they labor unions or public interest law groups, and the

plaintiffs in the cases through which these groups wage their political battles. For one of the critical features of litigation—one of several that set it
apart from other forms of policymaking—is that groups cannot simply
decide to seek relief through the courts without a live case involving
affected plaintiffs. Critics of public interest law have accused organizations
of seeking out clients to use in their litigation campaigns, depicting the
process as almost sinister at times (Wasby 1983). Litigation for policy
change invokes questions of representation on a number of levels, as the
litigating organization often has members that it represents on an ongoing
basis, as well as individual named plaintiffs in a discrete case. Amicus parties add yet another level of interests and individuals at least ostensibly
being represented in the process of litigating what is technically one dispute between the named parties.

In this case, at least, "seeking out plaintiffs" does not seem to describe
the process through which the UAW and AFL-CIO attorneys obtained the
aggrieved workers for this suit. Joan Bertin stated that once companies
implement policies like that of Johnson Controls or American Cyanamid,
it is easy for an organization like the ACLU or a sympathetic union to find
plaintiffs. In fact, the plaintiffs will find *them* once apprised of their rights
in a given situation. Bertin explained that she had been asked to address the
women at American Cyanamid concerning their rights to a cause of action;
once they were aware of their options, the women asked her to represent
them in such a case. Bertin then served as co-counsel with the workers'
union, the Oil, Chemical, and Atomic Workers (OCAW), on the litigation.
Bertin noted that public interest law critics characterize this process of
spreading information and informing workers of their rights, about which
they frequently are unaware, as "creating problems." But the *Johnson Controls* case began initially with grievances filed at the local level.

Susan Deller Ross depicted the process as even less orchestrated than
did Bertin. As she put it, a lot of major suits such as this occur via "happenstance—an employer passes a stupid policy, there are local women who
get upset and decide to do something and they happen to get in contact
with the right people. It's not lawyers finding an ideal plaintiff out there,
typically, rather it is women with a sense of grievance connecting up with
organizations; as it progresses up higher in the legal framework people see
what the issues are and run with it. . . ."[24] Ross's portrait of typical litigation
supports Wasby's findings regarding the seemingly orchestrated litigation
campaigns of the NAACP that were in fact much less controlled than is
commonly perceived.

In *Johnson Controls*, the case appears to have been quite worker-driven,
as it was the employees, upset by the company's policy, who approached

their union for a remedy. For all of the many reasons outlined above, the UAW was receptive to their complaint, and due to the presence of a legal staff eager to take on the challenge, was also well prepared to do so. Beverly Tucker, one of the involved UAW counsel, described how the workers themselves were adamant about pursuing the case even when she herself had doubts about their chances of prevailing.

Of course, once the case moves through several stages of appeal and additional counsel is brought in from as far away as Washington, D.C., and San Francisco, the ties between actual plaintiffs and attorneys grow more tenuous. At this point, it might be fair to say that the broader agenda—in this case, elimination of a type of discriminatory employment policy—takes over from obtaining relief for a particular group of clients. Of course, to the extent that they remain members of the class on whose behalf the case is being litigated, these plaintiffs will benefit from the outcome. But Marsha Berzon herself admitted that she did not meet any of the plaintiffs in this case until late in the process, and that eventually doing so helped her to somewhat redirect her thinking about the issue and her approach to the case. She was, in effect, reminded of who she was representing and why.

The UAW was, of course, not alone in its quest to eliminate fetal protection policies, nor was Johnson Controls alone in defending them. Both had allies of many stripes, with a range of constituencies and agendas of their own (see Table 3). The "friends of the UAW" will be the focus of the next chapter, while those supporting the company are the subject of chapter 5. It is worth noting some of the significant relationships here, however, as coordination between litigants and amici has become a common strat-

TABLE 3.

Amicus Curiae Briefs in *UAW v. Johnson Controls*

Amici for the UAW	Amici for Johnson Controls
American Civil Liberties Union*	Chamber of Commerce of the United States
American Public Health Association*	Concerned Women for America
Equal Rights Advocates*	Equal Employment Advisory Council*
State of Massachusetts*	Industrial Hygiene Law Project
NAACP LDF*	National Safe Workplace Institute
Natural Resources Defense Council	Pacific Legal Foundation*
New York City Bar Association*	U.S. Catholic Conference
State of California	Washington Legal Foundation
Trial Lawyers for Public Justice	
The United States and the EEOC	

* Indicates brief contained multiple parties; table shows lead group on each brief only.

egy with significant implications for the process of interest representation in the judiciary. Rather than "friends of the court," the true modern function of amici curiae is much more to be friends of the litigating parties, who often utilize outside groups to make additional arguments or present more information than they are able to do within the confines of their own briefs.

The closest relationship between the UAW and any of its amici was certainly with the ACLU, as Bertin, counsel of record for the ACLU brief, had actually been of counsel to the UAW in the early stages of the litigation and withdrew to perform the role of amicus coordinator, working closely with Berzon and the other AFL-CIO and UAW counsel. As outlined above, the traditional division between trade unions and women's rights activists has been bridged significantly in the past twenty to thirty years, albeit with various unions and the AFL-CIO progressing at different paces. In addition to the plaintiff United Auto Workers, nine other unions or union organizations were involved in the *Johnson Controls* case as amici: the Amalgamated Clothing & Textile Workers Union; the American Federation of State, County, and Municipal Employees (AFSCME), which had signed on in the *Wright v. Olin* case challenging fetal protection policies; the Coalition of Labor Union Women (CLUW); the Communications Workers of America; the International Chemical Workers Union; the National Union of Hospital and Health Care Employees; the Oil, Chemical, and Atomic Workers Union (OCAW); the Service Employees International Union; and the United Mine Workers of America. CLUW had adopted health and safety concerns as part of its agenda in the late 1970s, and was committed to fighting gender discrimination. OCAW had been down this same litigation path before in the early 1980s, to no avail. The Communications Workers, like the UAW, had been fairly progressive relatively early on (in the 1950s and 1960s) in its acceptance of women (Kenneally 1978), and supported the litigation effort against General Electric that led eventually to the PDA. The Chemical Workers Union had been an early ERA supporter and also was an amicus in *Wright v. Olin*. All of the labor union amici were co-signatories to the ACLU brief authored by Joan Bertin—an attorney with the amount of experience in this area like Bertin knew which sympathetic unions to tap as allies.

Berzon also worked closely with Susan Deller Ross, the author of the brief filed under the sponsorship of Equal Rights Advocates and several other women's rights legal organizations. Like the other technical issues focused on by other amicus briefs, Berzon and Ross felt that an in-depth treatment of the Pregnancy Discrimination Act, including its legislative history and intent, was necessary, as this was the primary statute relied upon in the lawsuit.

Berzon worked closely with Bertin throughout the litigation, and thus was quite cognizant of the arguments being presented by both the ACLU and the APHA (as Bertin crafted both documents—see chapter 4 discussion). But, in a case of this complexity and high profile, it would take more than one or two supporting briefs to fully round out the arguments that the UAW side wished to make, especially given the dearth of information in the lower court records. Looking back on the case, Berzon referred to the briefs by the Natural Resources Defense Council (NRDC), Trial Lawyers for Public Justice, and the state of Massachusetts as being critical in helping to advance the UAW's side in the case. These briefs set forth the scientific, tort liability, and public health impact arguments that provided essential context to the Title VII arguments being made by the UAW itself. The union, however, avoided alerting the Court to the degree of coordination among its amici, making only one reference to any of them in its own briefs. The reference, in the UAW's first brief on the merits, was to the NRDC's brief that focused heavily on the animal studies issue. The union referenced the issue in its own brief, signifying its importance, and referred the Court to the more detailed (and technically credible) explanation put forth by the NRDC.

When discussing amicus curiae briefs, Berzon offered that those filed by government entities can be particularly critical and influential. Of the ten briefs filed in support of the UAW, three were from governments (state or federal): California along with its Fair Employment and Housing Commission filed a brief, another was filed by Massachusetts and a host of other states, and the United States with the EEOC filed one as well. Of course, it is not possible to determine if these briefs influenced the outcome of the case, but it is significant that the plaintiff side had the support of several levels of government. Their positions and contributions to the overall effort will be examined in the following chapter, as will the roles and arguments of all of the amici for the UAW; the amicus supporters of Johnson Controls will be the subject of chapter 5. Those chapters will look at this litigation from a different vantage point, that of outside organizations who saw the case as a vehicle through which to pursue some aspect of *their* policy agendas. Their connections to the plaintiffs and company that were parties to the case were of course even less direct than those between the plaintiffs and some of their own attorneys in the later stages of the litigation. The amici each had constituents of their own who were the most removed of all from the parties, invoking intriguing questions about the nature of representation in public interest litigation.

WAGING THE BATTLE IN COURT

What actual arguments did the union present to the Court in order to advance its cause? Vose (1959) observed that minoritarian politics, a descriptor for group litigation, reaches past the limits of the political process for direct appeal to constitutional principles (or existing legislation) through litigation. This enables a group to bring its claim before a court, rather than having to attain an electoral or legislative majority to enact new policy. But it also serves to limit the bases on which claims can be made. To what extant law did the UAW appeal in advancing its case?

In the UAW's petition for a writ of certiorari to the Supreme Court (filed January 29, 1990), the union focused on the proper application of Title VII law, including who should bear the burden of proof, which defense is available to the employer, and the applicability of scientific toxicity studies on animals. The brief asserted that the lower courts had "left the law in total disarray," appealing to one of the most basic reasons that the Supreme Court would grant certiorari: reconciling conflicting circuit court decisions. But it also attempted to emphasize the significance of the case to women's employment opportunities, and even to the ability of the medical community and federal agencies to rely upon animal studies where necessary. Johnson Controls attempted to counter these arguments in its March 1 Brief in Opposition by stating that unanimous federal judicial precedent held that fetal protection policies were indeed permitted in certain circumstances, and that the disagreements over allocation of the burden of proof and the proper Title VII defenses allowed were inconsequential. The company also attempted to forestall some of the UAW's arguments procedurally (particularly the issue of possible less discriminatory alternatives to exclusion) by stating that they had been waived below, and undertook to portray itself as a model employer that had actually been ahead of the curve on industrial safety. The UAW, in its subsequent reply brief (March 15), stated that Johnson Controls was not taking issue with the central matters warranting review, and that indeed the defense allowed and the allocation of the burden of proof were quite material to the outcome. The union also used the opportunity to note the outcome of the now-decided *Johnson Controls v. California FEHC* case, which was not in the company's favor. The brief also noted the statement contained in the EEOC's most recent policy guidance that called for judicial resolution of the issue, thus further inviting the High Court to accept the challenge and intervene.

The Supreme Court granted certiorari on March 26, 1990. In its first brief to the Court on the merits of the case, filed on June 1, 1990, the UAW repeated the questions for review that it had put forth in its petition for certiorari—the proper application of Title VII and the validity of animal studies. The union then claimed that the policy in question was facial discrimination on the basis of sex, and that it could not be justified as a BFOQ. The brief went on to state that between their economic dependence upon their jobs and these exclusionary policies, women were put in a situation of having to choose between their livelihood and their right to have offspring, a choice that men were not required to make. The UAW cited the PDA as evidence that Congress expressly intended to forestall such a situation, thus using already codified policy to invalidate these employer practices that adversely affected their women members. Similarly, the union pointed to OSHA's express rejection of different lead exposure levels for men and women, and accused Johnson Controls of dismissing OSHA's conclusions. The UAW thus aligned itself with another government agency and existing regulatory as well as statutory law to bolster its claims against the employer. Even an allegedly benign purpose, such as protection of potential offspring, does not render an illegal policy legitimate, according to the UAW brief—the only relevant criterion is ability to perform the job. The brief also again mentioned the California case that ruled that fetal protection policies violated that state's equal employment opportunity laws, invoking additional existing favorable law.

Johnson Controls' reply brief of July 19 attempted to meet the UAW on the territory that it had staked out, by offering different interpretations of the same laws cited by the union. The company in fact went even further and cited several of the amicus briefs filed in support of the UAW, including the ERA, APHA, and U.S./EEOC's, thereby taking on not only the union but its litigation allies as well, and on the very issues to which they brought particular expertise. The company criticized the APHA for claiming that the *absence* of studies demonstrating an equivalent reproductive risk through men justified a presumption of such a risk, and challenged Equal Rights Advocates' assertion that the PDA specifically precluded all employer policies that excluded only women because of reproductive risk. Johnson Controls also noted its agreement with the U.S./EEOC's statement in their amicus brief that OSHA's lead standard was not dispositive of the issue in this case and with their framework for a BFOQ analysis. In contrast, it cited only one of its own amici, the Chamber of Commerce.

The primary argument of Johnson Controls' brief was that avoiding harm to third parties, including fetuses, is reasonably necessary to the manufacturer's normal business operation. Although it again claimed that the analytical framework and burden of proof allocation were irrelevant to the outcome of the case, the company conceded that its policy was indeed

an example of disparate treatment. It essentially asserted that its fetal protection policy was defensible even under the more stringent BFOQ defense
to facially discriminatory practices, because the BFOQ was not limited
strictly to ability to perform the job as petitioners were arguing. It also
argued that complying with Title VII would not necessarily preclude tort
liability for a damaged fetus. Subtle language differences are also notice-
able, as the company pointed to "rodent studies" (which had been termed
"animal studies" previously) relied upon by the union, claiming that the
results of such studies could not be extrapolated to humans.

In a follow-up brief filed on August 3, Johnson Controls called to the
Court's attention the decision in *Grant v. GM,* which had been decided on
July 20, one day after its prior brief had been filed. Although the decision
in *Grant* invalidated General Motor's similar exclusionary policy, Johnson
Controls nonetheless used it selectively to support several of its positions,
including language citing the need to take into account all interests affected
by fetal protection policies in a Title VII inquiry and the availability of the
BFOQ defense. The company then parted with the *Grant* decision's application of the BFOQ defense, criticizing it for being too narrow in not
allowing for instances in which individual risk assessment is impractical.

The final brief on the merits was filed on August 27 by the UAW in
response to the prior two briefs from the respondent Johnson Controls. In
this last brief, the union reiterated the company's concession that its policy
was facially discriminatory and therefore only defensible as a BFOQ. The
brief also noted that the company did not present any evidence that men
are *not* at risk for contributing to fetal injuries. The union then made three
major points. It argued that an employer cannot decide to have a policy of
zero risk for fetuses and not for adult workers, stating further that the claim
that no less discriminatory alternatives to fetal protection policies exist
rests upon the false premise that all women present substantial risk to real
children, and that women themselves are incapable of personal risk assessment. Finally, the UAW asserted that Title VII's BFOQ defense cannot be
broadened for fetal health and that adhering to Title VII requirements
would not leave a nonnegligent employer liable in tort.

The UAW thus kept most of the arguments in its briefs confined to Title
VII/BFOQ interpretation issues—that is, the arguments were fairly legalis-
tic and stressed adhering to previously articulated notions of Title VII
application. There was little rhetoric about sexism and stereotypes, much
about burden of proof and business necessity vs. BFOQ defenses. The
union seemed to be attempting to make it an easier decision for the justices
by rendering the case a matter of retaining the proper legal standard, rather
than portraying the case as vital to women's equality of opportunity to

pursue nontraditional employment. The company, on the other hand, conceded the initial legal point regarding whether the fetal protection policy was facial discrimination, and argued for a lenient reading of the BFOQ defense, relying on lower court precedent, potential tort liability, and a desire to "balance interests." While the UAW insisted on going by the letter of the law, Johnson Controls attempted to soften the issue by citing inconsistent precedent, unknown risks, and possible liability, and asking the Court to perform an essentially legislative function in weighing the interests of women's employment opportunity against possible risks to potential fetuses or to companies through lawsuits.

The oral arguments before the Supreme Court on October 10, 1990, gave the litigants their final opportunities to make their major arguments in the case. A key difference, however, at this phase of the litigation is that the attorneys are not unfettered and free to present their points exactly as they may wish—the justices freely and frequently interrupt the prepared argument with pointed questions, forcing the lawyers to address issues that they may have wished to avoid. During the arguments in *UAW v. Johnson Controls,* the justices were decidedly more aggressive in their questioning of Stanley Jaspan, the attorney for Johnson Controls, perhaps indicating their predisposition in the case and providing a harbinger of the outcome.

Marsha Berzon, representing the UAW and the class of affected workers, led off by reiterating the central tenet of the briefs, that fetal protection policies were fundamentally inconsistent with Title VII, especially as amended by the PDA, and not defensible under the BFOQ exception. She also asserted that the policies were misguided in their focus on only women workers, and that a policy aimed at all fertile employees would be able to pass Title VII muster. Berzon also to some extent waxed more rhetorical when speaking directly to the justices than in the written pages of the briefs, warning that sanctioning fetal protection policies would lead to resegregation of the work force, leaving some women to unemployment and poverty and others in toxic jobs in female-intensive industries that did not employ exclusionary policies.

Arguing for respondent Johnson Controls, Jaspan asserted that the central issue in the case was whether Title VII was meant to require employers to expose employees' offspring to harm. He reiterated the claim that Johnson Controls had been progressive in occupational health, and that in their view the ability to work cited in the BFOQ defense included the ability to perform the job *safely.* Again attempting to use the same laws as his opponents, Jaspan stated that one of the purposes of the Pregnancy Discrimination Act was fetal health (in that its original intent was health insurance coverage for pregnancy), a purpose *furthered* by policies such as those of Johnson Controls. He said that the BFOQ defense should apply because this was a situation in which it was not feasible for the employer to perform individualized risk assessments for each female employee. Jaspan also cited the amicus brief of the United States and the EEOC as being consistent with the company's position, even though they were filed in support of the UAW.

Berzon used her rebuttal opportunity to focus on the issue of risk assessment. She posed the semi-rhetorical question, "how do we determine how much risk is enough," asserting that insisting on zero risk for hypothetical fetuses was unreasonable when the same level of stringency was not applied to actual adults. Fetal protection policies, she stated, exclude an entire class of workers, substantially all of whom are not within the group that presents the risk (pregnant women).

The strategic rationale that led the UAW to court, therefore, was evident in the arguments that it presented once there. The union relied heavily on a straightforward interpretation of Title VII and the PDA (as well as OSHA rules), and secondarily on social arguments regarding women's employment opportunities and the unacceptability of pitting economic needs against childbearing. But, while established law provided the union with its *primary* basis for challenging fetal protection policies, it did not rest on this claim alone. The UAW carefully assembled a cadre of amicus allies who would put forth additional supporting arguments. These will be explored in the next chapter.

4

Friends of the Court and
Friends of the Plaintiffs

*T*he women and men of the UAW were not the only ones who felt they had a stake in the outcome of *UAW v. Johnson Controls.* When the U.S. Supreme Court agreed to hear the case, ten briefs amicus curiae were filed on behalf of the UAW, while another eight were filed supporting Johnson Controls. The number of briefs alone, however, does not fully convey the level of interest group activity. Ninety-three organizations and thirty-seven individuals signed the ten briefs urging reversal of the Seventh Circuit decision. Those supporting the respondent company contained far fewer co-signatories—only two briefs contained more than one party, and the eight briefs were signed by a total of ten groups.

While it is typical for conservative groups to coordinate less with one another in their amicus activity than more liberal groups (Epstein 1985), the low overall number of parties on the respondent side of the case may be indicative of a belief by those following the case that it was unlikely to be overturned, and so therefore those supporting Johnson Controls were not as inspired to join the fray. Indeed, when *UAW v. Johnson Controls* was taken up by the High Court, several appellate courts under every possible Title VII framework had upheld fetal protection policies, and thus those content with the status quo would likely have been rather confident that the Supreme Court would hold in their favor. Those fearing the codification of an adverse Title VII precedent, however, felt compelled to urge the Court to find for the union. They knew that much was at stake, as the Supreme Court's decision would become the rule of law on this issue throughout the United States. Several of the attorneys on this side recalled

TABLE 4.
Amici Supporting the UAW

American Civil Liberties Union
ACLU-Wisconsin
Amalg. Clothing and Textiles Workers Union
American Association of University Women
AFSCME
American Friends Service Committee
Asian Immigrant Women Advocates
Boston Women's Health Book Collective
Center for Constitutional Rights
Central NY Council on Occupational Safety and Health
Coal Employment Project
Coalition of Labor Union Women
Committee for Responsible Genetics
Comm. Workers of America (CWA)
Connecticut Women's Education and Legal Fund, Inc.
Employment Law Center
Intl. Chemical Workers Union
Maine Labor Group on Health
MassCOSH
Mexican American LDEF
National Abortion Rights Action League
9 to 5 National Association of Working Women
National Black Women's Health Project
National Council of Jewish Women
National Lawyers' Guild
National Lawyers' Guild–Mass. Chapter
National Organization for Women (NOW)
National Union of Hospital and Health Care Employees
Natl. Women's Health Network
National Women's Political Caucus
New York Coalition on Occupational Safety and Health
Nontraditional Employment for Women
North Carolina Occupational Safety and Health Project
Northwest Women's Law Center
Occupational Safety and Health Law Center
Oil, Chemical and Atomic Workers Union (OCAW)
PhilaPOSH

Planned Parenthood Federation of America
Rochester Council on Occupational Safety and Health
Santa Clara Center on Occupational Safety and Health
Service Employees Intl. Union (SEIU)
Silicon Valley Toxics Coalition
United Mine Workers of America
Western New York Council on Occupational Safety and Health
Wider Opportunities for Women
Women's Economic Agenda Project
Women Employed
Women's Law Project
Worksafe for Healthy Communities
eighteen individual workers

American Public Health Association
American Nurses Association (ANA)
Am. Society of Law and Medicine
Association for Women in Science
Environmental Defense Fund
Massachusetts Department of Public Health
Massachusetts Exec. Office of Labor
Occupational and Environmental Reproductive Hazards Clinic and Education Center
Society of American Law Teachers
Toxics Use Reduction Institute
Nicholas A. Ashford, J.D., Ph.D.
David Bellinger, Ph.D.
Eula Bingham, M.D.
Vilma R. Hunt, B.D.S.
Susan Klitzman, Dr. Ph.
Philip J. Landrigan, M.D.
Marc Alan Lappe, Ph.D.
Marvin S. Legator, M.D.
Donald R. Mattison, M.D.
David Michaels, Ph.D., M.P.H.
Herbert L. Needleman, M.D.
Anthony Robbins, M.D.
John F. Rosen, M.D.
Jeanne Stellman, Ph.D.
Directors of Occupational Medicine Programs:
  Eddy Bresnitz, M.D.
  Mark R. Cullen, M.D.
  Steve Hessl, M.D.
  Philip J. Landrigan, M.D.
  Linda Rosenstock, M.D.
  Laura Welsh, M.D.

Equal Rights Advocates
NOW LDEF
National Women's Law Center
Women's Legal Defense Fund

Massachusetts
Arizona
Connecticut
Delaware
Florida
Louisiana
Maine
Michigan
Minnesota
Nebraska
New Jersey
New York
Ohio
Oklahoma
Puerto Rico
Texas
Vermont
Virgin Islands
Washington

NAACP LDF
Natl. Black Women's Health Project

Natural Resources Defense Council

NY City Bar Association
Assoc. of Black Women Attorneys
Committee on Women's Rights–NY County Lawyers Association
NY City Commission on Human Rights

State of California
California FEHC

Trial Lawyers for Public Justice

The United States
The EEOC

their deep and genuine fear of an adverse precedent that would prove very damaging to Title VII. The motivations of the various amici will emerge in detail in this and the following chapter.

This case first attracted amicus briefs at the Seventh Circuit stage, when three briefs were filed (by the Employment Law Center, the ACLU, and the American Public Health Association). These three organizations then joined together, along with dozens of others, to file a single amicus brief urging the Supreme Court to grant certiorari. It was when certiorari was granted by the Supreme Court that amicus activity broadened considerably. While there were over ninety groups supporting the UAW's challenge to Johnson Controls' policy (see Table 4), not all of them played equal roles in the effort. Some, such as Joan Bertin and the ACLU, were close allies of the union from earlier stages, with prior involvement in the fetal protection policy issue, while others signed on to briefs as a show of support with little further involvement. All, however, played some role in moving the case toward the eventual outcome.

While at first glance the array of briefs and groups seems rather heterogeneous—and indeed it is—there exists a logical interconnectedness

TABLE 5.
Alignment of Amici Supporting Petitioner UAW

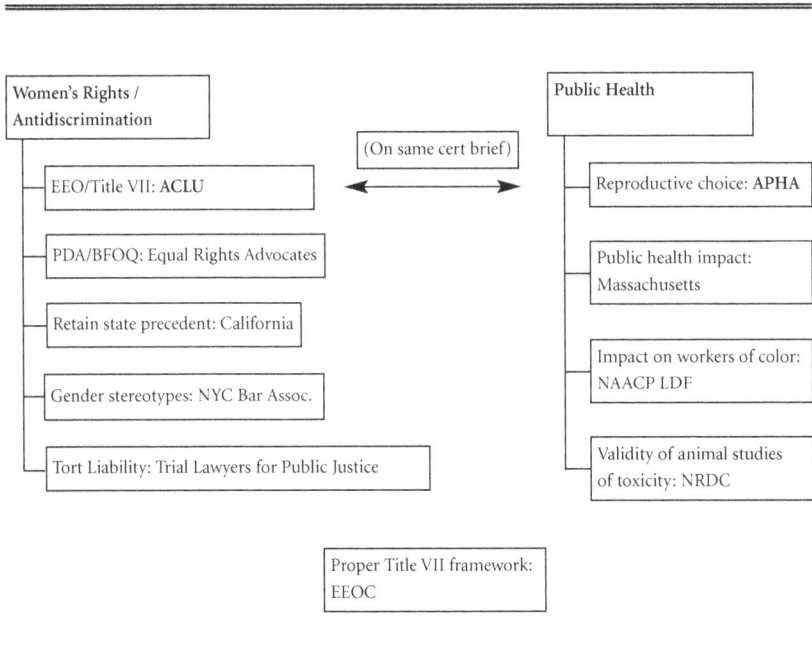

Women's Rights / Antidiscrimination		Public Health
	(On same cert brief)	
EEO/Title VII: **ACLU**	⟷	Reproductive choice: **APHA**
PDA/BFOQ: Equal Rights Advocates		Public health impact: Massachusetts
Retain state precedent: California		Impact on workers of color: NAACP LDF
Gender stereotypes: NYC Bar Assoc.		Validity of animal studies of toxicity: NRDC
Tort Liability: Trial Lawyers for Public Justice		
	Proper Title VII framework: EEOC	

between them all that becomes apparent after exploring the agendas and
strategy decisions of each. The interests that lined up in opposition to fetal
protection policies can be divided roughly into two general categories: those
seeking to advance an equality agenda and those focusing on health implications (see Table 5). Championing each cause were the expected interest
groups, as well as some less predictable backup players that provided extra
depth. On the whole, the amicus effort displayed on behalf of the UAW's
plaintiffs was a comprehensive and well-orchestrated campaign.

Again, one of the principal aims of this book is to illustrate how organized interests follow issues on their agendas across policy arenas, including
into litigation. In so doing, they often work with a consistent set of allies
who bring their expertise from prior policy skirmishes to bear on the issue
when it ends up in court. Not every party that signed onto an amicus brief
had prior involvement in this issue to the same extent but many were repeat
players and had sought legal change through legislation and regulation prior
to joining the UAW in this case. This chapter will reveal how these interests
organized for a decisive Supreme Court victory through strategic use of both
arguments and organizations. What this will also reveal is the extent to which
such strategic necessity might have changed the terms of the debate.

THE WOMEN'S RIGHTS COMMUNITY IN COURT

There were two briefs filed that represented what may be termed the
"women's rights" agenda to the Court. The brief for the ACLU Women's
Rights Project focused primarily on advocating a particular interpretation
of Title VII, while the one filed by Equal Rights Advocates was devoted to
the legislative history of the Pregnancy Discrimination Act, arguing that
fetal protection policies like Johnson Controls' were precisely what the Act
was designed to proscribe. As will become apparent, this division of parties
and arguments was part of a deliberate strategy to present the strongest
and most effective points to the Court.

The ACLU Women's Rights Project and Friends

The previous chapter demonstrated that the preeminent amicus organization in the *Johnson Controls* litigation was the American Civil Liberties
Union (ACLU), due to the work of Joan Bertin and the ACLU's Women's
Rights Project (WRP). The ACLU filed one of the three amicus briefs on
the side of the UAW at the Seventh Circuit stage, filed the only amicus brief
at the certiorari stage, urging the Supreme Court to accept the case for
review, and was the sponsor of one of the ten briefs for the UAW on the

merits at the Supreme Court level. The ACLU's brief on the merits in the Supreme Court litigation contained forty-eight additional organizational and eighteen individual signatories, rendering it the largest brief in terms of parties. The efforts of Bertin and the WRP in the area of fetal protection policies is consistent with O'Connor's (1980) characterization of the WRP as the only one of the women's rights legal groups that could truly be characterized as an outcome-oriented litigant, and the only one to have pursued systematic litigation.

There is some minor historical significance in the strong position taken by the ACLU in this case, as this organization was one (along with the AFL-CIO and many others) that back in the 1960s had favored the *retention* of protective labor laws for women (see chapter 2 discussion).[1] The ACLU, however, established a women's rights project in 1971 following Ruth Bader Ginsburg's ACLU-sponsored brief in *Reed v. Reed* (the case in which, for the first time, the Supreme Court declared a gender-based classification to be in violation of the Fourteenth Amendment). Indeed, pregnancy discrimination and reproductive hazards, both implicated in the *Johnson Controls* litigation, are among the WRP's areas of concentration. The WRP claims to be "the principal group responsible for systematic legal reform through the courts in the areas of women's equality and economic rights."[2]

Initially, the WRP focused on equal protection challenges to gender discrimination, in cases such as *Craig v. Boren,*[3] the case that, largely due to the WRP, set forth the intermediate level of scrutiny subsequently applied to instances of gender classification, and *Califano v. Goldfarb,*[4] in which discriminatory Social Security regulations were struck down. But, by the end of the 1970s, the Project had concluded that at that time the equal protection clause was of limited use, and that attainment of strict scrutiny for gender would likely not occur without a more sympathetic Court or a constitutional Equal Rights Amendment. Thus it shifted to statutory remedies such as Title VII, which had heretofore been used primarily to combat race discrimination. In the late 1970s and early 1980s, the Project "developed a litigation docket involving non-traditional jobs, such as truck driving, the skilled trades, and production line factory jobs," focusing on areas that would have greater impact on poor women and women of color. The WRP was also involved in a number of pregnancy discrimination cases, which "is, in many ways, at the heart of most employment discrimination against women." These agendas would lead it squarely into the fetal protection policy arena. The Project even coined a term for what it viewed as the intersection of the nontraditional employment and pregnancy discrimination issues, dubbing it the "new protectionism," and pointed to *UAW v. Johnson Controls* as the culmination of their work in this area.[5]

The WRP also pursued a series of cases that challenged sex-based actuarial tables that resulted in lower pensions and insurance benefits for women and attacked the undervaluation of work traditionally performed by women. The WRP describes these types of cases as "complex, requiring the use of statistics and experts, and highly experienced litigators," confirming the observations of much of the literature on group litigation that full-time attorneys and expertise are critical to a successful group litigation program (O'Connor 1980; O'Neill 1985; Tushnet 1987).

The ACLU's involvement in the *Johnson Controls* litigation was essentially preordained, as the Women's Rights Project had become an acknowledged repository of expertise on the issue. Bertin had represented the plaintiffs in the litigation against American Cyanamid in the early 1980s, and was of counsel in *Johnson Controls* at the district court level.[6] The ACLU was also involved as amicus in *Wright v. Olin* and had coordinated expert witnesses in other cases. The ACLU in fact had crafted a long-term strategy with regard to fetal protection policies, and during the 1980s devoted considerable effort to the issue and to developing legal arguments. It had identified such policies as a target issue in the 1970s, and part of the strategic plan was to have a case reach the Supreme Court. Thus, when *Johnson Controls* went forward, the ACLU was ready, having filed amicus briefs in other fetal protection cases such as *Wright v. Olin, Hayes v. Shelby Memorial Hospital,* and *Zuniga v. Kleberg County Hospital.* As stated by Joan Bertin, the organization felt that the Seventh Circuit decision in this case "did such violence to Title VII" that it was imperative that it be overturned. "The moving force," stated Bertin, "was direct representation in prior cases." Through filing an amicus brief, Bertin and the WRP essentially continued in an unofficial representational capacity, continuing the efforts begun in earlier, appellate level cases.

The coalition that she led was also a continuation of that earlier time, one that began as formal (CRROW) and became de facto (the various co-signatories to this Supreme Court brief). Bertin emphasized the value of this historical coalition activity, for by the time *UAW v. Johnson Controls* reached the Supreme Court, any disagreements between coalition partners had been resolved and there was a clearly defined strategy and consensus of opinion.

The ACLU generally participates more frequently as a direct party rather than as amicus, except at the Supreme Court level, where it has filed amicus briefs in cases with a direct bearing on the *Johnson Controls* case, including *Wards Cove Packing v. Atonio* (Title VII burden of proof framework), *Price Waterhouse v. Hopkins* (applicability of Title VII to sex stereotyping in employment), and *California Federal S&L v. Guerra* (how employers may treat pregnancy under the PDA). As the *Johnson Controls* case proceeded from the District Court to the Seventh Circuit, Bertin removed herself from direct representation to coordinate the amicus activity in the case. One reason for this move was to bring forth information and arguments to present to the Supreme Court, as there was no trial record below due to the summary judgment disposition at the District Court level. There was also a strategic decision made by the ACLU to encourage greater union involvement in the litigation to conserve resources, as the *Cyanamid* litigation had proved very costly.[7]

The ACLU thus presents a striking example of an organization with an institutional commitment to an agenda of eradicating barriers to gender equality that has systematically pursued that agenda over the years across many venues. While most of its work in this area has been through litigation, the ACLU was also a formal supporter of the Pregnancy Discrimination Act, the legislation that ultimately provided the statutory basis for the decision in *UAW v. Johnson Controls*. At times the group has taken the lead, and at others served as amicus. In both capacities, expertise and alliances were forged and developed. When the issue of barring women from what had the potential to be a wide range of jobs manifested itself in the *Johnson Controls* litigation, the ACLU was simply continuing along a well-defined path when it served, in effect, as the lead amicus organization.

When the ACLU (along with APHA) filed the brief amicus curiae urging the Supreme Court to grant certiorari in *Johnson Controls*, it stated two broad points. The first was that the case presented issues of great public importance, particularly to working women and their families, including: the range of health effects associated with lead; evidence of male reproductive harm; the validity of animal data; and individual rights to make risk assessments. The second point was that review was needed to resolve conflict among the circuits regarding the correct application of Title VII in this context, including clarification of the meaning of the Pregnancy Discrimination Act (PDA) and the BFOQ defense, and the type of guidance to provide the EEOC. The brief argued that the court below had departed radically from established Title VII law, and that the BFOQ exception related only to the ability to actually perform the job. The ACLU also claimed that fetal protection policies themselves had negative health effects due to income loss to women, that male reproductive risks were being ignored, and that the lower court decision generally undermined good public health policy.

As will be seen below, many of these latter arguments were taken up by the American Public Health Association at the merits stage. While the ACLU and the APHA joined forces on the lone amicus brief filed at the certiorari stage, when review was granted and it was time to file briefs on the

merits of the case, the APHA filed its own separate brief and took some of
the original ACLU co-signatories (primarily individual scientific and
health experts) with it.[8] This strategy was explained by Joan Bertin as an
attempt to separate and clarify the political from the scientific and medical
arguments, a distinction it was felt the Court needed to see. Thus the
ACLU's brief on the merits focused much more on Title VII and the PDA
(including the inappropriateness of cost increases as a sex discrimination
defense) and the importance of equal employment opportunity (including
the importance of eliminating decision making based on group characteristics), leaving the health arguments to the APHA in its separate brief
(which the ACLU cited in its own brief). These amici determined that the
best strategy was to divide the legal and public health arguments up and file
them in briefs under the names of organizations that possessed the requisite expertise to get them heard.

But even this division of labor and expertise was not clear cut. While
Bertin was the counsel of record for both of the ACLU briefs (at certiorari
and on the merits), and the spin-off APHA brief lists Nadine Taub of Rutgers University as counsel, Bertin actually was the principal author on all
three. Taub explained that she had written the APHA's brief when the case
went to the Seventh Circuit, but that her involvement at the Supreme
Court stage was "peripheral." While it is not uncommon to have a counsel
of record listed who was not the primary author on the brief,[9] in this case,
it is more significant as the two briefs shared a common origin and author
(Bertin) who served as an invisible link. The two attorneys had worked
together before—Bertin authored a chapter in a book edited by Taub that
came out just prior to the Supreme Court level of litigation in this case[10]—
and there have always existed close ties between the ACLU and Taub's
Women's Rights Litigation Clinic at Rutgers University. Taub has served in
an advisory capacity to the ACLU's Women's Rights Project (WRP) and to
a lesser extent the Reproductive Freedom Project of the ACLU. Thus
Bertin's role as coordinator of amicus activity extended even beyond the
actual briefs that bore her name. Bertin's knowledge of the issue was so
deep that she was used to craft both documents, while Taub was experienced at drafting amicus briefs for APHA. The APHA's brief will be discussed more fully below.

It is also interesting to note that the ACLU stated that the courts in this
case were essentially inappropriately performing a legislative function by
assuming the responsibility for the balancing of interests that the issue
required. The arguments put forth in its brief are, as expected, more conservative than the ACLU's public statements. While the WRP claims to be
a premier force in changing the law to expand women's rights, in this brief,

TABLE 6.

Parties to Brief Supporting Certiorari Filed by ACLU

ACLU

ACLU-Wisconsin

Amalg. Clothing and Textiles Workers

AAUW

AFSCME

American Public Health Association *

Am. Society of Law and Medicine *

Central NY Council on Occupational Safety
and Health

CLUW

Committee for Responsible Genetics

Communications Workers of America

Employment Law Center

Environmental Defense Fund *

International Chemical Workers

MassCOSH

NARAL

9 to 5 National Association of Working
Women

National Black Women's Health Project

NOW

National Women's Health Network

National Women's Law Center +

National Women's Political Caucus

Natural Resources Defense Council #

NY Coalition on Occupational Safety and
Health

Nontraditional Employment for Women

North Carolina Occupational Safety and
Health Project

NOW Legal Defense and Education Fund +

Occupational Safety and Health Law Center

Oil, Chemical and Atomic Workers

PhilaPOSH

Planned Parenthood Federation of America

Rochester Council on Occupational Safety
and Health

Santa Clara Center on Occupational Safety
and Health

Service Employees International Union

Silicon Valley Toxics Coalition

United Mine Workers of America

WNYCOSH

Wider Opportunities for Women

Women Employed

Women's Law Project

Women's Legal Defense Fund +

Nicholas Ashford, J.D., Ph.D. *

David Bellinger, Ph.D. *

Eula Bingham, M.D. *

Mark Cullen, M.D. *

Philip J. Landrigan, M.D. *

Marvin S. Legator, M.D. *

Donald Mattison, M.D. *

Herb Needleman, M.D. *

John F. Rosen, M.D. *

Jeanne Stellman, Ph.D. *

Directors of Occupational Medicine Programs: *

Eddy Bresnitz, M.D.

Steve Hessl, M.D.

Philip J. Landrigan, M.D.

Laura Welsh, M.D.

* Joined APHA brief at merits stage

+ Joined ERA brief at merits stage

Filed own brief at merits stage

it argued that *existing* law adequately addressed the issue at hand, and even stated that, in effect, this was not truly a matter for the courts.

Bertin proffered that once policies such as those at issue in this case are adopted by employers, finding a plaintiff for an organization like the ACLU is not difficult. In the *Cyanamid* case, she was invited to come and talk to the women employed there about a possible cause of action, at which point they asked her to represent them in such an action. Thus, she stated, although the ACLU will sometimes become involved in a case over a matter of legal theory, when *Johnson Controls* arose, she felt she was representing the workers that the ACLU had already represented over the years on this issue—distinct clients with serious legal claims. She was therefore representing individual women and men, but also the larger class of those similarly affected by fetal protection policies. The emphasis on representing the interests of workers was enhanced by including eighteen individual workers as parties on the briefs, as well as their statements of interest.

Litigation strategy decisions can have a direct impact on representational issues. While Bertin and the ACLU were of counsel in the initial stages, the fact that this was a labor union case created a different representational dynamic, and indeed affected the character of the case itself. While organized labor and women's rights advocates are both constituencies known to the courts, they often come from quite different perspectives on issues. Thus bringing this case forward as a labor issue rather than a "women's" issue makes for a different perception, both to the Court and the outside world. The distinction, however, may be more apparent than real, as the previous chapter revealed how closely those two sectors really are (at least on these issues). Nevertheless, appearance does matter. As explained by Nadine Taub, having the UAW as the litigant helped the issue be seen as one of workers' rights and not a narrower "women's rights" issue. Having a labor union present the challenge on behalf of both women and men, whose interests in a clean workplace were essentially the same, "helped get the issue across."[11] Taub added, however, that it also helped the UAW to have Joan Bertin and the women's rights community involved. She recalled a session in which Bertin and Carin Clauss worked with Marsha Berzon to prepare her for the Supreme Court oral arguments, each providing their unique and critical perspectives on women's rights and labor law, respectively.

While Joan Bertin characterized her decision to withdraw as necessary to the coordination of the amicus activity, Marsha Berzon, the AFL-CIO Associate General Counsel brought in for the Supreme Court level, cited some actual tension between the parties who were involved in representing the affected workers in this case. Berzon stated that there was some initial mistrust by the women's rights sector of organized labor and its commitment to this issue. These initial misgivings were eventually overcome, however, and Berzon cited the expertise of Bertin and others as indispensable to her efforts at the Supreme Court level. Affirming Bertin's belief in the importance of the earlier work that had been done on this issue, Berzon also cited the "institutional women's movement interest" that had developed extensive experience and expertise that would not have existed had it been solely the purview of private attorneys. The degree of direct coordination between the UAW litigators and Bertin's ACLU made for a high degree of congruence between the interests of each.

While it is neither feasible nor necessary to explore the involvement of each group that signed onto the ACLU's brief at the merits stage, the Employment Law Center (ELC) emerges as one of the more significant ACLU allies in this effort. This is largely because, while it was one of many groups to join the ACLU's brief, the organization had been directly involved in the parallel case involving Johnson Controls in the state of California (a case in which Bertin also served in an advisory capacity). The ELC is a project of the Legal Aid Society of San Francisco that focuses exclusively on issues of economic justice in the workplace, particularly legal issues affecting employment of poor and underrepresented groups. In this it is philosophically similar to the ACLU's WRP. As stated by Pat Shiu, a senior staff attorney with ELC, the organization faces no restrictions in the types of cases it can litigate, and thus takes on big issues to try and push the law, or clarify the law and establish favorable precedent.

The ELC represented Queen Elizabeth Foster, the plaintiff in the case of *Johnson Controls v. California Fair Employment and Housing Commission* (see discussion below). According to Shiu, the group got involved in the federal *Johnson Controls* case to assert the same points it had made (successfully) in the parallel California case, as the same legal challenge was present in both. The ELC was quite concerned about the Court altering the BFOQ defense in a way that would have "serious and huge ramifications for every other Title VII case."[12] Shiu said that she was quite surprised at the Supreme Court's decision, given the lower court decisions and the prevailing bias about protecting fetuses that seemed to be dominant at the time, a bias that "threatened to change the very landscape of Title VII."

The ELC joined the ACLU brief despite the fact that its frequent coalition partner (and neighbor within the same San Francisco office building), Equal Rights Advocates, was filing its own brief. Shiu stated that the reason for ELC joining the ACLU's brief was that while the arguments being put forth by ERA, which focused heavily on the proper interpretation of the PDA, were important, ERA was approaching the case "from a different slant," and ELC's experience with Queen Foster and Johnson Controls in

California made it a more natural partner in the ACLU effort.[13] Shiu also emphasized the importance in major cases like *Johnson Controls* of garnering as much broad-based support as possible for the position being taken, so that it is not viewed solely as the position of the women's rights community but of "a progressive coalition of civil rights communities." Demonstrating a significant "force of people who are united" behind a position brings valuable credibility to the effort.[14] She noted that it was particularly useful to have the support of organized labor, and indeed all of the unions involved as amici in this case were on the ACLU brief. Thus the strategy that ELC believed most effective and important was being pursued in the ACLU's brief, which listed dozens of diverse organizations, including nine labor unions. ERA's brief, in contrast, was joined by the NOW Legal Defense and Education Fund, the National Women's Law Center, and the Women's Legal Defense Fund, a more homogeneous set of groups.

One of the questions presented for exploration in this book was whether groups must present narrower or more conservative positions when their issues move to litigation, given the unique constraints of that process. While I initially speculated that such an approach would be manifested primarily through language used in legal arguments, it appears from studying the women's rights groups involved in *Johnson Controls* that this may have been effected through strategic partnering as well. Rather than tempering the arguments, groups might attempt to obtain a diverse set of organizations to support their position, making it seem less radical by its endorsement by a coalition of mainstream groups or groups spanning the political spectrum. Judith Kurtz of Equal Rights Advocates maintained that it was sometimes legitimate to question whether the presence of the women's rights community might sometimes hinder a litigation effort. In a slightly different vein, she also said that having certain groups join a brief may serve to lend "clout" to the brief, or to signify the unity of sometimes disparate interests, such as East and West Coast feminists (who have at times differed in their philosophical and strategic approaches to advancing women's rights).[15] ERA's brief in *Johnson Controls* indeed contained women's rights advocates from both coasts (itself and NOW). Pat Shiu of the Employment Law Center also stressed the importance of backing positions with broad-based coalitions for the sake of credibility. The efforts of Joan Bertin to secure such an array of co-signatories on the ACLU's brief further supports this view.

Shiu was emphatic in stating that the client's interests never get sacrificed in a public interest litigation effort such as this—that as attorneys their first duty is always to the client. But she also did say that there are ways to make the broader interests of the organization and those of the client align themselves. Since the ELC has the luxury of taking only those cases they wish, they can literally wait for the "public interest plaintiff," someone who shares their broader view of the issues at stake. Shiu also stated a strong belief in coalition activity, believing that it actually serves clients better as the ideas become more refined as they are bounced off of "smart people."

The rest of the groups that joined the ACLU's brief fell into several broad categories, but all "had a connection to the purpose of non-discrimination in the workplace" according to Bertin. These included: other civil rights organizations, including the Center for Constitutional Rights and the Mexican American Legal Defense and Educational Fund (a frequent coalition partner of the ELC); the nine unions listed above; religious groups (American Friends Service Committee, National Council of Jewish Women); numerous health groups, including the Boston Women's Health Book Collective, the National Women's Health Network, and occupational safety and health groups from various states and regions; reproductive rights groups (NARAL, Planned Parenthood); women's rights organizations that focused on employment and economic issues (9 to 5 National Association of Working Women, Nontraditional Employment for Women, Women Employed); and other women's rights groups (AAUW, NOW, the National Women's Political Caucus, the Northwest Women's Law Center). Many of these also had prior involvement in some of the precursor policy issues that came before Johnson Controls. NOW, for example, which was formed for the very purpose of effecting Title VII's nondiscrimination mandate for women, was also involved in the passage of the Pregnancy Discrimination Act and the *Cal Fed* litigation. The National Women's Political Caucus and NARAL were also part of the pro-PDA coalition.

Legislative History

While the ACLU Women's Rights Project's amicus brief represented the women's rights perspective and also included a host of diverse allies, there was another brief filed that also represented the women's rights legal community, authored by several other prominent women's legal groups. The Women's Legal Defense Fund (WLDF)[16] was the lead organization on the brief, for reasons that will emerge, while the brief's author was not formally affiliated with any of the groups. It was joined by the NOW Legal Defense and Education Fund, the National Women's Law Center, and Equal Rights Advocates (ERA).

The statement of interest of amici curiae in the brief states that the four sponsoring organizations "were leaders in the Campaign to End Discrimination Against Pregnant Workers (CEDAPW), the coalition which was the

principal proponent of the Pregnancy Discrimination Act. . . . Amici
believe that the decision below has the potential for causing great harm to
enforcement of the PDA." The National Women's Law Center, which began
as the Women's Rights Project of the Center for Law and Social Policy, represented amici curiae in the *General Electric v. Gilbert* decision that provided the impetus for the PDA (see chapter 2), and participated in the
development of this remedial legislation. The Women's Legal Defense
Fund, in addition to participating in the coalition to enact the PDA, was
active in pressuring the EEOC following the statute's adoption to issue
guidelines on the application of Title VII as amended by the PDA in light
of the proliferation of employer exclusionary policies based on reproductive hazards. WLDF formed the Coalition for the Reproductive Rights of
Workers (CRROW) to further this mission, and also participated as amicus in the 1983 *Newport News* case (the first at the Supreme Court level to
address the PDA) and in *California Federal S&L v. Guerra* (1987). Donna
Lenhoff of WLDF explained that, in the 1970s, WLDF had taken the "hard
line position" on the treatment of pregnancy in the employment context,
advocating equal treatment of the sexes by treating pregnancy the same as
any other temporary disability. In the context of reproductive hazards, this
philosophy meant cleaning up the workplace rather than excluding fertile
women, in effect using the pregnant woman as the OSHA yardstick for
determining employee vulnerability.

An interesting closing note to the interest statement states that "the
ACLU, which was also a major participant in the CEDAPW, fully endorses
this amici curiae brief, but is submitting a separate brief on behalf of itself
and other amici." This disclaimer was included to forestall any speculation
that there were divisions within the women's civil rights community over
this case, as had become evident in the *California Federal S&L* case. Susan
Deller Ross, the brief's author, noted that given the issues related to childbearing implicated in *Johnson Controls,* the case indeed had the potential to
have "heated up to be a rehash of the same old controversy but never did."
ERA's Judith Kurtz recalled that the ACLU's brief had been "well in the
works for some time" as it was an issue Joan Bertin had been working on for
years, and so therefore most of their arguments had been previously
decided upon. Thus, although there were in effect two "women's rights"
briefs, each had a different emphasis and it was a deliberate strategic move
to file both.

The legislative history brief was authored by Susan Deller Ross of
Georgetown University Law Center, one of the principal drafters of the
Pregnancy Discrimination Act (PDA), whose career reads much like the
modern history of the evolution of sex discrimination law. She was

involved in crafting the ACLU's brief in *Phillips v. Martin Marietta* as a law student, and while at the EEOC in 1971, she drafted the Commission's pregnancy guidelines that were effectively overruled in the *Gilbert* decision. Ross then served as Clinical Director at the ACLU's Women's Rights Project and co-chaired the Campaign to End Discrimination Against Pregnant Workers (CEDAPW), before moving into teaching at George Washington and then Georgetown University, where she continues her involvement with significant sex discrimination litigation.

Ross's brief presents a telling illustration of how a complex litigation campaign is formed. She noted that in Supreme Court litigation it is typical for litigating attorneys to assess the coalition of communities and organizations interested in the issue and to then assign roles in the litigation to those organizations to carry out through amicus briefs. As described by Ross, the groups "divvy up topics": "The level that the [parties'] lawyers are functioning on is figuring out what the legal arguments are that need to be made, which are the strongest and the weakest, where you need bucking up one argument versus another, and figuring out which group is going to fulfill each of those needs. There is a group of legal organizations on behalf of women that work loosely together and often informally divvy up who is going to play what role." Ross also noted that, in her experience, the subject matter needs and the appropriate drafters come first in consideration, with organizations added to provide the institutional backing. In this case, that institutional backing came from the four groups listed above. Donna Lenhoff of WLDF observed that because these groups often partner with the ACLU and some of the other groups that were on the ACLU brief, the fact that they were on this separate brief points to a probable "deal" that was struck with Joan Bertin, who in effect released several of them from her own brief to sponsor this additional brief. Without Bertin's consent, Lenhoff asserted, WLDF "would never have left" her brief. Here is further evidence of the high degree of coordination that was occurring between the various briefs and sets of groups on those briefs, with Bertin squarely placed in the central role.

While Bertin had taken on the responsibility of creating a coalition of amicus support for the UAW at an early stage, Ross related that somewhat late in the process, Marsha Berzon decided that a brief devoted to the legislative history of the PDA was needed. For this, she turned to Ross, a fellow drafter of the legislation, who already had a strong interest in becoming involved with the case. Ross said that they devoted an entire brief to legislative history because that history was so strong—"our real ace in the deck." Like the ACLU's desire to create a factual record in its amicus brief that was lacking from the lower courts, explicating relevant legislative history is another common goal of amicus groups (Wasby 1984; Scheppele and Walker 1991). As Ross describes the process, that realization was the impetus for the document, and while she concentrated on the content of the brief, Judy Lichtman and Donna Lenhoff of the Women's Legal Defense Fund worked on the strategy and mechanics of assembling a late-entry coalition. Lenhoff described WLDF's role in some of the earlier fetal protection policy cases as "the Washington segment" of the effort, performing policy work and "squelching some legislative skirmishes." Therefore, Lenhoff stated, it was logical that WLDF would take the lead on the legislative history brief once the issue reached the Supreme Court. Their goal was to influence what the Supreme Court framework should be by delineating the intent of the PDA. She echoed Bertin's observation that by this time the arguments of this community had been well established since the *Cyanamid* case.[17]

The brief was for the most part the work of the WLDF and Ross, but ERA, the NOW LDEF, and the National Women's Law Center were retained to give the brief additional organizational support and depth. All but Equal Rights Advocates had been parties to the ACLU's amicus brief supporting certiorari, but then moved over to Ross's brief. This particular collection of organizations also served to inform the Court and others that the notorious rift between the two different camps over the legal treatment of pregnancy that had surfaced in *Cal Fed* was not present in this case. Thus, beyond the substance of the arguments contained in the brief, the very composition of actors on the brief was itself part of the message, confirming another phenomenon identified in the group litigation literature— making a statement to the Court on the issue at stake in the pending case.

Like the ACLU and the Women's Legal Defense Fund, ERA's involvement in this case could almost be considered preordained. The organization was formed in 1974 as "a law firm specializing in issues of sex-based discrimination"[18] by a group of feminist attorneys that included Wendy Williams, now at the Georgetown University Law Center, who testified at the PDA hearings and authored an influential article on fetal protection policies in 1981, and Nancy Davis, who served as the organization's Executive Director until 1995. "Since 1974, the ERA has been involved in most major cases involving sex discrimination, particularly those involving pregnancy discrimination, an issue that has pitted traditionally allied women's groups against each other" (O'Connor and Epstein 1989, 71).

ERA also joined a brief amicus curiae with the NOW LDEF in the case *In Re A.C.*,[19] in which a pregnant woman was forced via court order to undergo a cesarean section against her will. ERA and NOW LDEF argued that a competent adult woman is entitled to make her own decisions about the course of medical treatment. The case also implicated broader philo-

sophical questions about women's autonomy when childbearing is introduced as a factor, the same issues at stake (if in somewhat less dramatic
terms) in *Johnson Controls*. ERA was also a party on briefs filed in several
key abortion cases: *Webster v. Reproductive Health Services*[20] and *Bray v.
Alexandria Women's Health Clinic*[21] (with the National Abortion Rights
Action League), and *Rust v. Sullivan*[22] (with NOW LDEF). The outcome of
UAW v. Johnson Controls was listed in ERA's 1990–91 Annual Report, in
which the organization describes the major cases in which it was involved
in the previous year.

Although ERA was founded as a "teaching law firm specializing in
issues of sex-based discrimination," the organization now stresses that it
has "evolved into a legal organization with a multifaceted approach to
achieving equality and economic justice for all women" (1992–93 Annual
Report). Judith Kurtz reinforced this by stating that while litigation is how
ERA began it certainly is not primary now—while they view it as necessary
and useful, it is but one of the "skills and weapons" that they have and
employ. Sometimes, she said, the experience gained through litigation provides necessary knowledge to advocate for public policy change in other
ways. Nonetheless, the group's annual reports are dominated by accounts
of the cases in which ERA is currently involved.

According to Kurtz, the organization participates predominantly as a
direct litigant, with amicus activity "almost incidental." She said that other
groups will do the amicus work and that ERA will not file additionally
unless they have a distinctly different point of view or other groups are not
fully focusing on a particular issue with which they are concerned. The key
legal issues in a case will be raised "with or without amicus briefs" she
stated, and what the briefs can do is bring forth broader implications.
Echoing many others, she said that amicus briefs are not effective if they
merely repeat the briefs of the litigating parties. She also said that there are
occasions when there is conflict between groups who are ostensibly on the
same side in a case, and a litigating party may have groups writing amicus
briefs that they do not want.

The ERA brief itself reads like a defense of the legacy of the PDA, focusing heavily on its legislative history, and makes three primary arguments.
First, it asserts that the PDA intended to classify any exclusion of fertile
women based on their pregnancy or potential pregnancy as facial discrimination under Title VII. Second, it argues that only ability to perform the
job, and not fetal health concerns, was relevant in determining whether a
challenged policy met the narrow BFOQ exception for disparate treatment.
Finally, to implement a fetal protection policy, an employer such as Johnson Controls would have to make it sex neutral, allowing it to comply with

Title VII and make the workplace safe for the children of both male and female employees. The brief also admonished the Seventh Circuit for not considering the PDA or its legislative history in its decision, and referenced testimony at the PDA hearings in favor of the legislation by the EEOC and by Laurence Gold of the AFL-CIO (who was of counsel for the UAW in *Johnson Controls*), as well as testimony against the PDA by the Chamber of Commerce.[23]

CALIFORNIA: AHEAD OF THE CURVE

There were two briefs filed in support of the UAW by states—one by California and its Fair Employment and Housing Commission, and the other by Massachusetts and several other states and territories. No states filed in support of the company. As will be shown, however, the two state-sponsored briefs took very different approaches to the case and became involved for different reasons, although both had prior involvement in the issue.

The brief filed by California properly belongs within the family of briefs and groups that were focused intensively on Title VII and the PDA and their applications in this context (that is, more on the employment discrimination than the public health side of the issue). A similar case involving the same company had arisen in the California state court system, and was actually decided before the Supreme Court oral arguments in *UAW v. Johnson Controls*. In that case, *Johnson Controls v. California Fair Employment and Housing Commission*,[24] the state had argued that fetal protection policies violated California's equivalent of Title VII and prevailed. The state did not want this ruling invalidated by the federal case and so filed a brief amicus curiae in *UAW v. Johnson Controls* before the U.S. Supreme Court.

There were many links between this state-court litigation and the parallel proceeding moving through the federal courts. Prudence Poppink of the California Fair Employment and Housing Commission (the state analogue to the EEOC) had been an attorney with the Employment Law Center (ELC) from 1975–1981; Pat Shiu of the ELC became counsel for the plaintiff in the California case, and the organization also joined the ACLU's amicus brief in the federal *Johnson Controls* case. On the other side, the same attorney who ultimately represented Johnson Controls at the U.S. Supreme Court, Stanley Jaspan, also litigated the *California FEHC* case.

Poppink stated that the sole reason for California filing in the UAW case was because of the prior case that had been decided in California, that the state does not pick and choose cases in which it would like to get involved but only does so if a case will affect its established law. Once California was on record and had been upheld by its appellate court, "we definitely felt we had something to say" as there was no other case law at that time support-ing a finding of sex discrimination on this issue. Poppink was insistent that it be noted that the case in California was decided *prior* to the UAW case, that they had already fought that fight and won and were thus ahead of the federal courts on this issue.[25] Echoing the rhetoric of the amicus brief, Pop-pink said that the state was concerned with the "disingenuous, results-oriented approach of the [federal] circuit court opinions." Manuel Medeiros of the State Attorney General's office, who was involved in both the California litigation and the Supreme Court brief for the state in the UAW case, confirmed this view and explained that the state will often become involved as amicus when a national case will affect California or states generally.[26] In this case, there was even greater impetus for California to file, as they had just established favorable precedent in the state court system for prohibiting fetal protection policies and did not want to see that policy overturned mere months later by the U.S. Supreme Court.

Poppink believes that even if the Supreme Court had affirmed the Sev-enth Circuit's opinion California's law could have prevailed in the state, as state law is allowed to be more stringent than federal law. Under this sce-nario, she said, there would have been an anomalous situation in which such policies would be outlawed only in California and not elsewhere in the United States. In that case, they predicted that the company would have likely moved its operations to another state, a potential economic loss for the state and the current employees of the company. The state thus had a practical as well as legal desire to have the Supreme Court concur with the state court's ruling on fetal protection policies.[27]

The California brief in *UAW v. Johnson Controls* was fairly strong in the presentation of its arguments. The two primary assertions of the brief were that "judicial treatment of sex discrimination predicated upon fetal pro-tection has been ill-reasoned and manifestly result oriented" and that "nei-ther society's interest in workplace fetal safety nor its interest in equal employment opportunity for women are adequately served by allowing employers to discriminate against women in purported furtherance of fetal safety." The brief also stated: that courts applying Title VII are not equipped to resolve fundamental policy disputes; that the history of the issue in the circuit courts has been one of attempting to circumvent the PDA; that Johnson Controls is making multiple erroneous assumptions about women; and that where concern for fetal safety would require exclu-sion of both male and female employees, the employer would "most likely ignore societal concern altogether in favor of economic self-interest." Per-haps as a state—one with considerable prior experience adjudicating this policy issue—California felt more able to use strong language than would an interest group attempting to gain the attention and favor of the Court.

As a state, California cannot be considered as an interest group per se. The state did have significant relationships with other parties to the litigation nonetheless, because of the previous litigation that had occurred in California involving the same company and policy. These relationships did not take the form of direct coalition activity in filing the amicus brief, but, as was observed above, Prudence Poppink of the Fair Employment Housing Commission was formerly with the ELC, which had litigated the Queen Foster case and was a co-signatory to the ACLU brief in the Supreme Court *Johnson Controls* case. She recalled having attended at least one strategy session over the federal *Johnson Controls* case at the Employment Law Center. Poppink said that the state, however, is unlikely to partner with private groups in litigation, as they cannot ally too closely with entities that could potentially come before the FEHC. In addition, she noted, the state will usually have a somewhat different perspective than a private interest group. Medeiros concurred, saying that while he was not aware of the state ever joining with private groups, it will join with other states. When this occurs, each state must of course review the brief to ensure that it comports with its own existing laws. He said that there was no consultation with the attorneys for the UAW when drafting their amicus brief, as "they [the UAW] were not involved in the California case."

THE PUBLIC INTEREST LAWYERS' BRIEFS: THE NEW YORK CITY BAR AND TRIAL LAWYERS FOR PUBLIC JUSTICE

Group litigation commonly involves organized interests allying with attorneys, as the former need the technical expertise of the latter, for the judiciary is the terrain of lawyers. In this case, several of the amicus groups followed this pattern (Ross and the Women's Legal Defense Fund, Taub and the American Public Health Association), but there were also two briefs filed by groups of attorneys themselves—the Association of the Bar of the City of New York, and Trial Lawyers for Public Justice.

The brief filed by the New York City Bar Association had one essential premise, which was that stereotypes about women workers are both outmoded and illegal under Title VII. The brief argues that the assumptions about women and their reproductive lives that underpin Johnson Controls' fetal protection policy are too reminiscent of the days of *Muller v. Oregon* (1908), and that such unwarranted exclusion of women results in women's economic harm and also in reproductive harm to men, who are left to work in unhealthy environments. The brief states that the company's policy clearly conflicts with Title VII as amended and clarified by the PDA. But, while the legal basis for invalidating fetal protection policies was certainly stated, the Bar's main emphasis was rather on the unfair stereotyping that led to the adoption of such policies. The brief referred to reinforcing notions that women should be childbearers and homemakers, the denigration of women's labor force participation, assumptions that only women are responsible for the health of future generations, and that they are incapable of making decisions about work and family for themselves.

The Association bills itself as having been founded for the purpose of eliminating corruption in the government and courts of New York in the 1870s, and as continuing to work for political, legal, and social reform. Among the Association's activities are a Study of Women's Advancement in the Legal Profession, intended to analyze the glass ceiling in large law firms; viewed in light of this project, the brief's emphasis on the traditional sexism of the legal profession seems quite consistent. The Association had also filed a brief in support of Ann Hopkins in *Price Waterhouse v. Hopkins,* a case dealing with gender stereotypes. Its *Johnson Controls* brief references an article by Joan Bertin, author of the ACLU amicus brief and a longtime advocate in the area of women's employment rights. So, while there may not have been direct collaboration between the Bar and the ACLU as far as amicus strategy, the brief linked itself at least indirectly to the broader amici coalition.

While there were three briefs filed in support of the UAW by governments or government agencies—California and its FEHC, Massachusetts and numerous other states, and the U.S./EEOC—this brief presents the rather anomalous situation of a partnership between public and private entities. The New York City Commission on Human Rights, the city agency charged with enforcing local antidiscrimination laws, signed onto the New York City Bar Association's brief, along with the Association of Black Women Attorneys and the Committee on Women's Rights of the New York County Lawyers' Association (NYCLA).

The other attorney association brief filed came from Trial Lawyers for Public Justice (TLPJ), a membership organization that comprises trial lawyers and law firms, which filed its brief alone. As stated by Arthur Bryant, the organization's Executive Director, the TLPJ was founded because there were not public interest lawyers doing damage-related suits. In the brief itself, TLPJ bills itself as "a national public interest law firm dedicated to using the skills and approaches of plaintiffs' trial lawyers to advance the public good."

The statement of interest goes on to explain that TLPJ is particularly interested in this case because it involves two policy areas in which it regularly works—sex discrimination and workplace safety—that should be viewed as complementary rather than contradictory. This brief thus presents another example of a group filing an amicus brief based at least in part upon its expertise and prior experience in at least one of the issue areas implicated in the case, again confirming the observations of much of the literature on group litigation that full-time attorneys and expertise are critical to a successful group litigation program (O'Connor 1980; O'Neill 1985; Tushnet 1987). TLPJ has participated in cases related to *Johnson Controls,* including *United States v. Virginia*[28] (challenging Virginia Military Institute's male-only admissions policy), as well as in the *Harris v. Forklift Systems*[29] case involving sexual harassment. The group also filed an amicus brief on behalf of the National Women's Health Network in *Silkwood v. Kerr McGee.*[30]

According to Bryant, TLPJ participates in "precedent-setting litigation," primarily through direct litigation but also through amicus briefs, and mostly below the Supreme Court level. The group's primary (but not only) issue area is tort liability, which positioned it perfectly to weigh in on one of the more contentious issues in *UAW v. Johnson Controls.* TLPJ's brief, authored by Lucinda Finley of the SUNY Buffalo law school, focused primarily on that issue, and Bryant said that they also vetted the briefs of other amici to ensure that they did not misstate tort issues. Marsha Berzon recalled Finley coming to California for a short stint and writing the brief in one concerted effort, and noted that TLPJ's work was particularly helpful to the litigation. Here was a clear example of specialized amicus backup. Like several other attorneys involved in amicus briefs in this case, Finley had previously authored a law review article on maternity and the workplace, in which she argued that "the fact that women bear children and men do not has been the major impediment to women becoming fully integrated into the public world of the workplace" (1,119).[31]

TLPJ used some of the strongest language of all the amici supporting the UAW in its condemnation of Johnson Controls' policies. The brief stated that the fetal protection policy "has little to do with fetal protection and a lot to do with sex discrimination," that it is "based on a web of speculation" about the adverse effects of allowing fertile women to work around hazards, and argued that such policies "trample on women's autonomy." The brief further claimed that the company's "professions of 'moral concern' are severely undermined by the amount of risk to worker and consumer health that the company routinely tolerates as an aspect of lead battery manufacturing."

It is only after leveling the above charges that the brief delves into Title VII and tort liability issues, warning that the proposed expansion of the

BFOQ defense would "eviscerate Title VII and undermine the safety-enhancing goals of tort law." The brief asserted that a fundamental tenet of tort law—that fear of liability will deter unsafe actions and create incentives to make improvements in safety—would be devastated if speculative tort liability could excuse discrimination. Finley argued that the social costs of dangerous workplaces are so open-ended that incorporating such considerations into Title VII litigation would "overwhelm" such trials with social policy judgments "better left to Congress." The brief further argues that concern about potential tort liability is an improper component of a Title VII defense. Finally, the TLPJ brief adds its imprimatur to the argument that animal study data should not be disregarded, and that the entry of such data by the plaintiffs below should have precluded the entering of summary judgment in favor of the employer. This argument, although focused on more extensively by the Natural Resources Defense Council (NRDC) was not merely incidental to the Trial Lawyers' brief, as a ruling on the validity of animal studies would affect victims of toxic torts, a key area for TLPJ.

Bryant said that TLPJ files approximately 75 percent of its amicus briefs solo, and that decisions regarding whether to participate in coalition briefs depend on the case at hand. He observed, as did many others, that the Supreme Court does not like to be overloaded, so there is an effort made by groups to combine efforts and file as few separate briefs as possible. If TLPJ agrees with a position being taken by an existing brief and has nothing unique to add, it will sign on in order to avoid the redundancy that is frowned upon by the Court.

THE APHA BRIEF: TAKING THE LEAD FOR SCIENCE AND PUBLIC HEALTH

As noted at the beginning of this chapter, the two dominant themes in the arguments for the union side were equal employment opportunity and public health. The American Public Health Association (APHA) most clearly symbolizes the public health faction within the pro-UAW amici, with its position as the oldest and largest public health organization in the nation and the highly regarded co-signatories on its amicus brief. While both equal opportunity and public health issues were cited within the ACLU's brief urging certiorari, which the APHA joined, when the case was accepted for review, the ACLU and APHA divided the two areas and fanned out with their respective allies to provide greater depth to each set of arguments. The briefs just reviewed placed greater emphasis on the legal and discrimination issues. As described by Joan Bertin above, APHA took the more scientific tack, and was in effect backed up by the state of Massachusetts, the NAACP LDF, and the NRDC, which provided depth to specific public health issues in additional briefs.

The APHA has a longstanding commitment to reproductive choice, dating back to *Roe v. Wade,* which provides part of the philosophical foundation for its involvement here. Beyond that, the organization was concerned in this case with the prospect of unsound public health policy being promulgated by scientifically and technically ill-equipped courts. The APHA has organized sections within its structure devoted to Occupational Health and Safety and to Population, Family Planning, and Reproductive Health. From the brief's statement of interest: "Amici do not believe that there is a sound scientific basis to focus attention only on women workers, because all workers face significant health risks from occupational exposures such as those at Johnson Controls. This kind of policy disserves overall promotion of workplace safety and health, as well as the health of women and children, who lose income and benefits that are essential to their health and well-being." And further: "APHA's reproductive health policy, adopted in 1979, 'condemns the corporate practice of forcing women to choose between their jobs and the right to reproduce [and urges governmental agencies to develop] occupational exposure standards that protect women, men, and the fetus.'"

The APHA does not have a formal litigation section or program, but has been quite active in the courts nonetheless, filing ten to twelve briefs per year. It has participated in every major abortion case, including *Roe v. Wade.* Katherine McCarter, the organization's Associate Executive Director for Programs and Policy in the early 1990s, stated that it is an important policy role for a group like APHA to be present in the judiciary, making clear statements to the Court on issues that figure prominently on the organization's agenda.[32] Interestingly, McCarter observed that the organization's general membership was for the most part unconcerned with and unaware of APHA's litigation activity, or might even question the group's involvement in some cases. Such work thus appears to be much more of a staff-driven activity that is seen as a necessary but relatively minor part of the organization's overall policy work. According to McCarter, litigation is solely a policy activity, as APHA is not a trade association with "pocketbook issues" of its membership at stake.

APHA's heightened litigation activity in fact dates to the mid-1970s, when a feminist health clinic in Florida approached APHA for amicus assistance in a case in which they were involved dealing with client access.

McCarter retained Nadine Taub of Rutgers University's Sex Discrimination Clinic to do the brief pro bono for APHA, and Taub has since remained active in litigation for the organization on women's rights issues. It was Taub, in fact, who was counsel of record on APHA's brief in *Johnson Controls*, although as explained above it was largely authored by Joan Bertin of the ACLU Women's Rights Project. Taub has been involved as counsel for amici in many important abortion and gender discrimination cases, including *Planned Parenthood v. Casey, Rust v. Sullivan* (1990), *Ohio v. Akron Center for Reproductive Health, Webster v. Reproductive Health Services* (1989), and *Price Waterhouse v. Hopkins* (1989).

In its public materials, the APHA, like other groups, describes its wide array of activities and emphasizes the impact that it has had on the policy process, but only refers to the legislative and regulatory processes and does not cite its litigation work at all. This combined with the observations of Katherine McCarter that the membership is in fact barely aware of the group's litigation efforts indicate that the APHA's purpose in working through the judiciary is not to enhance its public image or to even represent its members. This stands in contrast to other participants in the litigation—for example, the UAW and its employee members, or the various state health departments concerned about the health and financial status of its constituencies—where direct representation of member interests was more of an impetus for involvement in the case.

In its amicus brief supporting the UAW, the APHA uses strong language in its rejection of Johnson Controls' efforts to address its reproductive hazards problem via fetal protection policies, stating that "once again, women's biological role as childbearer is advanced as a rationale for discrimination that would deny women lucrative employment or, in a modern twist, require them to be sterilized to qualify for full employment rights. Johnson Controls' policy, sweeping in scope and virtually unlimited in its implications, treats all women as 'childbearing vessels' . . ." (3–4). The brief asserts that Johnson Controls has ignored the evolution in federal policy that reflects an understanding that reproductive risks are mediated through both sexes. Part of its argument, to some extent, actually concerned the forum more than the substance of the debate, as it contended that Title VII litigation was "not the appropriate forum for addressing workplace safety and health concerns which are addressed under other federal laws." The brief states that the legal issues involving application of Title VII are in fact straightforward, and that the "failure of the court below to enforce Title VII enmeshed it in a dispute over the scientific validity of a discriminatory policy. . . . the inevitable result of establishing workplace health rules as an accidental by-product of discrimination litigation would be to undermine the work of health and safety officials charged with assessing and regulating workplace hazards" (7–8).

In addition to arguing that Title VII was not the vehicle to fashion sound policy around reproductive health hazards, the APHA brief further contended that the solution proffered by the lower courts would seriously threaten public health. Citing OSHA's lead standard, the brief notes that Johnson Controls' stated position in the present case mirrors that taken by the Lead Industries Association in opposing the lead standard in the 1970s, a position rejected by OSHA.

APHA's final argument concerned risk assessment and risk management of workplace hazards, and the effects of such assessment on occupational health policy. The brief expressed concern that ad hoc case law would create poor and inconsistent policy, citing the divergence of the state of California in its case against Johnson Controls from the federal courts of appeal. The brief concludes that the judicial process is ill-suited to the creation of policy of this sort, that it should be left to elected representatives to balance the competing interests and to technical regulatory experts to fashion appropriate specific policies and regulations.

There was a great deal of strategic partnering on this brief—as with the ACLU and ERA briefs, the composition of the authoring coalition was an important part of the message. APHA included Dr. Eula Bingham as a party, who had been head of OSHA when the lead standard was adopted. Bingham explicitly worked to have nondiscrimination language included in that standard, and generally had taken a strong stance in opposition to fetal protection policies during her tenure at OSHA, including a letter to Fortune 500 companies.[33] Her statement of interest in the APHA brief notes that "[Dr. Bingham] was the Assistant Secretary of Labor for OSHA from 1977 through January, 1981, during which time OSHA's lead standard was promulgated. Thus, she was the government official responsible for reviewing and evaluating the submissions regarding OSHA's lead standard." Carin Clauss was Solicitor of Labor at that time and assisted in the development of the OSHA lead standard. She then went on to the University of Wisconsin–Madison, where she led the appellate-level litigation against Johnson Controls for the UAW (see chapter 3).

The APHA brief also provided a forum through which some of the occupational health experts cited by Johnson Controls in support of its position could contest what they viewed as misguided use of their research. The company had used a 1987 study published in the *New England Journal of Medicine* by Dr. Herbert L. Needleman and Dr. David Bellinger—a study that linked maternal blood lead levels and physical and neuropsychologi-cal development in children—to bolster the validity of its fetal protection policy. Even in that study, however, the authors had stated that they had not studied paternal exposure and "thus cannot rule this out as a contributing factor." The authors published a follow-up commentary in 1988 to protest the misuse of their work by Johnson Controls in the earlier phases of its lit-igation, and both appear as co-signatories to the APHA brief.

In the late 1980s, the Massachusetts Department of Health conducted a study of employers in the state, in part to determine what policies were in place relating to reproductive hazards. The study found that a significant number of manufacturers had some form of exclusionary policy in effect.[34] The Massachusetts Department of Health was one of the parties that joined the APHA brief. On the study of Massachusetts industry, Depart-ment of Health staff worked with private sector researchers, including Dr. Maureen Paul, who has published extensively in the area of reproductive hazards. Her 1993 book contains a chapter by Joan Bertin, as well as a chap-ter by Dr. Bellinger. A 1994 text by Needleman and Bellinger also contains a chapter by Bertin. There is thus a network of public health professionals who have continued to work closely together on these issues, a network that contains Bertin, a vital link to the civil rights side of the antifetal pro-tection policy alliance.

Several of the other signatories of the APHA brief had also published on the issue in the past. In a 1983 law review article, one of APHA's signa-tories, Nicholas Ashford, Ph.D., had written that, as workers become more aware of the reproductive risks that they face on the job, "they will begin to focus on legal mechanisms for reducing reproductive hazards in the work-place" (abstract). Ashford and his co-author go on to explore the use of compensatory remedies, worker protection laws, and antidiscrimination law to push employers to provide safer workplaces. Donald R. Mattison, M.D., had a chapter in the same 1993 Paul text cited above, and Marvin Legator, M.D., had published a book on the subject in 1984. Jeanne Stell-man, Ph.D., had written on some of the policy aspects of fetal protection policies (see literature review in chapter 1).

While the APHA split from the ACLU to develop the public health arguments against employer fetal protection policies, there were several other briefs that also explored public health angles, in a sense further divid-ing up these issues and providing even greater depth and expertise. Two of these briefs took population-based and epidemiological approaches to demonstrate the impact of these policies, while a third focused specifically on the science of toxicity assessment.

THE PUBLIC HEALTH IMPACT OF FETAL
PROTECTION POLICIES

The Commonwealth of Massachusetts, along with a large number of other states and territories, filed a separate amicus brief in *Johnson Controls* in support of the plaintiff employees. In many respects, this brief is atypical as compared with many of the others in this case (with the exception of California and the U.S./EEOC), as Massachusetts and the other states are not interest groups in the traditional sense. As is demonstrated by the content of the brief, however, these states nonetheless had a substantial stake in the outcome. Massachusetts had in fact already demonstrated a special interest in the issue through its study of employer practices referenced above.

Massachusetts' brief combined straightforward legal reasoning with health arguments akin to those of the APHA, as well as pragmatic concerns of a state charged with safeguarding public health. While APHA expresses the concerns of public health professionals, as a state, Massachusetts is responsible for the health of its population and the financial implications of threats to public health. The state argued that not only could the challenged fetal protection policy not meet the BFOQ test, it also could not be justified on public health grounds, as it undermined both Title VII's goal of equal economic opportunity and the goals of workplace health and safety.

The brief gave the most emphasis to the adverse public health effects of the types of employer practices at issue in this case. The state outlined economic problems associated with gender discrimination in employment, including the continuing wage gap and poverty of female-headed households and how lack of health insurance exacerbates poverty problems. It went on to note that exclusion of women from jobs with good benefits has negative long-term effects on public health, and especially on children. And, the brief argued, the state is faced with significant costs of resulting occupational illness, including lost tax revenue and welfare costs. Thus, while the brief grounds its opposition to fetal protection policies safely in a straightforward legal interpretation, it clearly is intended to perform just the type of function that is considered typical and even critical of amici— informing the Court of the broader implications of the issues in the case.

The brief asserted that the Pregnancy Discrimination Act makes it clear that only the ability to work is relevant in assessing whether a challenged policy qualifies as a BFOQ, and that women must not be treated as if they are always potentially pregnant. In addition, the brief cast doubts on the company's claimed fears of tort liability, pointing out that Johnson Controls had presented no evidence of litigation or a threat thereof related to lead exposure. It was also noted that the pattern of fetal protection policy implementation raises doubts about their true motivation, as they are only found in traditionally male-dominated occupations where women have only recently begun to attain employment (often in the face of employer resistance).

UAW v. Johnson Controls also inspired the involvement of the pioneer civil rights litigating organization, the NAACP Legal Defense and Education Fund (LDF). Best known for challenging racially discriminatory policies in court, the Fund also participates in litigation that may not on its face seem to be about race, in order to present the impact of a particular case on people of color.[35] The LDF was also involved in drafting the 1964 Civil Rights Act that included Title VII, and has been active in major subsequent cases interpreting it. In its 1994 Annual Report, the LDF listed *Phillips v. Martin Marietta,*[36] the first Title VII gender discrimination case, among its historical victories.

Marianne Lado, an attorney with the LDF who authored the *Johnson Controls* brief, explained how the case came to be on the Fund's docket. The LDF functions as a law firm and is not a membership organization, and so it generally becomes involved in cases through outside requests. Individuals or groups, such as the National Black Women's Health Project (its partner on this brief), will request the LDF's involvement in cases deemed relevant to its mission. The Fund often works in coalitions in its litigation efforts. For some time, a segment of the NAACP's constituency had been pressuring the LDF to become involved in the abortion cases, which at first the organization perceived to be outside its area of concern. *UAW v. Johnson Controls,* says Lado, served as a "bridge case into the reproductive rights area," as it involved both discrimination and reproductive rights, and the Fund came to see this set of issues as "squarely within its area of expertise."[37] Finally, the Fund would be able to get involved in abortion cases on behalf of the women who had been asking because it could build on its experience in this fetal protection policy case. Because, for poor African American women, reproductive health is not merely access to abortion but the entire range of reproductive care, and, as outlined below, there is extensive data indicating that black women are at greater risk from workplace reproductive hazards. Since its involvement in *Johnson Controls,* according to Lado, the LDF now has "a whole docket of reproductive health cases."

The LDF's brief in *Johnson Controls* began as did many others with statements regarding the facially discriminatory aspects of Johnson Controls' policy and why it therefore needed to be judged according to the disparate treatment–BFOQ framework. The brief did, however, add a novel argument not put forth by any of the other parties, one that clearly demonstrates the utility of interest groups participating to articulate the needs of a group that might otherwise be overlooked, even by sympathetic allies. The LDF observed that the BFOQ was not available as a justification for racial discrimination, as it is for sex. Allowing the business necessity defense to be used to evaluate fetal protection policies, the brief asserted, would in effect allow a defense for racial discrimination that did not previously exist, as it would open the door to treating facially discriminatory practices as a less serious infraction.

The majority of the brief, however, was devoted to demonstrating that African American workers are disproportionately affected by unhealthy workplaces because of their concentration in dirty jobs, and particularly in jobs with high female concentration. Additionally, the document argued, excluding all potentially pregnant women from these better-paying jobs, where fetal protection policies have been found, places African-American women at greater risk of poverty and poor health. This was illustrated by noting that the earnings of these women are vital in supporting their families, and that most low-wage jobs lack employer-provided health coverage.

Lado explained that the brief had two basic parts: the legal portion and the extralegal policy portion. The legal theory was straightforward, and LDF was making no new legal claims but rather supporting the arguments being made by the women's groups. But the LDF strove to go beyond that to demonstrate to the Court the impact of these employer policies on poor women of color—this was the primary emphasis of the brief. The LDF's brief here reads much like a modern-day Brandeis brief, as it is rife with empirical and epidemiological data on the prevalence of toxic working conditions and health problems of African Americans, particularly women, as well as evidence of reproductive risks to men from toxic exposure. As stated by Lado, the Fund was clearly "appeal[ing] to the Court as a major policymaker." The brief also cited several pertinent public policies, including the PDA, the recent decision of the California court of appeals, and the EEOC's updated guidance, which stated that the BFOQ was the correct defense for fetal protection policies. Like the New York City Bar Association brief, Lado's brief also referenced an article by Bertin, indicating at least a level of awareness if not direct connection between amicus parties. This brief therefore expanded on the public health emphasis of the APHA brief, providing support to the public health arguments and expanding on the impact of those issues on a particular segment of the population.

The final public health-oriented brief came from the Natural Resources Defense Council (NRDC), another organization that was on the ACLU's brief supporting certiorari and then branched off to more fully develop its own specific arguments. The sole purpose of the NRDC brief was to argue for the validity of animal studies, which formed the basis for what scant research existed at the time on reproductive risks to men from toxic exposure (a cornerstone of the argument on the plaintiff's side that excluding only women from reproductive hazards is only a partial solution to the problem). Thomas McGarity of the University of Texas Law School wrote NRDC's brief at the request of Al Meyerhoff in the organization's San Francisco office. McGarity explained that filing the brief was a "defensive move," as NRDC was quite concerned over the Seventh Circuit's "frightening language" denigrating animal studies. At that time, there was little Supreme Court language on animal studies in the public law context, and the NRDC was afraid of the Seventh Circuit's view becoming national precedent. McGarity conceded that, while the organization was sympathetic to the plaintiffs, protecting animal data validity was its primary concern. This brief thus presents the clearest example in this litigation effort of an amicus party using an existing case to advance its agenda, even when the issue on which it is advocating is not central to the parties to the case. The stance taken was, however, also philosophically consistent with the NRDC's overall political agenda.

NRDC's brief made two arguments. The first was that an established body of scientific opinion supports the use of laboratory animal studies in assessing the reproductive toxicity of chemicals. The brief asserted that judges lack the requisite expertise in toxicology to be drawing conclusions about the worthiness of scientific data. The second main argument was that courts and administrative agencies have consistently relied upon such animal studies in assessing the risks of chemicals to humans. NRDC noted that the 1990 revised EEOC policy guidance said that its investigators should not reject animal studies. According to McGarity, the brief was deliberately narrowly focused on the animal studies issue, and was designed to "flag" the issue for the justices. So, again, a brief was filed that backed up the public health side of the UAW's amicus coalition but provided depth on one particular aspect of that side's position.

THE FEDERAL GOVERNMENT WEIGHS IN

Although three of the ten briefs supporting the UAW were filed by governments (California, Massachusetts, and the United States with the EEOC), the EEOC's clearly stands as unique among the amicus briefs supporting the UAW, as it was filed by the federal agency charged with enforcing the law in question (Title VII as amended by the PDA), and its policy guidances on the

issue were directly implicated in the legal dispute. Its interest in the outcome is thus quite evident. According to Charles Shanor, then General
Counsel with the EEOC, the Commission will file amicus briefs (on the
merits only, seldom at the cert stage) if a case involves EEOC policy or a law
it is charged with enforcing. Shanor stated that "the Commission feels it
ought to speak on the issues in which it is involved."[38]

The EEOC had a somewhat checkered history with the reproductive
hazards issue going into this Supreme Court litigation, dating back to the
late 1960s (see discussion in chapter 2). The Commission's first chairman
was publicly dismissive of the sex discrimination portion of its mission,
and throughout its history the EEOC has not taken definitive stances on
sex discrimination issues or had significant enforcement muscle to support
its policy statements. Its 1971 pregnancy guidelines were disregarded by the
Supreme Court in *Gilbert,* and its attempt to regulate employer practices
around reproductive hazards in 1980 foundered. When litigation emerged
and progressed in the early 1980s, the EEOC tended to follow the courts
when crafting its own policies, rather than the reverse.

It was not until just before the certiorari petition in *UAW v. Johnson
Controls* was filed at the Supreme Court that the EEOC came out in opposition to the Seventh Circuit's ruling on fetal protection policies in the form
of new policy guidance. There was speculation on the part of the AFL-
CIO's Marsha Berzon regarding the politics of the timing of that revised
policy guidance. She thought it far too coincidental that the new guidelines
were released just two days before the petition for certiorari in *Johnson
Controls* had to be filed, and believed that it was timed deliberately to influence the Court's decision to take up the case. She noted that, as the government generally does not file amicus briefs on certiorari petitions (this
observation was echoed by Shanor), this was an alternative means of con-
veying the agency's opinion to the Court. Berzon opined that if the Court
had requested an opinion from the solicitor general (as it will do in cases
involving an interest of the federal government), that amicus brief would
have said essentially what was in the new guidelines, but that it "would have
become a much bigger political mess. I don't know who generated it and
why, but find it hard to believe it was an accident—somebody there
decided to get this out so it could be used."[39] The UAW cited the EEOC's
new guidance in a footnote (p. 19) and included the policy "for the Court's
convenience" as an appendix.

Shanor confirmed that the EEOC had generally pursued a course of following the lead of the federal courts in crafting its policy guidance on fetal
protection policies. The EEOC was "simply restating the judicial position,
solidifying it, providing a national sweep to that view."[40] The Commission

had thus adopted the more lenient business necessity framework as the proper defense in its 1988 guidance. But, when the controversial decision in *Wards Cove Packing v. Atonio*[41] significantly broadened that defense by crafting a burden of proof scheme heavily favoring defendants, the EEOC was "left in an awkward position with a policy it didn't really want" with regard to these employer practices. This, combined with the Seventh Circuit's opinion in *Johnson Controls,* provided the internal impetus for the EEOC to revise its policy in January 1990.

The arguments presented by the EEOC in its brief take on special significance as they have the status of a policy statement from the enforcement agency for Title VII. The importance of the EEOC's opinion on how to evaluate Johnson Controls' policy is evident, as Johnson Controls itself and several of its amici cited the EEOC's brief in their own briefs (only those on the respondent side would have been able to do so, as their briefs were filed after all of the amicus briefs on the UAW side were filed).

The U.S./EEOC brief stated that Johnson Controls' fetal protection policy constituted facial sex discrimination and that the only available defense to a sex-based, facially discriminatory employment policy is the statutory BFOQ defense. This much nearly all of the parties, litigant and amicus, conceded. The brief went on, however, to assert that it is possible for a sex-based fetal protection policy to meet the BFOQ test, as nothing in the language or scope of the BFOQ provision precludes its use to defend such a policy. The EEOC also said that the BFOQ was not limited to mere ability to adequately perform the job but that it included safety concerns for third parties, including fetuses. Additionally, the brief stated that there was no existing determination that either federal or state law immunizes employers for injury to fetuses caused by workplace conditions, or that state tort liability would be preempted by Title VII compliance.

These statements were seized upon by the company and several of its amici to support their position that the challenged policy did indeed meet the BFOQ provision. The EEOC brief, however, qualified the concession regarding the possibility of meeting the BFOQ standard by noting that the employer "bears a rigorous burden" in justifying its use of a sex-based policy, and went on to state that the court of appeals below had in fact misapplied the BFOQ defense. The lower court's "most glaring error," the EEOC brief commented—an error significant enough to warrant reversal—was its failure to consider reproductive harm mediated through men. The Commission urged adherence to OSHA's gender-neutral lead standard.

Shanor explained that the EEOC can participate in litigation independently at all levels except the U.S. Supreme Court, at which point it must act through the office of the solicitor general. The participation of the solicitor general (SG) in this case merits specific attention, as the SG possesses unique status as a litigator before the Supreme Court, representing the position of the current presidential administration. As described by Salokar (1992, 1995), the solicitor general occupies a multifaceted position at the nexus of law and politics, functioning as an advisor to the Supreme Court while advocating for the administration that the office serves. Caplan (1987) argued that under Ronald Reagan the office of the solicitor general became politicized as never before, an assertion challenged by Salokar and others who noted that the office has always been political in nature. "That the solicitor general professionally presents the government's case and adeptly employs the norms of precedent and legal reasoning, should not be taken to minimize the office's role as an advocate who wants to prevail on the merits for a client (namely, the executive branch and its interests)" (Salokar 1995, 60).

Salokar goes on to observe that "the solicitor general can be a valuable operative for an administration seeking policy change through the courts" (Salokar 1995, 61). Thus the United States, in a sense, behaves in a manner similar to the private interest groups that bring suit or file briefs. Like interest groups, the SG participates both as direct party and as amicus curiae before the Court. Amicus submissions are filed at the discretion of the SG, but often the Supreme Court invites such briefs, as do other outside parties such as interest groups or members of Congress. The SG enjoys considerable success before the Court in both direct party and amicus capacity. Salokar found that in the Supreme Court terms from 1959 through 1986, the government's position was upheld in nearly 72 percent of the cases in which it filed as amicus. The success rate was higher when the SG supported the petitioner in a case (78 percent) than when it backed the respondent (58 percent).

O'Connor (1983) determined that the government's amicus activity was indeed influenced by the political preferences of the sitting administration. This is borne out by the tack taken in the U.S./EEOC brief filed in *Johnson Controls.* Although filed in support of the petitioners, the Republican Bush administration brief was far less strident in its condemnation of the employer's policy, and clearly allowed for the possibility of similar policies, differently tailored, passing Title VII muster.

CONCLUSION

The amicus effort on the UAW side of this litigation was a highly integrated campaign. Marsha Berzon, the UAW's Supreme Court litigator, described asking the NRDC to file the brief on the animal testing issue, having meetings and conversations with the authors of the APHA and TLPJ briefs, extensive work with Joan Bertin of the ACLU, the importance of the Massachusetts brief, and holding a press conference following the ruling that was organized by Nancy Davis of Equal Rights Advocates. Clearly, part of Berzon's strength as a Supreme Court litigator was not only in effectively presenting legal arguments to the Court but also in working to ensure that a reputable cast of supporting players was assembled. But when it came right down to it, said Berzon, "without the ACLU Women's Rights Project and the AFL-CIO's Supreme Court litigation project it would have been damn hard to do this."[42] The institutional knowledge developed by Bertin, combined with the Supreme Court expertise of Berzon, presented a formidable challenge to employer fetal protection policies. While many attorneys interviewed for this study (particularly those on the side of Johnson Controls) made observations concerning the value of filing amicus briefs at the certiorari stage, seemingly supporting Caldeira and Wright's (1988) conclusion that such briefs can affect the Supreme Court docket, there was only one brief filed supporting cert in this case. That brief, however, represented years of experience in prior litigation and policy work around fetal protection policies, and on it the ACLU was joined by forty organizations and fourteen scientific and public health experts. A brief with that many parties urging the Supreme Court to take up a case quite strongly assumes the appearance of a lobbying campaign, which in effect it was, continuing through the merits stage of the litigation.

One of the most striking revelations of the foregoing examination is the degree of shared goals and cooperation between the labor and women's rights communities. In the previous chapter, the emerging ties were shown at the founding of the Coalition of Labor Union Women (CLUW), ties that strengthened through the remainder of the 1970s, as the two sectors worked together on comparable worth, in the Campaign to End Discrimination Against Pregnant Workers (CEDAPW) for the Pregnancy Discrimination Act, in the Coalition for the Reproductive Rights of Workers (CRROW) for the failed EEOC reproductive hazard guidelines, and in the early 1980s in litigation around fetal protection policies.

What the table in chapter 2 indicated that was illustrated more fully in this chapter is the extent of prior experience the amici in this case brought to the effort. Several of the most active organizations—the ACLU, the Women's Legal Defense Fund, Equal Rights Advocates—were not only veterans of previous policy battles related to women's equal employment opportunity, they were accustomed to working with each other. This facilitated a high degree of coordination and cooperation among these key players. Other groups, while not necessarily veterans of this same de facto coalition, were nonetheless experienced in working on many of the component issues in the case. Thus the NAACP's expertise in illustrating the adverse impact of discrimination on African Americans, and Trial Lawyers for Public Justice's experience in taking on issues of tort liability provided additional dimensions to the litigation effort. Whether working in concert or individually, these well-organized interest groups, as outlined in the first chapter, continued to press their agendas through litigation when important issues surfaced in this case.

Johnson Controls had its own amici, of course, some of whom also had extensive histories in this area. Their efforts are examined in the following chapter.

5

Friends of the Status Quo

*T*he number of amicus briefs filed on the plaintiff and respondent sides was nearly the same—ten for the former and eight for Johnson Controls. But there were far fewer total amici (individuals and groups) on the briefs filed on the side of Johnson Controls than were found supporting the UAW. Despite the documented rise in conservative interest group litigation (O'Connor and Epstein 1983b; Epstein 1985), supporters of the employer were numerically far outnumbered in this litigation. The company's sympathizers may have thought that an adverse outcome was unlikely and that their additional advocacy was not needed, since all prior court cases had upheld the legality of fetal protection policies. The positions taken by those who did file on behalf of Johnson Controls were essentially: pro-business (the Chamber of Commerce, National Association of Manufacturers, and Equal Employment Advisory Council); profetal rights (U.S. Catholic Conference and Concerned Women for America); industrial hygiene (National Safe Workplace Institute, Industrial Hygiene Law Project); and conservative free-market oriented litigation groups (the Washington, Pacific, and New England Legal Foundations).

While free enterprise and opposition to regulation are frequent issue areas in which conservative groups litigate, in this case, the field was made more complex by the layering of fetal rights and occupational health issues on top of employer autonomy and economic interest. Despite the fact that these groups fall neatly into the major categories of issues implicated in this case, there was not nearly as much coordination of amicus activity on this side of the case. A few groups stepped forward to articulate their views on the component issues of importance to them, but there was no deliberate designation of organizations to develop specific arguments, as there was on the plaintiff side. While there was a much larger number of fairly heterogeneous organizations supporting the UAW, there was actually a more striking range on the *employer* side when it came to prior experience and expertise with litigation. For while on one end of the spectrum there were groups like the Chamber of Commerce with a formalized litigation arm, at the other end were the industrial hygiene briefs with no prior litigation experience at all.

Another notable difference in the litigation approaches of the two sides in this case is seen in the stage at which the various amici became involved. No amicus briefs were filed on the employer side at the Seventh Circuit stage, the point at which amici first emerged supporting the UAW, and no groups filed amicus briefs at the certiorari stage urging the Supreme Court to deny review. This is despite the fact that many of the attorneys for amici that eventually filed in support of Johnson Controls on the merits professed a strong belief in the utility of filing briefs at the certiorari stage. Their absence at the certiorari stage in this case, however, stems largely from the fact that these groups were on the winning side in the lower court. Because the presence of amicus briefs serves to notify the Court of a case's salience, those content with the status quo are better off *not* filing a brief and drawing the Court's attention to a case that they would rather not see taken up. In their stated belief in the efficacy of amicus briefs influencing the Court's plenary docket, and in their opting not to file at the cert stage

TABLE 7.

Amici Supporting Johnson Controls

Pro-business	Fetal rights
U.S. Chamber of Commerce	Concerned Women for America
Equal Employment Advisory Council/National Association of Manufacturers	U.S. Catholic Conference
Free market	**Industrial hygiene**
Pacific Legal Foundation/ New England Legal Foundation	Industrial Hygiene Law Project
Washington Legal Foundation	National Safe Workplace Institute

TABLE 8.
Johnson Controls Amici with Prior Activity on Pregnancy Discriminatiuon and/or Fetal
Protection Policies

	Geduldig v. Aiello	*GE v. Gilbert*	*OCAW v. Am. Cyanamid*	*Wright v. Olin*	*UAW v. JC* (merits)
Chamber	x	x			x
EEAC				x	x
NAM	x	x			x
PLF	x				x
WLF			x		x

in this case, these amicus attorneys confirmed what Caldeira and Wright (1988) concluded in their study of amicus filing—that the number of briefs filed, and not whether they advocated granting or denial of certiorari, positively affected review being granted.

By definition, the company in this case was in a reactive position, unlike those on the plaintiff side who purposefully brought this suit to both vindicate the claims of the affected workers and clarify the application of Title VII in this context. Nonetheless, the amici who stepped forward to support Johnson Controls followed a similar pattern to that of their counterparts on the other side. Many of the groups had many years of experience advocating in various policy venues around issues that formed the basis for this lawsuit (see Table 8). These precursor issues include legislation such as the Equal Pay Act, Title VII and the Pregnancy Discrimination Act, EEOC guidelines interpreting these statutes, and court cases from the early 1970s onward in which the law's application was challenged and refined.

THE BUSINESS ADVOCATES

As one would expect, several groups committed to furthering business interests came to the support of Johnson Controls in this litigation. There were two briefs filed that specifically took the position of advocating for employers: one was filed by the Chamber of Commerce, the other jointly by the Equal Employment Advisory Council (EEAC) and the National Association of Manufacturers (NAM).

In actuality, it was the Chamber's litigating arm, the National Chamber Litigation Center (NCLC), that filed the amicus brief in *Johnson Controls.*

In describing the workings of the NCLC, Stephen Bokat, the center's Executive Vice President, was candid in pointing out that it is a public *policy* law firm and not a public *interest* law firm. That is, the center does not profess to advocate in the public interest, but rather is avowedly devoted to furthering business interests. He echoed an observation of many academic court watchers that, while liberal groups have traditionally used the courts more, conservative groups have increasingly done so in response. The NCLC was formed in 1977, partly to counter increasing litigation activity by liberal interests. According to Bokat, the Chamber began to engage in litigation out of necessity—it could not ignore it, and its membership demanded it.

Bokat and Timothy Dyk,[1] the outside attorney who served as the counsel of record for the Chamber's *Johnson Controls* brief, both stated that NCLC does more amicus activity than direct litigation, although it does engage in both. The two agreed with many other amicus attorneys interviewed that filing briefs at the certiorari stage can have a great deal of significance, with Bokat asserting that this is where "a great winnowing out of the issues occurs." In Bokat's view, the NCLC is most effective when it can indicate to the Court that a case has far greater implications than other cases under consideration for review. As a broad-based group, the Chamber carries weight with the Court, as it can demonstrate that a case affects a broad segment of its membership and not just the company before the Court in the instant case.[2] On the other hand, because of its separate structure, the NCLC can represent other parties besides the Chamber, although it does not do this frequently. There might, however, be occasions in which, for strategic reasons, the business community's litigation posture would be better served by having an individual business as the plaintiff than the full Chamber of Commerce.

Timothy Dyk offered a more subdued assessment of the impact of amicus briefs in general, maintaining that their impact is diluted because there are so many of them, causing the Court to pay more attention to what the parties themselves say. In his view, there are so many "me-too" briefs that a creative brief may often get lost in the shuffle.[3] Dyk stated that he believed that the Chamber's brief in *Johnson Controls* presented a "novel" argument and did not fall into this redundant category. He did, however, agree with the observations regarding the certiorari stage. By the time the Court grants review to a case, in his view, many groups are drawn in "automatically" as they feel that they must have their say, and there is less strategizing involved. At the certiorari stage, more complicated judgments must be made, including whether a group wants the Court to hear a case at all. Dyk agreed that amicus participation at the cert stage makes a difference because it in effect alerts the Court that the parties to the case are not the only ones interested in it.

Bokat said that the NCLC will always consult with the litigating parties at least minimally when filing an amicus brief, as there could possibly be sensitivities involved in the case of which the NCLC's attorneys would not otherwise be aware. Dyk speculated that he "probably" consulted with the Johnson Controls attorneys, but that the Chamber was presenting a different theory and remained autonomous. Bokat did profess awareness of some instances where amici file briefs against the wishes of the litigating party, but said that it did not occur often and was not a large problem. Dyk again professed a somewhat different view, asserting that such unwanted amicus activity occurs more often than people admit. This, of course, was not an issue on the UAW side, as virtually all of the amici were part of what was in essence a team effort to back the union's claim with additional legal arguments and symbolic support. But the notion of "renegade" unsolicited amicus activity in a case such as this again points to how litigation comes to take on facets of a more public lobbying effort, rather than an essentially private dispute between named parties.

Both Bokat and Dyk expressed ambivalence about coalition activity in filing briefs. While both stated that it can prove a more efficient use of resources to combine with other groups, Bokat noted that it can also be difficult if too many parties are involved ("too many chefs").[4] Dyk offered additional reasons to combine forces on a brief, including having greater impact on the Court and attempting not to burden the Court with too many briefs, and said that it is more typical in general to have several parties on a brief. He noted that the Chamber probably files approximately two-thirds of its briefs with others and the remaining one-third solo. The Chamber will frequently take its own position, he said, because its view is different from the litigating parties or other amici on their side.

Unlike some of the other groups that filed or joined onto briefs in this case, the decision to become involved was not an easy one for NCLC. Despite the outcomes in the lower courts, he said that there was a feeling that the case would be difficult to win, as well as a recognition that it was emotionally charged, since it implicated issues of gender discrimination, fetal rights, and industrial safety. There was also a pragmatic fear of alienating women business owners, the Chamber's fastest-growing membership, although this fear was more theoretical than real (as Bokat did not recall hearing objections voiced by women members). The Chamber's main reason to think twice about getting involved was thus the same as one of the primary reasons that the UAW chose to pursue the issue: responsiveness to an increasingly significant female constituency. Bokat agreed with the speculation that responsiveness to women members was indeed what prompted the UAW's actions in this area, noting that "unions have a horrible history as protectionist societies for white men," a history that even exceeds that of business, while adding that real change has occurred and that unions are no longer that way.

The Chamber's brief argued that the federal government has repeatedly expressed concern over the dangers of birth defects due to maternal exposure to toxic substances, including lead. The brief's main argument, however, was that the Pregnancy Discrimination Act (PDA) does not bar protective actions taken by employers such as Johnson Controls and does not foreclose employee and fetal health considerations. It argued that since fetal protection policies do not constitute impermissible disparate treatment, the issue of whether they could meet the BFOQ defense was irrelevant since they need not be judged under that strict standard. The Chamber thus attempted to use the existing law with the greatest potential to *invalidate* fetal protection policies to demonstrate that they were actually lawful and in fact even desirable. The brief similarly attempted to use the OSH Act as well, noting that OSHA encourages employers to institute voluntary programs to protect the health of their employees and their unborn children.[5]

As was hypothesized, there is a notable contrast between the arguments and even the statement of interest presented in the Chamber's brief and its rhetoric outside the courtroom. In its statement of interest, the Chamber billed itself as the largest federation of business, trade, and professional organizations in the United States whose members are subject to Title VII and the OSH Act. The Chamber stated that it was filing because of its belief in the right of the employer to adopt fetal protection policies and other voluntary policies to safeguard the health of employees, and its view that such policies reflect both sound business practice and good corporate citizenship and are consistent with—indeed, serve—goals of applicable federal legislation.

In its promotional materials, however, the NCLC is less kind to federal policy aimed at controlling business practices. From its fifteen-year anniversary annual report (1992):

> Every day the U.S. business community is challenged by disgruntled consumers, workers, and citizen action groups . . . and burdened by excessive regulation, taxation and litigation. In the halls of government, the voice of business is the U.S. Chamber of Commerce, lobbying on behalf of the 220,000 organizations that are its members. But when action is required in the courts—to overturn unfair requirements or protect against unfair charges—the voice of business is an affiliate of the Chamber, an organization

independently funded by the business community it so ably represents. That organization is the National Chamber Litigation Center.

In a membership brochure, the NCLC's language is even stronger in its defiance of what it views as unfair and burdensome policy mandates: "In the case of The Government v. Business, NCLC is your strongest ally." In its newsletter *The Business Counsel,* under a headline declaring that "Aggressive Litigation Pays Off," rhetoric such as "NCLC won two major victories over [OSHA] . . ." and "In its fight to protect the right of employers and employees to negotiate wages and benefits without government interference . . ." is commonplace.[6]

The Chamber took advantage of its position as amicus for the respondent (filing later in the process) by referencing two of the amicus briefs for the UAW. The Chamber's brief notes that the petitioners (and by extension their amici) "cannot dispute that preventing birth defects by reducing or eliminating occupational exposure to certain substances is a 'legitimate and significant' societal interest" (3) and cites the brief amicus curiae of the state of California to support this contention. In referencing the brief of Equal Rights Advocates, however, the Chamber instead took issue with that brief's arguments relating to the Pregnancy Discrimination Act, noting that "we . . . reach diametrically opposite conclusions as to the purpose and scope of that statute" (7). This disagreement, as depicted by the Chamber, was because the UAW and ERA were asserting that the Act rendered all pregnancy or childbearing-related distinctions illegal, while the Chamber held that it simply applied the disparate treatment theory to pregnancy. Interestingly for the present case, during the debate over the PDA in 1977, one of the few references to the impact of the PDA on exclusion from toxic workplaces was made by the Chamber of Commerce in a prepared statement submitted for the record during the debate and also referenced during oral testimony.

Although there does not appear to have been much coordination of amicus activity on the Johnson Controls side, the NCLC may have had one of the strongest links to the respondent company; John P. Kennedy, general counsel for Johnson Controls, served at the time of this case as a member of NCLC's Constitutional and Administrative Law Advisory Committee, which guides the litigation activity of the Litigation Center on cases falling within that domain. The employer side of the case also had engaged in some "law review lobbying" in the past. David Copus, co-counsel on the NCLC brief, had co-authored an article in 1978 in the *Industrial Relations Law Journal* that held that the status of exclusionary fetal protection policies under OSHA and Title VII was unclear, and concluded that if it can be demonstrated that a hazard causes fetal harm disproportionately through maternal exposure, such policies could be lawful (Crowell and Copus 1978).

The other probusiness brief was filed jointly by the Equal Employment Advisory Council (EEAC) and the National Association of Manufacturers (NAM). Although the Chamber of Commerce filed its own solo brief, while the EEAC and NAM filed a separate brief, these three organizations are frequent partners in litigation activity. Each, however, is organized and focused in unique ways.

In some respects, the EEAC is similar to the NCLC, in that it was formed in the mid-1970s to advocate the business point of view in litigation.[7] It also differs in some significant ways. EEAC is not an arm of a trade association but is itself a membership association of employers concerned with equal employment opportunity issues. EEAC also does not sponsor direct litigation but limits its litigation work to the filing of amicus briefs. The amount of amicus activity performed by the EEAC contrasts vividly with some of the other groups that filed in *Johnson Controls*. The EEAC files nearly twenty-five briefs each year, while, for example, the Industrial Hygiene Law Project (IHLP) has only filed one brief during its existence.

The EEAC filed an amicus brief in *Wright v. Olin,* one of the first legal challenges to fetal protection policies in the early 1980s, and filed comments in opposition to the proposed EEOC reproductive hazards guidelines in 1980. It is indeed one of the few groups, like the ACLU, that has repeat player status in terms of litigation over this particular issue. This prior involvement, and the organization's definitional commitment to precisely the types of issues implicated in *UAW v. Johnson Controls,* made it a logical amicus participant in this case. Indeed, as described by Doug McDowell, the EEAC's General Counsel, the group's primary issues have been Title VII, the Americans with Disabilities Act, and burden of proof; two of these were central in *Johnson Controls.* McDowell did note that the facts in this case were rather unusual, and that the EEAC does not see many BFOQ cases. The case also did not have wide application to a lot of companies, he said, because not many firms reserve jobs by sex anymore (the very reason that the UAW attorneys relished the opportunity to pursue this case). Nonetheless, the decision to enter a brief was fairly straightforward, according to McDowell.

The National Association of Manufacturers (NAM) was the other organization on the EEAC's brief. As a manufacturing trade association, NAM clearly had its members' economic interests in mind when deciding to become involved in *Johnson Controls.* Quentin Riegel, NAM's General Counsel, stated however that when deciding whether to engage in litigation, the organization's first consideration is the impact of the case on *all* manufacturers, not only those that are members of NAM. He said that NAM got involved in this case in order to represent all manufacturers using known reproductive hazards that wanted to exclude any class of workers. In keeping with this generalized notion of interest representation, NAM does not represent individual members in cases.[8]

Riegel asserted that NAM was also concerned with "harm to babies" in addition to the issue of the expenses to its members associated with accommodating women. In his view, employers should be held to a standard similar to that contained in the Americans with Disabilities Act—that of reasonable accommodation—in this case, applied to pregnancy. He did also note awareness of the pressures on employees in jobs such as these to retain those jobs. He said that the question is one of how much society wants to spend protecting anyone, which becomes an economic issue.

NAM's litigation activity is structured somewhere in between that of the Chamber and the EEAC. It is a membership association that engages in litigation among other things, like the Chamber, but it does not have a separately defined organization that conducts its legal work. Riegel in fact indicated that NAM's legal staff had been significantly reduced in recent years, and that the organization often utilizes outside counsel, with internal legal staff performing more review and oversight than actual drafting of briefs. He observed that NAM's stature allows it to obtain high caliber legal services because the firms themselves benefit from doing work on the group's behalf. Despite the reduction in internal legal staff, the organization is still filing briefs "at a record pace" of ten to twelve per year, according to Riegel. These briefs require significant effort, he said, because NAM wants them to be of high quality and will only engage in a case involving issues that are the most important to business. Consequently, NAM turns down many requests to file briefs in cases. NAM will also decline to become involved if the business point of view is already being well represented, in part out of a desire not to burden the court with superfluous briefs.

NAM's litigation activity should also be viewed in the larger context of its other political activities. Riegel stated that NAM emphasizes lobbying Congress more than it does litigation, largely for the practical reason that Congress can always override a Court decision. It is less likely, however, to override the Court on constitutional matters, so that is where NAM focuses the litigation activity in which it does engage (as its litigation budget is small).

Like Bokat and Dyk above, both Doug McDowell and Quentin Riegel agreed that there is value in filing amicus briefs at the certiorari phase of litigation, although McDowell was less emphatic than others, stating that the EEAC files most of its briefs on the merits. Riegel, while cautioning that

generally it is difficult to assess the impact of amici on the Court, nevertheless believes that amicus briefs have more impact at the certiorari stage,
and NAM concentrates there accordingly because it is more cost effective.
Once the case moves to the merits, there are generally one or two legal
issues to be decided, and the litigating parties address those issues pretty
thoroughly; amici at this point "add color" in his view. Riegel asserted that
it is important for the Court to know the issues and groups interested in a
given case, and that amici assist with this information. He added that most
groups, however, lack the legal monitoring mechanism to enable early
involvement.

In their brief, the EEAC and the NAM posited that following the
Supreme Court's decision in *Wards Cove Packing v. Atonio,* the various theories used to analyze discrimination claims had essentially merged and
now simply required the employer to demonstrate a business justification
for the challenged practice. They further argued that the business justification defense was not limited to employee ability to perform the job but
encompassed legitimate safety interests of employees and third parties. In
addition, the brief asserted that the burden of persuasion remained on the
plaintiff at all times to create a record, establish a prima facie case of discrimination, rebut the employer's showing, and provide a reasonable alternative to the employer's policy. These amici also claimed that since the fetal
protection policy equally protected the offspring of all employees, it was
not facially discriminatory. They dismissed the evidence offered by the
UAW of male-mediated reproductive risk, "based on rodent studies," as
speculative at best, and mentioned the potentially astronomical tort liability to which manufacturers could be exposed. To rebut accusations of discrimination, the brief stated that exclusion of a substantial section of the
workforce actually leads to a smaller pool of qualified workers available to
the company and complicates administration of the workforce, and so
would not be in a company's best interests.

In its statement of interest in the amicus brief, the EEAC described itself
as "a nationwide association of employers and trade associations organized
in 1976 to promote sound approaches to the elimination of discriminatory
employment practices . . . [whose] members are committed firmly to the
principles of nondiscrimination and equal employment opportunity." The
organization thus made an attempt to employ some rhetoric favoring
equal employment opportunity, even though McDowell was frank in stating that the EEAC is nearly always on the opposite side of the U.S. EEOC,
the agency charged with ensuring equal employment opportunity, in litigation. Interestingly, in its annual report, the EEAC seems to strike a quite
conciliatory tone toward government regulators, including the EEOC,

emphasizing its role as a resource both to its members and the public. The 1995 Report even boasted of the EEAC having provided the forum for new EEOC Chair Gilbert Casellas's first major outside speech as chair, going on to proffer hopes of working even more closely with the regulatory agencies in 1995. The Report describes the EEAC's activities in benign terms, such as "serves as a legal resource for its members," "consistent emphasis on developing positions that are legally sound and that offer practical solutions," and "highlights for officials at all levels of government the practical impact of their decisions." NAM billed itself in the brief as "a voluntary business association of over 13,000 companies and subsidiaries, employing 85 percent of all manufacturing workers, and producing over eighty percent of the nation's manufactured goods . . . [who] are vitally interested in workplace safety and health issues, as well as the *proper* interpretation of civil rights legislation" (emphasis added).

The organizations thus cited both the classic and modern functions of the amicus curiae, describing themselves as both equipped to furnish the Court with valuable information and also as directly affected by the policy outcome of the case. "The members of EEAC and NAM, and the constituents of their association members, are employers subject to various employment and labor laws, including Title VII. . . . In addition, many of the EEAC and NAM member companies manufacture or process goods that involve chemicals or substances that have the potential to harm an unborn fetus. As a result, some companies have adopted fetal protection policies, much like the policy adopted by Johnson Controls in the instant case."

When interviewing representatives of all three of these business interest groups, each cited the other two as frequent litigation partners. NAM's Riegel said that because NAM is a broad-based organization, its choice of litigation partners is significantly affected by the issues implicated in the case at hand. Regarding coalition activity in filing briefs in general, Doug McDowell stated that the EEAC will partner with other groups "if someone wants to come on," but that they try to limit the number of parties on a brief to four or five—after that point, such coordination becomes "counterproductive" and the returns diminish. This view stands in direct contrast to that taken by Joan Bertin, Pat Shiu, and others on the multiparty ACLU amicus briefs, who cited a wide array of diverse interests on a brief as an asset.

While the amicus activity for Johnson Controls was not orchestrated by the respondent company, the attorneys for these business groups all indicated that they at least consulted with the Johnson Controls lawyers, and that such consultation is the norm. The EEAC's McDowell said that their brief's arguments were pretty close to what Johnson Controls itself was arguing, except for the claim that the burden of proof was always on the plaintiff, where the EEAC went beyond the company's position. He also said that while the EEAC will always consult the litigant in whose support they are filing the brief, if that litigant is not cooperative and willing to review the EEAC's brief, the EEAC will file it anyway and the party simply forgoes an opportunity for review and input. On the other hand, he said that at times the EEAC ends up virtually writing *for* the litigant if the party's own attorneys do not adequately represent its interests. McDowell added that that was not the case here, as Stanley Jaspan was "very strong" in his role representing Johnson Controls.

Like the U.S. Chamber of Commerce, the EEAC and NAM also referenced UAW amici in their brief. Since the EEAC focused heavily on EEOC policy in its brief, it also cited the amicus brief filed by the EEOC in support of the UAW. In a footnote in their brief, EEAC and NAM politely disagree with the EEOC depiction of the difference between the EEOC's 1988 and 1990 policy statements on fetal protection policies. The EEOC brief states that the key difference is that in the latter policy, the employer bears the burden of establishing the BFOQ; the EEAC and NAM assert that the employer "ought to be able to meet its burden with identical criteria regardless of the theory," in keeping with its overall argument that the disparate impact and disparate treatment theories had in effect merged into one framework.

The other attempt to reference opposing amici appears to have been done rather hastily, as it contained some inaccuracies. In the process of taking issue with the UAW's contention that only pure ability to perform the job—and not safety of employees or third parties—can be taken into account by employers, the EEAC/NAM brief cites a UAW brief and "Brief of the National Organization of [*sic*] Women." NOW, however, did not file its own brief: the organization was one of dozens of parties to the ACLU's brief, while the NOW Legal Defense and Education Fund was one of the parties to the brief of Equal Rights Advocates. Based on the page citation in the EEAC brief, it appears to be the ERA brief that is being referenced. While this may have been a mere technical error, there may also have been a desire to cite an opposing organization with a higher national profile (and one sometimes categorized as espousing more "radical" feminist views), hence the citation to NOW instead of to ERA.

While the three business groups discussed here shared goals and even credit on briefs, and do so frequently, each fills a different niche in representing the interests of business. The Chamber and NAM represent businesses as businesses, with the Chamber having a more diverse membership in terms of size and commercial activity, while the EEAC has a more narrow membership and purpose, representing businesses *as employers.* Thus, while the issues at stake in *Johnson Controls* fell within the broad spectrum of issues on the agendas of the Chamber and NAM, they formed a large part of the issue base of the EEAC, which concentrates on equal employment matters from the employer perspective. Doug McDowell explained that while the EEAC represents the business view in equal employment matters, its members do support the laws and their goals and wish to comply. The EEAC thus serves as a sort of broker, informing policymakers of the impact of employment laws on its members and in turn assisting its members in understanding and abiding by policy mandates.

THE DILEMMA OF WORKPLACE HAZARDS: THE INDUSTRIAL SAFETY BRIEFS

Like the pro-UAW side that had the APHA brief to lend scientific credence to its position, there were scientifically oriented briefs on the employer's side as well, filed by the National Safe Workplace Institute (NSWI) and the Industrial Hygiene Law Project (IHLP). While they are two very different entities, they were similarly positioned on this case and there are indirect connections between them. Both groups, while filing on the side of the employer, were not in fact strong advocates of fetal protection policies at all but were concerned that outlawing them would be harmful in the short term.

Founded in 1987, the NSWI is very much the creation and mission of one man, Joseph Kinney, who founded the organization after losing a brother in an industrial accident. The loss of his brother inspired Kinney to adopt workplace health and safety as his personal cause, and he created the Institute to further it. He takes a very systemic view of industrial hazards, asserting that we as a society have created extensive problems with workplace exposure to hazards, causing real potential problems for future generations. The country, however, in his opinion, lacks the willingness to depart from old paradigms and to engage in dialogue to devise true solutions, including ways to compensate victims and accommodate those clearly more at risk.[9]

Perhaps in an attempt to appease NSWI's natural constituency, the group's brief cites praise from both OSHA and the United Steelworkers in its introduction. The brief even states that although the NSWI is filing in support of the respondent company, in many respects it agrees with the petitioners and the amicus brief filed by the EEOC, particularly with regard to the need for further research on reproductive hazards, the acknowledgment that there has been a bias in research to date, and the admission that fetal protection policies are often a pretext for discrimination. The document goes on to say that on some of the implicated issues, NSWI would even go beyond the positions taken by the petitioners and their amici.

Moving to the legal arguments, the brief concedes that Johnson Controls' policy is indeed facially discriminatory, and that the lower courts' attempts to apply the business necessity defense when only the BFOQ was applicable was inappropriate. It is at this point, however, that the NSWI's position diverges from its pro-employee counterparts on the UAW side. The brief states that in narrow circumstances, policies such as those of Johnson Controls should be allowed, for if we as a society are going to hold companies accountable for workplace safety and health, we must give them the authority to take such steps as are reasonably necessary to ensure it. NSWI argued that, while the burden of proof did indeed rest with the employer, the fetal protection policy in question met the BFOQ requirements of being reasonably necessary and related to the normal operation of the company's business.

In addition to citing several different authorities to establish its credibility, NSWI also references opposing amici in the course of laying out its arguments. NSWI's brief in fact cites the ACLU's depiction of the dubious choice presented to women employees, the choice between "an uncertain risk of injury to unborn and perhaps uncontemplated children on the one hand, and a substantial reduction in income, economic well-being, and possibly even health (due to loss of health insurance) on the other." The NSWI brief validates this position as well as that of the employer community, thus attempting to establish its position on the moderate middle ground. Like several other amici on this side of the litigation, NSWI also outlines its agreement with the EEOC's amicus brief in which the agency asserts that the BFOQ exception is not necessarily limited to performance-related concerns.

Kinney's postlitigation assessment of the NSWI's involvement in *UAW v. Johnson Controls* was brutally frank—while he believes in the position that NSWI took, he nonetheless regrets having taken it. This is because the Institute's traditional allies within the public interest community viewed filing in support of the employer in this case as little short of betrayal and, in Kinney's opinion, rendered him and his organization "persona non grata." His bitterness over this experience left him with the belief that "there is no reason any public interest group should take a pro-business position" as they (business) give no credit or sense of respect in return. NSWI's support of Johnson Controls gained it little vis-à-vis industry, thus earning it no friends while alienating former allies. Staff, friends, and hundreds of thousands of dollars in foundation money were all lost following this litigation, and these former friends became enemies "over symbolic reasons" and not the reality of the issue, according to Kinney.

James Holzhauer, the NSWI's counsel on the brief and a member of its board at the time, offered a similar if less impassioned assessment. He noted that it was very difficult for an organization working for the rights of employees to file a company-side brief, and that Kinney worried, apparently with good reason, that it would damage the organization's emerging ties with organized labor. Both men, however, believed that a difficult and important policy issue was at stake, and that the issues were more complex and serious than other groups filing in the case made them appear.

Kinney professed cynicism that politics, rather than public interest or science, were driving the positions taken in the case. The AFL-CIO was part of the larger public interest community interested in this case that distanced itself from the NSWI as a result of the position it took, but Kinney asserts that the AFL-CIO itself was not pursuing the case because of a true belief in the issue but rather as a means of building bridges with feminist organizations. This is an outsider's view of labor's motivation that somewhat supports one of the hypotheses of this study, albeit from a cynical angle. While this may be largely a matter of opinion, it does cast a different and interesting light on the dynamics and relationships detailed earlier involving the ACLU Women's Rights Project (and other women's organizations) and the UAW and AFL-CIO.

The NSWI brief provides a striking illustration of what can be quite disparate interests between the sponsoring organization and its legal counsel. Not only did the Institute's brief in *Johnson Controls* cost it allies and funding, it also resulted in a permanent rift between Kinney and Holzhauer, who were essentially cofounders of the organization. Holzhauer served as the primary lawyer for NSWI and was on its board at the time of this case. The two were actually a somewhat unconventional team to begin with, as Kinney is a rather unabashed activist while Holzhauer is a corporate employment attorney with a large national law firm, Mayer, Brown, and Platt. By his own admission, Holzhauer more frequently represents the employer than the worker, while the interests of the latter are the main constituency of the NSWI, which is for the most part much more aligned with the interests of the petitioners in this case.[10]

Kinney openly expressed bitterness over the actions of Holzhauer following the case, accusing his former counsel of losing his public interest spirit and essentially selling out to corporate interests. Kinney believes that Holzhauer could have used his considerable influence in the business community to help the NSWI when it encountered trouble as a result of this litigation that *supported* business, but that Holzhauer failed to do so.

Litigation has not been a primary undertaking of the NSWI, and its only foray into this arena proved quite costly. The organization has focused more upon business practice than public policy, functioning as "a thorn in the side of corporate America" and using the media and publications rather than trying to influence policy.[11] The group felt, however, that *UAW v. Johnson Controls* was an important test case and a natural one in which to become involved given the organization's institutional concern with safety issues. Following the case, Kinney said that given the damage done to the organization's reputation and the destruction of its relationship with similar groups, NSWI was forced to strike a very different course or cease to exist. As a result, the Institute now focuses exclusively on occupational violence issues. This case, therefore, *caused* a major agenda shift for this organization.

The NSWI brief amicus curiae thus presents a case of a group that struggled mightily with its public position on the issue being litigated, ultimately deciding in favor of filing against its natural constituency. This ambivalence was reflected in the document submitted to the Court, as the brief is rife with references that attempt to assuage those allies that Kinney was in fear of losing. The result, however, would indicate that the attempts at moderation were insufficient to retain those allies, nor did they win any new friends on the other side. Indeed, the NSWI's foray into public interest litigation nearly proved fatal for the organization and caused a permanent rift between two of the organization's founders. Clearly, no single group or constituency has a universally accepted view of what constitutes the public interest, for in this case, while most groups organized to further the rights of workers saw the company's actions as contrary to the public interest, one group did not, and its dissent proved quite costly.

The other amicus brief filed in support of Johnson Controls from a workplace safety perspective came from the Industrial Hygiene Law Project. Like NSWI's brief, the IHLP's brief was largely the result of a collaboration between two people, one attorney and one industrial hygienist. Dr. Margaret Phillips brought the expertise of her profession, while Ilise Feitshans, then of Columbia University, provided the legal acumen. This brief provides a unique example of organizational amicus activity, for the IHLP did not exist prior to *Johnson Controls* and has not participated in litigation since. The Project was, in fact, formed for the express purpose of filing an amicus brief in this case. While it has not been formally dissolved, it has no ongoing activities and its creator, Phillips, has no specific plans to restart it.

The IHLP's brief strongly asserted that Title VII litigation was not the proper vehicle for resolving workplace health and safety issues, that it was not at all designed for such a purpose. If any government entity is appropriate to address such matters it is OSHA, according to the brief, and any regulatory lapses by that agency should be dealt with by Congress rather than the courts. In fact, the brief stated, Congress had at that point clearly stated its intention to address reproductive health hazards. The brief further held that health and safety concerns essentially trumped equal employment concerns, citing the government's obligation to protect health under the doctrine of *parens patriae.*

According to both Phillips and Feitshans, the IHLP was formed largely to provide a forum through which Phillips could safely express her views on the *Johnson Controls* case, as she was employed at the time by U.S. Steel and could not file a brief in her capacity as the company's industrial hygienist. She felt strongly, however, that the view of the industrial hygiene community needed to be heard along with those of business, labor, and women's rights groups, and the profession's own associations (such as the American Industrial Hygiene Association) lacked the will to take stances on controversial political issues.[12] While filing the brief under the IHLP name thus afforded some cover, Phillips also created the IHLP out of a recognition that an organization (or at least an organized interest) would carry more weight before the Court than would any one individual. Phillips thus underscored a similar point made by Susan Deller Ross (see chapter 4), that the issues and arguments that need to be made come first, and the organizations to carry those arguments forward come afterward. In the case of Ross, she was best qualified to author a legislative history brief, which was needed, and the Women's Legal Defense Fund and others were called upon to provide organizational vehicles for the message. In this case, Phillips actually felt that it would have been preferable to have the established industrial hygiene organizations file the brief, but they were unwilling to take a stand—therefore, she created her own organization.

Phillips was frank in her admission that filing on the side of Johnson Controls was a strategic decision based on the way she thought the Court would rule in the case. Since it was a conservative Court, she reasoned that it would be more sympathetic to the company's position, and filing on the side of the company would increase the chances that the brief would be "read and heard." Her view of the case was less one of two opposing sides than of an opportunity—or indeed a need—to speak for industrial hygienists whose work would be directly affected by the outcome. The constituency that the IHLP brief was representing was the professional industrial hygiene community, not necessarily workers themselves, or women, or employers. Indeed, although the IHLP "supported" the employer in this litigation, Phillips stated that she was glad that the Court rejected Johnson Controls' reasoning, although she viewed Blackmun's opinion that companies were immune from liability if they conformed to safety regulations as naive.

Feitshans, the attorney on the brief, also mentioned several strategic decisions made by the group, including their citing of Dr. Morton Corn of Johns Hopkins University as a toxicology expert because he had a more conservative reputation than Dr. Eula Bingham, who would also have been a logical choice given her past tenure as head of OSHA.[13] So, like several of the briefs on the UAW side, the composition of the team advocating a position on a brief is often as much a part of the message as the legal arguments contained within. The IHLP also deliberately kept its statement of interest in the brief as innocuous as possible in order to mask the fact that they were representing the views of that "renegade" industrial hygiene faction.

In a bit of a reversal of the situation in the National Safe Workplace Institute, with the IHLP it was the attorney of the pair who was more zealous. While Phillips and Feitshans made several of the same points in discussing the case, Feitshans was more dramatic in her depictions of the circumstances facing the Project and the faction of the industrial hygiene profession that IHLP represented. While Phillips cited the desire to appear before the Court as an organization instead of an individual as primary in leading her to form IHLP, Feitshans cited only the need for a "safe" forum through which to speak out safely on the absence of scientific risk assessment being employed in the debate over fetal protection policies. Feitshans asserted that the traditional male industrial hygiene community was simply not interested in the issue, and that the women's movement was only interested in the political aspects.[14] She viewed the work performed through the IHLP as epitomizing how movements are created and function, the essence of grassroots, single-issue politics. She saw her role as attorney as being the "translator of the voice of this renegade faction of the industrial hygiene profession." Feitshans went so far as to characterize the politics of the *Johnson Controls* case as a "conspiracy of silence," speculating that OSHA did not want this case to go forward because of the preexisting "blemish" of the *Cyanamid* case, in which several women wound up sterilized.

Feitshans corroborated Phillips's depiction of the IHLP's kind of neutrality as to the outcome of the specific case. Feitshans had spoken extensively with Marsha Berzon, counsel for the UAW, who thought that IHLP should be filing on the UAW side. Feitshans did, however, cite a more broadly "public interest" reason for the IHLP's involvement in the case than did Phillips, claiming that they were "without question representing the needs of working women, from which all else followed." While this might indeed seem to place the group with the petitioners, as Berzon wished, Phillips and Feitshans believed that simple adherence to nondiscrimination doctrine without valid scientific risk assessment was unsound public health policy.

There was at least an indirect relationship between the two industrial safety amici beyond their similar circumstances. Feitshans in fact revealed that she nearly went to work for Joseph Kinney at the National Safe Workplace Institute but ended up choosing a position at Columbia University instead. She stated that she advised Kinney on what to do in this case, advice that he might reconsider in retrospect. In any event, these two groups that filed workplace health and safety-oriented briefs had similar characteristics and informal connections.

IHLP's brief, like several others on the Johnson Controls side, cites the EEOC's amicus brief to support its own position, specifically the EEOC's statement that the BFOQ is not "absolutely unavailable for a sex-based fetal protection policy." This it is able to do in good faith, as IHLP's own argument takes a middle-ground position: neither wholesale exclusion of women nor complete dismissal of the known reproductive risks are wise policy choices with regard to the toxic workplace. While the EEOC did file on the side of the petitioners in this case, the agency nonetheless did not adopt the position that fetal protection policies are simply illegal in all forms, a fact that IHLP sought to highlight for the Court.

Thus both briefs that focused primarily on the technical and scientific aspects of the company policies in question were filed by organizations that were largely the efforts of a few key individuals. But the IHLP clearly falls on the far end of the spectrum in terms of experience in the litigation arena. Standing in contrast to organizations like the Chamber of Commerce's fully staffed and active Litigation Center, the IHLP's brief was signed by Feitshans's father, Jack Levy, as he was currently a member of the Supreme Court bar, a requirement for the counsel of record on an amicus brief. Phillips marveled at how accessible the litigation process was: "What impressed me about the process was that a handful of people could do it. . . . Filing a brief is within the reach of a small group, which is quite remarkable, given how expensive other types of political action can be." This presents an interesting twist on the notion that the courts are available to and used primarily by groups disadvantaged in other political forums (Birkby and Murphy 1964; Cortner 1966; Wasby 1984), for in this case a segment of a well-established professional community broke off and formed an independent faction in order to express a dissenting view, and found the judicial process amenable.

It is interesting to note that a case that centered on workplace health hazards generated so little amicus activity on the part of established industrial hygiene organizations, and also that the federal Occupational Safety and

Health Administration (OSHA) was not involved either. Other health and
safety groups that did participate, all on the side of the UAW, included: the
Central New York Council on Occupational Safety and Health; the Massa-
chusetts Coalition for Occupational Safety and Health; the New York
Council on Occupational Safety and Health; the North Carolina Occupa-
tional Safety and Health Project; the Occupational and Environmental
Reproductive Hazards Clinic and Education Center; the Philadelphia Area
Project on Occupational Safety and Health; the Rochester Council on
Occupational Safety and Health; the Santa Clara Center on Occupational
Safety and Health; the Silicon Valley Toxics Coalition; the Toxics Use
Reduction Institute; and the Western New York Council on Occupational
Safety and Health.

FETAL RIGHTS

While the notion of fetal rights played a central role in *UAW v. Johnson
Controls,* unlike the expected probusiness interest group amicus participation that materialized, there was not a parallel reaction by the traditional
pro–fetal rights organizations. The groups that stepped forth to articulate
the fetal rights position were not single-purpose pro-life organizations.
Groups like the National Right to Life Committee, that are dedicated to
eliminating abortion and advancing the cause of fetal rights, did not weigh
in. Instead, it was the U.S. Catholic Conference and Concerned Women for
America (CWA) that carried the fetal rights banner to the Court. During
the debate over the Pregnancy Discrimination Act in the late 1970s, a
strange alliance of feminist and pro-life interests had emerged, the former
supporting the legislation to eliminate barriers to women's employment,
while the latter saw penalties against pregnancy in the workplace as creating an incentive for abortion. To the extent that the fetal protection policy
issue invoked many of the same concerns, pro-life interests may have opted
out of this litigation because they could not support the elimination of a
concern for fetal health but were wary of supporting what could be perceived as an "antipregnancy" position.

   According to Jordan Lorence, then head of its legal department, the
CWA entered this litigation primarily to ask the Court to recognize that
there are legitimate nondiscriminatory situations in which women are
treated differently than men—thus the specific merits of the case were of
secondary concern.[15] Lorence also allowed that an additional motivation
was the potential to have a non-abortion case that would undercut the reasoning of *Roe v. Wade* that fetuses had no legal standing. In this aspect, the
organization was seeking both an incremental and a more philosophical

victory, and one more in keeping with its overall organizational mission. Jane Hadro, the brief's author, explained that her role was to craft the brief after the decision to become involved had been made by others (Jordan Lorence and Beverly LaHaye, the organization's president). Hadro surmised that CWA joined this litigation because the organization is "very pro-life" and it wanted the Court to affirm that it was legitimate for employers to "consider the child."[16] In fact, she said, since Johnson Controls had won at the lower court levels, CWA "may have simply wished to get the perspective of the child put forth." Their primary goal may not have been to influence the outcome, which they thought was likely to be a victory anyway, but rather to espouse a policy position not being articulated by any other groups. In Hadro's view, CWA would be providing the Court with yet another reason to uphold the judgment below. This confirms an observation made in the group litigation literature, that the outcome is not always the central concern of parties that litigate—sometimes putting a particular position on the record is considered a sufficient victory (Epstein and Rowland 1991).

At the time of *UAW v. Johnson Controls,* CWA had a Legal Department of four attorneys, including Lorence and Hadro, and engaged actively in litigation. The group's newsletter at the time contained a regular Litigation Report feature, updating members on cases in which CWA was involved. When CWA had this department, Lorence stated, litigation was a major emphasis and was quite effective. The group's strategy was to carve out particular policy areas, such as religious liberty or equal access, work to set favorable precedent in a region or judicial circuit, and then move on. For the most part, CWA attempted not to duplicate the efforts of other groups but rather to support them and focus elsewhere. When asked if raising the organization's profile could have been (or was ever) a motivation to file a brief in a major case, both attorneys dismissed this possible goal as both impractical (Hadro) and a "low class tactic" (Lorence). Lorence conceded that other groups do this, filing briefs simply to show off to their constituents and overemphasizing the significance of their participation, but he expressed disdain for this use of the amicus process.

CWA's was the more adamant of the two fetal rights briefs in its stance regarding rights of the unborn. Hadro explained that she wrote the brief to represent the interests of the child, which she considered to have been overlooked by the other participants in the litigation, including those on the employer's side. CWA thus "took up the gap" in the interest representation function by championing fetal rights. CWA's brief was the only one to substitute the term fetal protection policy with "child protection policy" throughout the document. Hadro stated that it would have been inconsistent with both the organization's beliefs and her own not to alter the language that way, as language is very important in the legal arena and since they believe that fetuses are children.[17]

The brief on the whole attempts to blend an argument that government and society are increasingly recognizing the rights of the fetus with legal arguments relating to Title VII, asserting that protection of the unborn itself qualifies as a BFOQ. The brief further states that policies that treat men and women differently are not as a rule discriminatory, and refers to the lower court decisions that upheld fetal protection policies. The brief thus achieves a mix of strong pro-life rhetoric with technical legal arguments made by courts and other parties in the case.

Beyond that, Hadro and Lorence both agreed that there was not much to be gained in using impassioned rhetoric with the Court. Hadro said that not only was it unwise but, in this case, she also felt it to be unnecessary, as the case was strong enough on the facts. Lorence more adamantly stated that it indeed would be "crazy, imprudent" not to tone down rhetoric because the Court is institutionally conservative and infrequently institutes major paradigm shifts. Restrained legal arguments are more suited to the kind of incremental change fostered by the judiciary.

The language of CWA's amicus brief confirms the perspectives of the two attorneys. From the statement of interest:

> [CWA's purpose is] to preserve, protect and promote traditional Judeo-Christian values through education, legal defense, legislative programs, humanitarian aid, and related activities which represent the concerns of men and women who believe in these values.

> CWA is concerned with the unwarranted employment discrimination against women, as well as the health and well-being of children, both born and unborn. The child protection policy at issue in this case is very important in an industry which has demonstrated ill-effects on unborn children due to prenatal exposure to lead. CWA believes that Title VII of the Civil Rights Act of 1964 was broadly enacted to proscribe discrimination in employment, but that it is not so broad as to prohibit employers from adopting policies which protect unborn children from work-place hazards. Based upon the record in this case, CWA supports the child protection policy at issue and urges this Court to affirm the ruling of the Seventh Circuit Court of Appeals.

The statement attempts to strike a judicious balance between women's employment rights and the rights of potential fetuses.

Interestingly, in its own literature, CWA asserts that the autonomy of parents in the rearing of their children is being increasingly threatened by the federal government. From a 1991 newsletter: "There is a battle being fought over who should have greater control of the children—mom and dad or the government. But God's Word clearly states that parents are responsible for the care and instruction of their children. We must fight and stand strong to maintain our rights as parents."[18] In the debate over fetal protection policies, however, parental (and particularly maternal) autonomy was an issue raised by the *plaintiffs,* who argued that company fetal protection policies denied freedom in childbearing decisions to women employees.

When asked about the opportunities and challenges presented by ami-cus coalitions, Lorence observed that his attitude about working with other groups has changed over time. While initially he favored working solo (perhaps more out of "ego" than anything else, he confessed), Lorence now prefers coalition activity (what he termed a more "mature" attitude). In his opinion, the Court is impressed by coalitions, particularly those that cut across traditional ideological lines. In this regard, he professed agreement with the ACLU attorneys who also stressed a belief in diverse coalitions. Lorence said that frequently in high-profile cases, parties to litigation that want to say more than they are able in their own briefs will solicit amicus support and coordinate such activity so that there is comprehensive cover-age of all relevant issues. Jane Hadro concurred, offering that the job of the amici is to take one point within the larger case and elaborate on it, pre-senting extra information ("beefing up a point") for the Justices that the parties cannot make themselves. However, this seems to have occurred on the plaintiff side in this case, and not on the employer side.

Lorence did also note, however, as did Stephen Bokat of the NCLC, that coalition briefs can be difficult from a practical standpoint because of the need to accommodate many diverse views. Because of this, he said that CWA often adopted a "take-it-or-leave-it" attitude with would-be allies, as there was frequently little time to "quibble over details." Lorence also offered a quite candid view of CWA's relationship with other parties in lit-igation in general, which he termed the "ugly relative principle." CWA, he said, is viewed by some as being an extreme right-wing organization, and not one that all litigants want supporting them publicly. While he ran the group's litigation department, he would as a matter of policy consult with the attorneys for a party on whose behalf CWA intended to file an amicus brief. Lorence was frank in stating that there were occasions when CWA was asked not to file, and that they complied with such requests. This could be one reason that the organization is more frequently a litigant itself than an amicus party. This is the flip side of the observation made earlier that who is on a brief often matters nearly as much as what the brief says: sometimes, a group's absence can prove more beneficial than its presence, simply due to its public ideological profile.

Like its fellow organizations supporting Johnson Controls, CWA challenged not only the UAW itself but also one of its supporting amicus briefs, that of Equal Rights Advocates. As several other pro-employer amici did, CWA took issue with ERA on its own terrain, interpretation of the Pregnancy Discrimination Act (PDA). In this instance, CWA disputed ERA's contention that Congress had fully explored the issue of exclusion of women from toxic work environments during its deliberations over the PDA in 1977. ERA asserted that Congress was aware that passage of the legislation would proscribe exclusionary fetal protection policies, while CWA argued that this particular policy outcome was only briefly touched upon during the PDA hearings.

The U.S. Catholic Conference (USCC) was Concerned Women for America's unofficial partner in articulating the pro-life position in *Johnson Controls.* The USCC is rather unique among the organizations that filed in the case, as it is not an interest group in the traditional sense. Its members are the Catholic Bishops in the United States, making its formal constituents quite a narrow class. Affiliated with the National Conference of Catholic Bishops (NCCB), the U.S. Catholic Conference is the arm under the General Secretariat charged with "carrying forward the Church's work in society," while the National Conference deals with the internal concerns of the Church.[19] The USCC is, in fact, described as the "public policy agency of the bishops." The committees of the USCC that develop policy and programs for the USCC have nonbishop members, including lay people.

According to Mark Chopko, General Counsel to both the USCC and the NCCB, *Johnson Controls* was an unusual case in that it involved conflict between policy issues in which the conference is usually engaged. The conference strongly supports workplace rights, unions, and collective bargaining; indeed, strengthening the rights of workers has been a "strong historical interest of the Conference." In this regard, the USCC would many times not be fully in accord with some of its fellow amici in this case, the overtly pro-business Chamber and NAM. It is rare, Chopko said, to find a case in which these various issues of concern to the USCC collide—why should anyone's health be risked at all? The case caused significant "soul searching," Chopko admitted, "because of the gut-wrenching, life and death issues, not just for unborn children but for women [economic security issues]." Thus, while it espoused a pro-life position, the USCC displayed considerably more conflict about its involvement on the fetal rights side of the equation than did Concerned Women for America, which viewed it as vital that the voice of the fetus be heard through its brief.

According to Chopko, the USCC has a "long tradition of seeking to persuade the courts on matters of importance to the Church and its people . . . engaging in litigation as needed."[20] The form of engaging, however, is limited almost exclusively to filing amicus briefs—the conference is almost never a litigant itself. The USCC's internal process, according to Chopko, is such that it first tries to decide why the Court has taken a case when it is considering its own involvement as an amicus party. The Conference attempts to determine which issues are central to the Justices, and then how those issues are relevant to the USCC and how the Conference can contribute to the case's resolution. As a result, Chopko said, the USCC does not file in every case, does not "lend its name to causes" and is "very particular about what we write on." He views its role as amicus as that of alerting the Court to questions contained in the case that are not obvious. Chopko described his role as Counsel as that of a "translator," communicating the views of the bishops to policymakers. This process of communication, he claims, is "the essence of effective lawyering." His goal, he says, is to "try to create public policy receptivity to the bishops' arguments" wherever needed. Again, both the classic and current functions of the amicus are invoked—advising the Court and advocating for an outside interest.

The Catholic Conference's brief, like CWA's, makes supportive statements about equal employment opportunity for women and attempts to strike a conciliatory tone, "rejecting absolutist approaches" that completely favor one imperative (equal opportunity or protection of the unborn) over the other. The overall argument made by the USCC's brief is that health and safety of the unborn must be considered as legitimate as other concerns when resolving this complex issue. The following is from the statement of interest in the brief.

> The Conference advocates and promotes the pastoral teaching of the Bishops in such areas as domestic social development, fair employment and anti-discrimination policies, family life, and the rights of the unborn. . . . Values of particular importance to the Church are the protection of the dignity of work, family life, equal opportunity, and unborn life. These interests are implicated in the instant case.

> This case presents novel, sensitive, and complex public policy concerns for the Court. This amicus has long supported efforts here and elsewhere to oppose employment discrimination; all persons must have full opportunity to work with safety and dignity. In addition, when unborn lives are threatened with injury, this amicus has supported efforts to protect them. Here, some would propose the Court create conclusive presumptions favoring one or the other interest. . . . This amicus rejects both absolutist approaches.

> Rather than engage in a discussion about whether and to what extent rights
> are in conflict, this Court should seek ways that oblige employers to take into
> account the lives and safety of workers *and* their unborn children. We insist
> that equal employment opportunity for all individuals cannot come at the
> expense of threats to their children.
>
> The particular purpose to which this Brief is addressed is limited. . . . With-
> out compromising any of our traditional policies and interests, this amicus
> writes only for the limited purpose of showing that such a policy may be not
> only reasonable but lawful under the Title VII bona fide occupational qual-
> ification defense.

To support its contention that protection of fetuses should qualify as a
BFOQ, the brief cites selected public policy examples (sometimes going
back as far as 1959) that are meant to demonstrate a strong public interest
in protecting the health and safety of the unborn. The brief includes a discussion of abortion as the "main exception to this public policy."

In a press release issued the day of the decision, Chopko again reiterated
the USCC's commitment to "the importance of the rights of women in the
workplace" and "equal employment opportunity for all individuals." Echoing the theme of the amicus brief, the statement continued by stating that
"we are concerned about the consequences of workplace and products hazards and protection of the environment. I am disappointed that the Court
did not include the safety of unborn children—our future—as a legitimate
consideration in deciding Title VII cases. I hope that, in the future, courts
and legislatures can find ways to accommodate both of these concerns."[21]

Chopko stated that USCC generally does not participate in coalitions in
its litigation work but rather that it has a tradition to do things itself. The
primary reason, he said, is "selfishness"—a concern with how decisions are
made, how strategy is set—and thus more a matter of practicality than
doctrine. There is a postulate in some academic treatments of interest
group litigation that control over litigation activity is directly related to
success, and that groups prefer to participate as direct parties for that reason (O'Connor 1980; Epstein 1985; Tushnet 1987). Chopko's statements
would indicate that some group litigants agree, and that it applies to amicus brief activity as well. Of course, "success" can be defined many ways,
even when discussing direct litigants with a real stake in the outcome of a
case—sometimes, the goal is publicity or credibility, or the establishment
of credentials within the judicial forum.

The USCC addressed two of the UAW's amici in its brief—the EEOC
and Equal Rights Advocates (ERA). The EEOC brief is referred to in a foot-

note in which the USCC states that it agrees that fetal protection policies are "more logically scrutinized under the BFOQ defense," and again in another footnote in which the Conference cites the EEOC brief's acknowledgment of the "social value of fetal protection." ERA, in contrast, has its arguments challenged in a lengthy footnote on essentially the same issues contested by CWA. ERA had contended in its own brief that the Pregnancy Discrimination Act (PDA) should be interpreted as prohibiting employer fetal protection policies. The USCC specifically takes issue with ERA's argument that because the PDA can be interpreted as prohibiting employers from firing or refusing to hire women who have independently elected to undergo abortion, then it also should be read to prohibit employers from attempting to minimize the risk to the unborn from its own manufacturing activities. The USCC argues that since the PDA allows employers to exclude abortion from health benefits plans, it follows that the PDA cannot be read to require that an employer cannot prevent an employee from exposing unborn children to harm in its workplace.

Perhaps in an attempt co-opt some of the stature of the opposing sides' amici, the USCC's brief also cites an American Public Health Association publication that urges attention to parental health and safety prior to conception in order to ensure giving birth to healthy children. The USCC brief even references statements by "union officials [that] have specifically recognized the importance of safety measures for the unborn: 'Investments in children and their families are essential to this nation.... As important, our prevention principle has the greatest meaning here: a dollar spent early in life to prevent early damage yields substantial savings for the society and for the individual downstream. The investment must begin before the child is born.'" The brief continues by citing law professor Wendy Williams's seminal 1981 article analyzing fetal protection policies, but merely the part that states that fetal health must become a corporate concern. She does not state that corporate concern be manifested through exclusionary policies. The brief thus cites experts and stakeholders from the "other side" of the case, but in a selective way, so as to appropriate these individuals' authority and lend it to the USCC's own arguments. And so, while the Catholic Conference may be somewhat unique in the world of organized interests, it does not hesitate to engage other groups on their own terrain.

FREE MARKET ADVOCATES

The final group of participants on the company side consisted of the conservative legal foundations. Their issues overlapped somewhat with those that brought the other pro–Johnson Controls amici to the case, but their arguments had a distinct flavor. These groups do not have "constituents" per se who would have been adversely affected by a ruling for the union, as one could argue was the case with the pro-business groups and the industrial hygiene and workplace safety advocates. Rather, their reasons for supporting the company were more ideological. These organizations also exist with virtually no other purpose than to engage in litigation, in contrast to fellow amici like the Catholic Conference or the Chamber of Commerce, which have numerous other functions.

One of these groups, the Pacific Legal Foundation (PLF), was the first and is considered a model of conservative public interest law firms (O'Connor and Epstein 1989). Just as the Chamber of Commerce entered the litigation arena in the 1970s in response to what it saw as increasing anti-business litigation, groups like PLF formed to counterbalance the groundswell of liberal public interest law. PLF urges the concept of limited government and makes opposition to regulation its primary focus. For example, the group helped to invalidate gender and racial minority preferences in city contracts in San Francisco in the late 1980s, representing white males whose equal protection rights, it argued, were being infringed upon by such governmental preferential treatment.[22]

The New England Legal Foundation (NELF) was created not long after PLF and was modeled on the California group. Among its purposes are to "assure that economic considerations are appropriately represented in judicial and administrative proceedings."[23] As described by Stephen Ostrach, NELF's Legal Director, the two foundations are "in the same kingdom but different species." While PLF did inspire the formation of NELF, he said, the latter is more focused on business issues (such as tax law, labor law, and property rights) than on political issues. In this sense, according to Ostrach, *UAW v. Johnson Controls* was "more up NELF's alley than PLF's," even though the "driving force [for their joint brief] came from Sacramento [PLF]."[24]

The Pacific Legal Foundation was one of the repeat amicus players in the area of gender discrimination in employment litigation. PLF, along with the Chamber of Commerce and NAM, was an amicus party in *Geduldig v. Aiello,* urging the Court to allow the exclusion of pregnancy from disability coverage. In that litigation, it faced two of its adversaries in *UAW v. Johnson Controls:* the EEOC and the ACLU. According to Anthony Caso, Director of Litigation for PLF, the organization got involved in *Johnson Controls* because it thought that business was being placed in an "untenable position," having to protect its employees from injury but being sued for taking what it saw as necessary steps to do just that. Ostrach displayed less conflict over the issues at stake in the case than did Caso, who allowed that it was at least a "delicate issue." Ostrach proffered that it was "lunacy that a company would have to go out of business because a woman wants to work with lead."

When asked who he envisioned himself and PLF as representing in this case, Caso responded that the organization "really takes to heart the moniker of public interest." They viewed their position in this case as furthering that philosophy, which includes a belief in individual rights and limited government. In this case, the rights being championed were those of employers vis-à-vis the government's regulatory authority over employment practices. Ostrach further put the organization's litigation into context, explaining that NELF and other similar organizations are increasingly looking to the agency rule-making process as the point at which to try to influence policy. The rationale, he described metaphorically, is that it is "easier to shape the law when it is still clay than to ask the courts to smash the vase later."

Ostrach was yet another public interest attorney to note the value of amicus filing at the certiorari stage. In his view, once a case is before the Supreme Court, "the Justices know what they need to know." Filing an amicus brief at the certiorari stage can really demonstrate the importance of a case, he asserted. Ostrach applied his reasoning about rule making to the litigation context, offering that it is advantageous for groups to become involved as early as possible, as one is better off defending a judgment than attempting to reverse it. Ostrach stated that the courts see that their job is to affirm decisions—otherwise, they would invite too many appeals. Therefore, he concluded, appellee is the desired position in which to be. He also noted that lower court judges truly appreciate amicus briefs, as they do not see many of them and briefs demonstrate that there is significant interest in a case.

The brief filed jointly by PLF and NELF urged a departure from normal Title VII analysis in cases involving the prevention of reproductive harm, as "this case fits neatly into none of the traditional modes of analyzing Title VII claims." They conceded that fetal protection policies are not facially neutral—and therefore not eligible for a disparate impact analysis—but asserted that the BFOQ framework that only allows for ability to perform the job would be at a socially unacceptable cost in this case. "Reproductive health cases," the brief argues, "are a class unto themselves." In their view, the issue before the Court was "whether an employer is required to put aside concerns about its employees' children's health."

The brief relies heavily upon citations to EEOC policy to support its contention that the Court should allow fetal protection policies to be judged under the business necessity defense usually reserved for disparate impact cases. The EEOC policy that it uses, however, is that issued in 1988, and not the revised 1990 policy that stated that the BFOQ was the proper defense. The PLF brief relegates this distinction to a footnote and characterizes it as mere relabeling of the policy, and also does not mention that the EEOC is itself an amicus party in support of the UAW in this case. (PLF's was in fact the only amicus brief on the side of Johnson Controls not to cite at least one opposing amicus brief.) Thus the PLF brief attempts to co-opt the authority of the very agency whose power it wishes to curtail, by attempting to use the EEOC's own policy statements to support the PLF/NELF position.

PLF's statement of interest in its brief exhibits the expected restraint of Supreme Court briefs and emphasizes its public interest orientation: "PLF is a nonprofit, tax-exempt organization incorporated under the laws of California for the purpose of participating in litigation affecting public policy. Policy for the Foundation is set by a Board of Trustees composed of *concerned citizens,* the majority of whom are attorneys. The Board of Trustees evaluates the merits of any contemplated legal action and authorizes such legal action only where the Foundation's position has broad support within the *general community*" (emphasis added). But, like other groups involved in this litigation, PLF's promotional materials convey a different tone than that used when addressing the Court. From a membership brochure, dire warnings such as "Regulatory Horrors—Are You Next?" and "government at all levels has always acted to limit our freedoms, intrude into our lives and narrow our rights" are meant to appeal to potential supporters. Notably, the list of things that PLF opposes includes both "discriminatory practices based on race, sex, or national origin" and "unreasonable regulations which lack common sense." Although it does not make an explicit statement in its brief, PLF is on record as supporting nondiscrimination, as are most groups filing on behalf of Johnson Controls.

Caso said that it was more typical for PLF to file briefs solo, but that, in general, groups banding together on briefs is common. He also asserted that often the value of a brief lies more in who files it than in the substance of its arguments, a notion that was supported by the strategic alignments crafted by many of the amici on both sides of this case. The purpose of the brief thus becomes one of indicating to the Justices who is affected beyond the instant parties more than highlighting previously unseen issues. Stephen Ostrach of NELF was forthright in admitting that NELF became a co-signatory to the brief with PLF "because we were asked" by PLF, who thought the brief would be more effective with multiple signatories.

Indeed, Ostrach observed that "95 percent of the time groups get involved with briefs because they are asked, either by a party in the litigation or by other amicus groups looking for names."

The other brief in this category was filed solo by the Washington Legal Foundation (WLF), which is similar to the above two groups in that it was founded during the same era (mid-1970s) for the same purpose: to provide a counterbalance to the increasing presence of liberal public interest law firms. WLF both participates directly in litigation and files amicus briefs. According to Daniel Popeo, the organization's founder, WLF files briefs "to counter the ACLU and NAACP LDF,"[25] both of whom were present as adversaries in *Johnson Controls*. The organization describes itself (within its amicus brief) as "promoting the free enterprise system and the economic and civil liberties of individuals and businesses." WLF was one of only two amici in *OCAW v. American Cyanamid*, one of the first cases involving employer fetal protection policies. WLF filed in support of the company, while the Coalition for the Reproductive Rights of Workers (CRROW) filed for the plaintiff. Thus WLF was one of the few repeat amicus players in fetal protection policy litigation on the employer side (see Table 8). Its interest in the issue having been established early on, it is not surprising to find the organization participating as the issue moves to the High Court.

In its brief, WLF focuses almost exclusively upon the issue of tort liability to a company that exposes fetuses to hazardous chemicals. From the statement of interest: "Amicus will present arguments supporting tort liability as a BFOQ defense to a charge of sex discrimination; those arguments will not be presented by the other parties." The brief contends that not only is "catastrophic" tort liability a very real possibility, but also that such liability can be a defense to a Title VII charge (and that neither OSHA nor Title VII compliance would preempt a toxic tort liability suit). The language employed in the brief is in fact noteworthy: WLF asserts that "Johnson Controls' fetal protection policy protects it from a very real threat of tort liability that could put [the company] out of business" (5). The Foundation thus turns around the notion of "protection," applying it to the company as well as to potential offspring.[26] WLF argues that tort liability should be both a business necessity and a BFOQ defense, obviating the issue of which legal framework is used to evaluate fetal protection policies. The brief attempts to dismiss certain of the points raised by the UAW side, such as risks to the male reproductive system ("irrelevant to the case at bar") and discriminatory intent ("one can assume that the marketplace places an equal value on men and women as employees").

WLF cited several opposing amici in its brief, including the NAACP (one of its self-proclaimed traditional rivals), Trial Lawyers for Public Justice, and the brief filed for the state of Massachusetts. WLF cites the NAACP to actually bolster its own position, noting that the NAACP and the National Black Women's Health Project "wax eloquent in their brief on the dangers to employees and their offspring posed by exposure to toxic chemicals" (5). WLF thus uses the NAACP's tactic of presenting extensive evidence of toxic harms to workers, and in particular minority workers, and portrays it almost as a concession to one of WLF's points (that workplace toxic exposure is a gravely serious problem for employees). Where the two groups differ, of course, is in their prescribed remedy for the problem.

WLF also takes on the pro-UAW amicus brief that functioned as its most direct counterpart, that of Trial Lawyers for Public Justice, which also focused primarily on the tort liability issue. While TLPJ argued that a toxic tort claim would be difficult to win because of problems of proof and causation, WLF countered that because Johnson Controls has admitted that lead exposure poses a risk to fetal health, a potential plaintiff would have less difficulty establishing cause. Finally, WLF challenges both TLPJ and Massachusetts in their assertions that male-mediated fetal damage poses an equally significant threat in the workplace. They do not, however, take issue with the substance of that argument, but merely assert that the UAW did not establish a record regarding this issue below and therefore waived the opportunity to do so.

CONCLUSION

Given the declarations of support for equal employment opportunity in all of these briefs supporting the employer, it is clear that groups favoring exclusionary fetal protection policies do not feel comfortable stating simply that women's childbearing function legitimates a form of employment discrimination. Rather, they feel obligated to affirm their own commitments to equal employment opportunity before explaining why *this* type of employer practice should be nonetheless condoned. While the rhetoric is thus different from the era in which women's childbearing roles automatically trumped other endeavors, the outcome, exclusion from jobs, remains the same.

Even without a concerted strategy to garner amicus support, or even any effort at all, Johnson Controls had nearly as many briefs filed in its support as did the UAW, albeit with fewer co-sponsors. Like the UAW side, the employer's amici fell along certain issue dimensions, providing the Court with more extensive arguments favoring retention of fetal protection policies. There was far less coordination on the company side between organizations, which is not unusual for conservative groups, and each side obviously desired opposite outcomes. But there were also many similarities between the two sets of organized interests that lined up on either side. Both sides: utilized strategic coalitions on their briefs (whether as sponsoring organization or expert witness) as part of the message they took to the Court; seized upon similar subissues like tort liability and the intent of the PDA (while adopting opposite postures); recognized the need for organizational backing for individual viewpoints; and saw the outcome as important to others besides the parties to the case.

As Epstein (1985) observed, the litigation campaigns of conservative groups, many of whom formed for avowed reactionary reasons, "have evolved from emotional exercises to professional, well-planned drives" (xii). Because of this, she notes, the courts are increasingly adjudicating claims between competing groups rather than discrete parties, as there is now more likely to be an array of organized interests on both sides. This has implications for the role of the judiciary as a policy-making forum, rather than an arbiter of narrow disputes.

6

Litigating for Political Change

*B*y now, it is well documented that interest groups participate extensively in the judicial process, pursuing their policy goals through litigation as well as through more traditional legislative or electoral means. The literature on interest group litigation has grown in recent years as scholars have paid increased attention to what Bentley and Truman noted and groups have recognized for some time—that lobbying the judiciary is one of the many options available to organized interests. For the most part, the literature tends to look at sponsorship and amicus activity separately, and has struggled with defining group "success" in litigation. The foregoing account of *UAW v. Johnson Controls* has attempted to integrate the activity of litigating parties and amici together to more accurately reflect how cases are actually pursued, as these parties often work closely together. Even when there is not a great deal of direct coordination between parties, the efforts of the amici supporting one side in a case cannot be viewed without considering the role of the litigating party and the dynamics of the case at bar, for this context is what provides amici the opportunity to step forth and articulate their positions, whether they are doing it to assist the party or for their own gain.

Students of politics have long referred to the "countermajoritarian difficulty" presented by unelected, life-tenured judges in effect engaging in policy making when courts exercise their power of judicial review (Bickel 1962). But it is also increasingly true that courts routinely make policy when rendering decisions in a wide range of public law cases—the courts' policy-making role in our three-cornered political system is not limited to instances in which they strike down legislative acts as unconstitutional. Studying interest group litigation thus merits our attention because courts do make policy, albeit through very different means, and if groups are influencing that policy it is important to understand which interests are represented in the judicial forum and how that representation occurs. With loosened standing requirements and increasing use of litigation by both private interests and the government, it becomes critical to understand this form of policy making.

THE UAW AS LABOR UNION AND GENDER DISCRIMINATION PLAINTIFF

When an interest group launches a comprehensive litigation campaign, spending seven years pursuing it all the way to the Supreme Court, it is logical to ask what prompted the action: how did the group come to adopt the issue in question onto its agenda, and why did it decide to use the courts? When a labor union is the organization bringing suit and the challenge involves sex discrimination in employment, these questions take on added significance, as gender issues have historically not figured prominently (if at all) on the agendas of organized labor or individual unions. Thus the case of *UAW v. Johnson Controls* provides a vehicle through which to explore not only the dynamics of interest group litigation but also a rather fundamental change in the labor force as women have come to play greater roles within both the work force and organized labor.

The review of the behavior of the UAW and that of the AFL-CIO and other unions in chapter 3 revealed that organized labor is not a monolithic entity. After observing the marked differences between the UAW and the AFL on gender issues on numerous occasions, and realizing that it is inaccurate to depict all unions as harboring discriminatory or "protective" attitudes toward women, it becomes less surprising that it was the UAW that brought suit over fetal protection policies. Although the UAW was not around in the late nineteenth and early twentieth centuries, when the battles around protective legislation began, even in the modern era it has been consistently ahead of the rest of organized labor on gender issues. Historically, the AFL opposed protective legislation for men, preferring that workers depend on the unions for protection, while favoring such laws for women for either competitive or paternalistic reasons, or both. Once the OSH Act and similar policies extended government protections to all workers, and gender discrimination had been outlawed for both employers and unions, organized labor had little choice but to drop its support for exclusionary laws and policies. The UAW, however, was much quicker to move in this direction. The AFL did of course join forces with the UAW as the *Johnson Controls* litigation progressed, but it was the UAW that initiated the proceedings and brought the case to a point where a Supreme Court challenge was viable.

A frequent conception of public interest litigation is one of aggressive attorneys taking advantage of individual plaintiffs to pursue test cases, in effect using or even creating actual cases to afford the interest group the requisite standing to gain access to the judicial arena. But several of the attorneys interviewed for this study indicated that quite often that is not how cases such as this develop, and *UAW v. Johnson Controls* presents an example of a case whose genesis lay in the plaintiffs themselves. Certainly, these plaintiffs were linked to personnel and resources that facilitated taking their challenge as far as it went, but the workers themselves do not come across as unwitting pawns in someone else's game: they may have been somewhat minor players by the time the case made the Supreme Court docket, but their very real grievances provided the initial impetus for the litigation.

By the late 1970s, when the issue of reproductive harm from workplace exposure first became a public issue, a confluence of both external and internal factors led to the adoption and litigation of the issue by the UAW and organized labor. Environmental factors included the existence of favorable legislation (Title VII and the PDA), the resurgence of the women's movement and a political environment more favorable to reproductive choice, and the increasing availability of the courts as an additional forum through which to contest policy disputes. Among the internal factors were: the existence of aggrieved employees insistent on seeking redress; the emergence of women as a voice within organized labor; the adoption of health and safety in general as part of organized labor's agenda; the presence of committed antidiscrimination attorneys within the UAW and the AFL; and the practical need of the union to respond to the needs of its fastest growing constituency—working women.

In pursuing its challenge to fetal protection policies through litigation, the UAW seemed to be emulating the policy pattern of the late 1960s and early 1970s over the implementation of gender discrimination legislation. Having found regulatory solutions unattainable, women's rights and union activists in both eras turned to the courts for favorable interpretations of recently passed legislation. This raises important questions regarding whether litigation is an inevitable part of the policy process and the limitations of regulatory policy making. The tack taken by the UAW in its briefs to the Supreme Court when the case was granted certiorari further supports the view that the union was firmly resting its appeal on what it saw as the intent of Title VII and especially the PDA. The union argued for a strict, narrow reading of the BFOQ exception, while its adversary, Johnson Controls, urged a more flexible approach to allow for accommodation of third party (fetal) safety interests.

There were interesting differences of opinion among the many attorneys who worked with or for the UAW on this case concerning how deliberate, focused, and coordinated the litigation effort was. Wasby's (1984, 1995) research has to some extent disabused outside observers of the notion that the highly successful—indeed, paradigmatic—litigation campaigns of the NAACP LDF were tightly controlled and planned efforts. Quite often, Wasby discovered, the organization has had to be reactive rather than proactive, as many factors that influence a litigation campaign are beyond any one party's control. Attorneys who worked within the UAW, such as Marley Weiss and Ralph Jones, depicted a much more calculated, controlled process, as did Joan Bertin of the ACLU, who herself had a master plan for just the sort of litigation outcome that did in fact occur. Others outside the UAW and the ACLU, but who were nonetheless closely involved, such as Susan Deller Ross and Judith Kurtz, and Marsha Berzon as well, spoke more of happenstance, saying that it was not necessarily the grand design of the UAW to change the law in this area—it just happened that a company adopted a policy that was highly objectionable to many of its women members and the union simply responded appropriately. The truth is undoubtedly some combination of these impressions, for Johnson Controls was neither the first nor the most visible employer to implement fetal protection policies. Other cases had been tried and resolved already when this one went forward, so the UAW was not acting randomly in a brand new area of workplace policy. The union knew what it was venturing into, but nonetheless may not have had a preexisting master plan in this policy area.

The UAW's lawsuit drew in a host of outside parties who also saw important issues at stake for their own constituencies. Some were actively sought out by the litigating parties, while others came of their own accord, using the amicus curiae function as a vehicle for their own political expression. Among the friends of the court who supported the UAW position were many states and the federal government; these combined with the range of private interests that joined the plaintiffs' side proved too formidable a group of adversaries to the company trying to defend its exclusionary policy.

While there was a large array of very diverse groups supporting the UAW, it is clear that it was labor and women's rights attorneys who were the driving forces in this litigation. This case in fact symbolizes well the new era in which these political and social movements truly joined forces as allies, not only on this issue but on the related issue of comparable worth as well. The cement holding that alliance together may very well be necessity, as both movements had their difficulties throughout the 1980s, but there are a number of areas of common interest, and this litigation has demonstrated the utility of closing ranks to overcome powerful business and conservative interests. The most consistent actors in policy struggles around pregnancy discrimination and fetal protection policies have been primarily labor unions and women's rights legal groups, which have effectively transcended the rift that has at times existed between the labor movement and the pre-dominantly middle-class feminist movement. Numerous participants in the *UAW v. Johnson Controls* case noted the existence and importance of this vital coalition. The Women's Legal Defense Fund's Donna Lenhoff recalled how "feminist lawyers at the UAW reached out to the women's rights com-munity," and Susan Deller Ross recalled "labor unions working very closely with the women's movement on the protection of women's right to work and not be fired under these fetal protection policies." Pat Shiu of the Employment Law Center had also stressed the value and importance of hav-ing organized labor as part of progressive coalitions.

The repeated activity of these two important sectors serves to illustrate one of the central assertions of this study—that organized interests with a clearly defined interest and investment in a particular issue will frequently follow that issue as it is taken up in various policy venues, including litiga-tion. Cases that involve interpretation or application of the law cannot be viewed solely from the technical perspective of a discrete dispute between well-defined and identified parties. These parties and their case become vehicles through which organized interests can defend or advance a posi-tion that they might already have pursued in a legislative or regulatory forum.

AMICUS ACTIVITY

When a case has a relatively high profile, numerous organizations can latch on as amici, lending the appearance of a highly integrated lobbying cam-paign to the litigation. Again, the case is the vehicle through which these organizations can further a preexisting agenda. Like providing testimony for a congressional committee, or submitting comments on proposed agency rule making, groups can provide input to the court via amicus briefs. As was illustrated in the foregoing chapters, organizations will often engage in all of these means of articulating their positions.

Group Agendas

It became evident that it is quite possible for many different interests to see very different issues at stake in the same case. What appears upon initial examination to be a case concerning one manufacturer of automobile batteries and its employees of childbearing age became a large-scale contest over the balancing of women's employment rights with fetal safety, as well as related issues such as legislative intent, the validity of animal studies in determining human vulnerability to toxins, tort liability, and the public health impact of reproductive hazards and lost employment opportunity. The amici for the UAW primarily emphasized equal employment opportunity and public health arguments, while those supporting the employer were defending the economic interests of business and the rights of the unborn (and unconceived) and arguing for different and competing readings of tort and occupational safety and health law. Some briefs invoked a range of issues, while others focused on one or two.

There were several groups that had participated in the past in contesting cases or policies dealing with gender discrimination in employment specifically around pregnancy and childbearing capacity. On the employer side, these stalwarts included the Chamber of Commerce and some of the conservative legal foundations, while on the plaintiff side, the ACLU, ERA, and the UAW itself have continually been central players. As described in chapter 2, the lines of cleavage around these employer policies formed in the early 1960s, as women's roles in the workforce were undergoing dramatic changes. They began with the Equal Pay Act, when the ACLU and the AFL-CIO supported the legislation as the Chamber of Commerce worked against it. All three were major actors in the *Johnson Controls* case. The cleavages continued on through the passage of Title VII and the struggles over EEOC enforcement, and persisted through the litigation and legislation around pregnancy in the 1970s. The ACLU and AFL-CIO were again opposed by the chamber in cases such as *Geduldig* and *Gilbert,* key catalysts for the 1978 Pregnancy Discrimination Act, over which they also sparred. They faced each other again in the first Supreme Court case applying the Act, *Newport News Shipbuilding,* and in debate over passage of the Occupational Safety and Health Act and then the promulgation of OSHA's lead standard. These same adversaries and others (the UAW and other unions, the Lead Industries Association, the EEAC) carried their missions through the attempted EEOC regulation of 1980 and the first fetal protection policy cases of the early 1980s, and finally on into this case.

The picture that emerges then is of well-organized interests squaring off against one another repeatedly over similar issues as those issues evolve and emerge in diverse policy forums. Sometimes, the groups themselves are responsible for the emergence of an issue in a particular place and time, other times they react when an issue surfaces due to other circumstances. At times, in fact, groups will intervene in an amicus role to in effect "protect their turf"—to ensure that issues of importance to the group and on which it might have achieved some policy successes are addressed "properly." This was illustrated in the present case, for example, by Trial Lawyers for Public Justice, which not only filed a brief to delineate its view of tort liability but also reviewed the briefs of other parties to ensure that they did not inadvertently undercut TLPJ's position. The reality now is that if and when an issue moves to court, it is not unusual and the players in that arena are not different than those working the issue elsewhere. Going to court has become an almost routine part of the policy process, and contesting issues there is now a matter of course for many organized interests.

The Amicus Strategy

The groups that filed briefs amicus curiae in this litigation varied widely in their structures, purposes, and degree of involvement in litigation in general. On one end of the spectrum were groups that had been in existence for some time and continually monitored judicial activity for cases touching upon their interests, such as the National Chamber Litigation Center and the ACLU. On the other end were groups like the Industrial Hygiene Law Project, an "organization" that was formed solely for the purpose of filing a brief in this case that would not have the ability to litigate directly on its own.

The most significant amicus party in this case was the ACLU, in the person of Joan Bertin, who offered a straightforward explanation as to why her organization was involved in this case as amicus curiae and not as a litigant. The principal reasons, she stated, were that allowing the union to litigate the case conserved the scarce resources of the ACLU, as prior litigation on the same issue had proved costly, and that the lower court disposition had left the case with a sparse record, which she set out to remedy through amicus briefs, both her own and others. For Bertin and the ACLU, the outcome was a longstanding goal and considered critical. There were also other groups, such as the Natural Resources Defense Council and Concerned Women for America, for whom the specific outcome was of only secondary concern. They were interested in the legal status of animal research and fetal rights respectively, and saw either a threat or an opportunity in this case to advance their agendas in these more narrow areas. Filing an amicus brief thus allows a group to focus only on a specific issue without incurring the costs of a litigation effort, for which it may also lack the requisite standing.

It is not possible to determine with certainty whether the efforts of the UAW's amici played a part in its victory (see below for a discussion of the Supreme Court decision), but the joining together of such a multitude of professional, political, and social interests, as well as several government entities, seems likely to have affected the Justices' perception of the case and the issues. This is of course precisely what litigating lawyers and their amici hope, as many of them have notions about how the Court operates and how their own tactics affect that operation. Challenging fetal protection policies in court had never proved successful before, and so the UAW expanded the scope of conflict: first through class action certification and even more so through the retention of a wide array of supporting groups. This is an interestingly paradoxical strategy, at least on a theoretical level, as the judiciary renders interpretations of either the Constitution or existing law—it does not promulgate new law. Groups appealing for judicial resolution of a conflict must frame their appeal in terms of extant policy, rather than ask for a new balancing of interests and the creation of a new law. For a policy *change*, groups must seek legislative relief, grounding their claims in popular support and appealing to majority rule. By retaining a large and diverse spectrum of interests to back a claim in court, a litigant is essentially introducing an element of popular will into what is designed to be a process dictated only by existing rules and their effects on the parties to the case at hand. It would be difficult to find a more telling illustration of the politicization of the judicial process, as these groups essentially lobbied the Court for a particular interpretation of the bona fide occupational qualification (BFOQ) exception under the Pregnancy Discrimination Act.

Judith Kurtz, Managing Attorney for Equal Rights Advocates, and Pat Shiu of the Employment Law Center, observed that when an organization is participating directly in litigation and representing a plaintiff, that plaintiff's interests are always paramount and cannot be compromised in order to make a political statement. As a result, while groups may have more control over the progress of a litigation effort as a direct party, in some sense they are more constrained when there is an actual plaintiff with discrete interests involved. Kurtz said that as an amicus organization, there is greater freedom to "urge political points that you want to push."[1] So, while much of the interest group litigation literature has cited a preference by groups to participate in litigation as a party rather than as amicus in order to retain control, this preference may not be universal, and is in fact strongly affected by a group's purpose in a particular case or issue area. If a political statement is more important than the actual case outcome, participating as amicus is in fact *more* advantageous, as a group then has freedom to state its views without the constraint of plaintiffs' interests.

An interesting phenomenon to observe when studying interest group litigation is how groups spar with one another in the judicial arena. The litigation process is far more constrained than other political forums, and as a result the interplay between interests is also more muted. Moves in this process are carefully controlled by the Court itself, with firm deadlines by which briefs must be filed and page limits on those briefs, which represent the only form of participation and communication, even by the involved parties. The parties in the litigation continually file briefs and then more briefs in response in a back-and-forth process, taking on and countering the arguments made by their opponents. They thus engage in a sort of legal dialogue with each other through their briefs to the Court. Amici, however, are limited to one filing and, depending on which party the brief supports, have a certain deadline by which the briefs must be filed. This process lends a tactical advantage to the amici for the respondent, as they are able to address points made by the petitioners' amici in their briefs, as they have already been filed. The "dialogue" thus becomes more of a limited debate, with one side making arguments to which the other side is free to respond, while the first side lacking an opportunity for rebuttal.

The amici supporting Johnson Controls took ample advantage of the opportunity to counter assertions by the UAW's supporters.[2] All but one brief referenced at least one of the briefs filed for the UAW, with some mentioning two or three. The brief most commonly cited in this way was the U.S./EEOC brief, which is not surprising given its status as the controlling regulatory agency and its partial support for some types of exclusionary policies in some circumstances. Although the EEOC is not widely viewed as a particularly formidable regulatory authority, both sides in this case cited the EEOC whenever possible in order to enhance the credibility of their arguments.

There emerged in the amicus process in this case a set of adversarial counterparts on each side, organizations or groups of organizations that focused on a particular aspect of the case but with opposing interpretations. And so, while the UAW and Johnson Controls sparred over that company's policy, other rivals took up various related issues. The brief of Equal Rights Advocates in a sense "debated" the correct interpretation of the legislative history of the PDA with the Chamber of Commerce's brief; legal staff involved in the ERA brief had been involved in drafting the PDA, and the Chamber had testified against it. Trial Lawyers for Public Justice, an organization committed to using mechanisms like tort liability to advance socially progressive causes like environmental protection, occupational health, and employee rights, was challenged in its opinion regarding the potential tort liability of employers like Johnson Controls by the Washington Legal Foundation, a politically conservative organization committed to business interests. The American Public Health Association's opinion on risk assessment was met with opposition by the Industrial Hygiene Law Project. These sparring groups were taking on the same issues but approaching them from different perspectives, representing very different constituencies—this was a battle of the experts on several quite important policy areas taking place around a case ostensibly involving but one company and one union. Just as a congressional hearing on proposed legislation assembles panels of witnesses to represent various interests, here the interests assemble themselves, as there is no formalized process within the judiciary for ensuring that all potentially affected parties are heard, beyond allowing the filing of amicus curiae briefs.

Amicus Coordination

"Don't annoy the Justices!" This was a familiar mantra among the Supreme Court attorneys queried about their involvement in this and other policy-oriented litigation. The tactics employed and the disparity in the level of formality between legislature and judiciary give this admonition heightened importance in the latter arena. In Congress it might prove productive to have as many constituents and groups as possible contact legislators to influence a vote, since more communication is taken as indicating more interest, but such tactics are actively discouraged when dealing with the Court. Many amicus attorneys with Supreme Court experience spoke of "me-too briefs" that are explicitly frowned upon by the Court. While the Court is interested in knowing who, beyond the litigants, is affected by the issue in question, it does not want a brief from each group with something at stake that has no additional information to offer.

While many attorneys allowed that there was some value to letting the Court know just how many groups felt themselves to be affected by a given case, Jordan Lorence echoed many in stating that the Court does not appreciate amicus briefs that merely reiterate the arguments of the litigants. Such briefs, he stated, which simply inform the Court that a group supports a certain position, are of minimal value to the Justices. Rather, they prefer briefs that explain other implications beyond the instant case, or that provide additional factual background. In his words, "this is how you lobby the Supreme Court, this is the official way to do it; you don't write them letters like you do Congress, you file an amicus brief."

Several attorneys referred to this imperative as encouraging more coalition activity between groups filing briefs. Bertin's theory was that it is better to give the Court fewer but better briefs. In addition to decreasing the load on the Justices, there were other advantages cited for coordinating amicus activity. By parceling out various points or arguments to outside groups, parties to a case can conserve precious space within their own briefs, focusing on the facts or issues most vital to them, while ensuring that other points will still be presented to the Court. Having outside groups file amicus briefs thus serves to afford litigants additional pages through which to advance their causes, as well as to alert the Court to the extent of interest in the issue being litigated. Using amici also allows the parties to have certain arguments presented by entities with greater credibility or expertise. It in fact became evident through the foregoing analysis that often the composition of parties on a brief, or even those cited within its pages, can be an important part of the message.

The two sets of amici in *UAW v. Johnson Controls* were decidedly different from one another in terms of amicus coordination. Stanley Jaspan, the attorney representing the respondent company, professed that he played no deliberate part in coordinating amicus support, while Berzon and Bertin spent considerable effort lining up dozens of organizations friendly to the UAW's cause. This case was somewhat remarkable in terms of the large number of amici that participated, but the numbers alone may be misleading, particularly with regard to those on the UAW side. While some of the amicus groups certainly had real interests at stake and were involved in the drafting of their briefs, many of these groups were asked to participate by the union or were asked to sign on to a brief in progress. The ACLU brief alone contained forty-nine organizational co-signatories, representing 53 percent of the total organizations on this side of the case. The APHA's contained ten groups, which constituted 11 percent of the total. The remaining eight briefs carried the balance of organized interests for the UAW. Thus the two briefs that were directed by Joan Bertin accounted for 64 percent of the groups, most of whom simply signed on. So, although they endorsed the position being taken by the UAW and its lead amici, many of these groups did not step forward of their own accord out of an internally driven sense of need but were in fact recruited to lend greater diversity or weight to the effort, or to provide additional credibility.[3]

THE FINAL DECISION

On March 20, 1991, seven years after the first EEOC charges were filed against Johnson Controls by the UAW in Wisconsin and following two adverse decisions in the district and appellate courts, the U.S. Supreme Court validated the union's claim that fetal protection policies were in direct violation of the legal proscription against sex-based employment

classifications contained in Title VII as amended by the Pregnancy Discrimination Act. While it is not possible to discern with certainty which
arguments made by the parties or their amici influenced this outcome,
inferences can be made from the framing of the Court's decision.

After reviewing the adoption of fetal protection policies by Johnson
Controls and the subsequent litigation that they inspired, the Court states
in its opinion that it granted certiorari in order to "resolve the obvious conflict between the Fourth, Seventh, and Eleventh Circuits on this issue, and
to address the important and difficult question whether an employer, seeking to protect potential fetuses, may discriminate against women just
because of their ability to become pregnant" (196).[4] In its petition for certiorari, the UAW had indeed stated that the three lower courts had "left the
law in total disarray." Resolution of lower court conflict was also one of the
two broad reasons given by the ACLU in its amicus brief supporting certiorari. On the other hand, the brief for Johnson Controls opposing certiorari asserted that "unanimous federal precedent holds that Title VII
permits an employer in narrow circumstances to adopt a fetal protection
policy." The conflict in the lower courts actually concerned the burden of
proof scheme to be applied to these policies and not the outcomes of these
cases, which were indeed consistent with one another. In its brief opposing
certiorari Johnson Controls attempted to minimize the importance of
these inconsistencies, arguing that they were "immaterial" to the outcomes,
which the UAW directly disputed in its subsequent reply brief to the Court.
Before explicating its decision, the Court acknowledges in a footnote the
recently decided cases of *Grant v. General Motors* and *Johnson Controls v.
California Fair Employment and Housing Commission*, both of which for
the first time invalidated fetal protection policies.

There were four primary components to the Court's opinion, which
was written by Justice Harry Blackmun and joined by Justices Thurgood
Marshall, John Paul Stevens, Sandra Day O'Connor, and David Souter.
While it did not cite directly any of the briefs of either the parties or amici,
many of their arguments are evident in the decision.

First, the Court stated that the fetal protection policy in question constituted facial discrimination, or a case of disparate treatment, holding that
because the policy classifies on the basis of the potential for pregnancy it
constitutes "explicit sex discrimination under the PDA," a point made by
the ACLU in its amicus brief on the merits. The lower courts were criticized
by the high court for applying the disparate impact/business necessity
framework and the *Wards Cove* burden of proof scheme (which several of
the amici supporting Johnson Controls explicitly endorsed). The Court
further stated that the policy was not neutral because it did not apply to

males, and that a benevolent motive such as protection of potential off-spring "does not cancel out discrimination." Both of these arguments were made explicitly by the UAW in a brief, and the nondiscriminatory motive point was also made by the ACLU. This conclusion, noted the Court, is bolstered by the PDA and by the new EEOC enforcement policy promulgated in response to the Seventh Circuit decision in this case. Because the employer's policy constitutes disparate treatment, the Court determined, the BFOQ standard must apply.

Second, the Court stated that Title VII's BFOQ provision, the PDA, legislative history, and case law all prohibit employer discrimination based on the capacity to become pregnant. The BFOQ safety exception, the Court declared, is limited to interference with ability to perform the job in question (this was also argued by the UAW, as well as by the ACLU, ERA, the state of Massachusetts, and the APHA), and unconceived fetuses are neither customers nor third parties whose safety is essential to business. The PDA's own BFOQ standard is invoked, which states that pregnant employees must be treated the same unless they differ in their ability to work. Here the Court cites the House and Senate legislative reports on the PDA, indicating that the emphasis on the PDA's legislative history by ERA and the Women's Legal Defense Fund through the brief by Susan Deller Ross may have had an impact. The Court concurred with their depiction of the intent of the PDA, and not with the interpretations offered by the Chamber of Commerce and others who offered competing versions of the PDA's meaning.

Third, the decision held that the respondent company could not establish a BFOQ, as "professed moral and ethical concerns about the welfare of the next generation do not suffice to establish a BFOQ of female sterility" (206). Here the language used by the Court is similar to that employed in the amicus brief of Trial Lawyers for Public Justice, which stated that "expanding the BFOQ defense to include considerations of moral concerns and social costs . . . will eviscerate Title VII." The decision further held that Title VII and the PDA mandate that decisions about the welfare of children be left to parents and not to employers or courts, disallowing employment decisions based on reproductive capacity. Since only a small minority of women might even become pregnant, a fear of prenatal injury does not show that substantially all fertile women are incapable of doing their jobs. Here the language and arguments are similar to those employed by Trial Lawyers for Public Justice, whose brief claimed that "Johnson Controls' policy is based on a web of speculation about the number of women who might get pregnant and who might have children adversely affected by lead."

Finally, the majority opinion added that employers' tort liability and increased costs "do not require a different result." For if Title VII prohibits fetal protection policies (as this Court has determined) and the employer informs employees of existing risks and does not act negligently, the basis for tort liability "seems remote." In its final brief to the Court, the UAW had argued that "a non-negligent employer would not be tort liable." In any event, the opinion continued, the incremental cost of hiring members of one sex cannot justify discrimination. Marsha Berzon stated in her oral arguments that a monetary factor like tort concern cannot establish a BFOQ. The Court notes that OSHA has stated since 1978 that there is no basis for female exclusion. The opinion further holds that Title VII forbids discrimination as a means for diverting attention from the employer's obligation to monitor the workplace for hazards.

The majority opinion concludes by minimizing its own decision, stating that the holding is "neither remarkable nor unprecedented," since "we do no more than hold that the PDA means what it says." Observing that concern for offspring has been a historical excuse for denying women equal employment opportunity (which was noted by the APHA, Trial Lawyers for Public Justice, and the New York City Bar in their briefs), the opinion states that it is not for either the courts or employers to make choices regarding employment and reproduction for women.

Justices Byron White, William Rehnquist, and Anthony Kennedy authored a separate concurring opinion. In their opinion, these Justices agreed with the majority in finding that the policy at issue here was facially discriminatory and overly broad, that summary judgment below was improper, and that the burden of proof had been misapplied below. But the concurrence claimed that the Court erred in determining that fetal protection policies could *never* pass muster under the BFOQ defense, thus agreeing with the view adopted by the United States and the EEOC in their amicus brief (although the brief is not cited directly). They also specifically disagreed with the majority that tort liability could not be part of the equation, and held that compliance with Title VII and OSHA would not necessarily protect an employer from such liability.

Justice Antonin Scalia wrote his own separate concurring opinion, in which he stated that the discussion of evidence of harm to males was irrelevant, because even without such evidence, treating women differently on the basis of pregnancy constitutes discrimination. He also held that whether or not all pregnant women place children at risk is also irrelevant, as Title VII leaves that decision to parents. He disagreed slightly with the other concurrence by agreeing with the majority holding that any action required by Title VII could not give rise to tort liability—this does not answer the question, however, of whether an action indeed is required by Title VII even if it renders one subject to liability under state tort law. Scalia also asserted that cost considerations *could* be relevant to a BFOQ defense.

Whether the Court was swayed by some of the more political or social arguments against fetal protection policies is difficult to tell, as it predictably confined its decision primarily to legal arguments related to the proper application of statutory law (with the exception of the acknowledgement that childbearing has been a traditional rationale for gender discrimination). The UAW and each amicus brief in its support all made the straightforward claim that fetal protection policies violated Title VII and the PDA, and this is what the Court held in its decision. It is therefore not possible to determine if any brief managed to convince the Court that this was the appropriate reading of the law. Many of the points that distinguished individual amicus briefs from one another were not invoked in the decision, such as the broad public health impact (the state of Massachusetts), or the disproportionate impact on people of color (NAACP LDF), or the validity of animal studies in determining human risk (NRDC). Nonetheless, the amici whose roles emerged as dominant in chapter 4—the ACLU, the APHA, and Equal Rights Advocates—are the ones whose arguments appear most prominently in this decision. Since these groups' involvement with the issues at stake predates this decision—in fact reaching back to the emergence of fetal protection policies as a policy issue—this is not terribly surprising. Whether it was the organizations' and attorneys' stature or the merits of their arguments that swayed the justices cannot be determined with certainty, but in fact the line dividing the two may be somewhat artificial, as it has been largely their work in these areas, developing the legal arguments and a track record, that had earned these groups their credentials.

Overall, the tone and content of the opinion comported most closely with the positions of the UAW and its closest amici—the ACLU and the PDA legislative history coalition brief—while the White/Rehnquist/Kennedy concurrence matched up more closely with the position adopted by the Bush administration's solicitor general and EEOC.

LITIGATION AS PART OF THE POLICY PROCESS

As interest group litigation lies squarely at the nexus of law and politics, a typical pattern that emerges when studying interest groups that engage in litigation is a sort of symbiotic relationship between legal expertise and the political will of an organized interest. A group filing a brief brings with it the presence of the constituency that it purports to represent, while attorneys provide the technical expertise and language that allows the group to engage in the highly formalized process of litigation. Both sides of the partnership are necessary, as neither seems to be sufficient alone. Indeed, the counsel of record on a Supreme Court brief must be a member of that bar, which precludes just anyone from filing a brief. But simply being a Supreme Court attorney is not enough either. The Court has truly become a forum for group politics, and attorneys recognize the need to present themselves as representatives of larger interests. Even groups with their own internal legal staff may go outside the organization if a particular view or expertise is needed—the matching up of Susan Deller Ross, a legal expert on the PDA, with Equal Rights Advocates and the Women's Legal Defense Fund, provides a clear example of this strategy. Groups without established legal mechanisms must rely solely on outside counsel—examples include the partnering of Margaret Phillips, the industrial hygienist, with Ilise Feitshans on the Industrial Hygiene Law Project, and Joseph Kinney of the National Safe Workplace Institute working with attorney James Holzhauer.

Some of the attorneys for organizations that are active participants in the litigation arena explicitly stated that the judiciary actually was *not* an appropriate forum for the resolution of many issues that are nonetheless disputed and decided there. Several of the amicus briefs in *Johnson Controls* asserted within their pages that the issues at stake in the case were better left to Congress or regulatory experts than to the courts for resolution. They cited the lack of expertise of judges to resolve issues of this complexity, and the fact that the balancing of interests required by conflicts such as this is the job of a legislative body, particularly when the law governing the particular issue, such as fetal protection policies, is unclear.

The brief filed by the Industrial Hygiene Law Project made this point strongly. The brief stated that Title VII litigation was quite ill suited to resolve such technical issues, arguing that occupational health policy was the purview of OSHA, and that any lapses in OSHA's policy making should be addressed by Congress and not the courts. This was especially pertinent in the extant case, the IHLP stated, as Congress had at that time expressed an intention to address reproductive health hazards. Even the ACLU brief, with its impressive array of organizations, stated that the courts in this area were performing a legislative function by balancing interests. But rather than stating that the issue needed to be taken up by Congress, the ACLU brief asserted that this matter had already been addressed and settled by the PDA, which in the ACLU's view was plainly intended to prohibit policies such as that of Johnson Controls. Despite these admonitions, these organizations nonetheless recognize that for good or bad, the Court will often be the final arbiter of a policy dispute. They therefore feel compelled to articulate their interests in the outcome, just as they would if there were pending legislation.

Margaret Phillips of IHLP, while criticizing judicial resolution of occupational and public health issues, was nonetheless rather positive in her evaluation of the litigation process itself. She noted that filing an amicus brief was remarkably affordable, especially as compared with how expensive other types of political action can be, and was thus within the reach of even small groups. She also viewed the process as more focused, providing a single point of contact, whereas the legislative process can be quite diffuse. The formality and narrowly defined methods required of groups addressing the Court actually serves to reduce groups' costs, in her opinion. Her partner on the IHLP's brief, attorney Ilise Feitshans, had a similarly enthusiastic if mixed view of the process. She saw tremendous value in the ability of groups that might not otherwise have a voice in the political process being able to participate in this way, characterizing it as the "essence of truly grassroots, single-issue politics." It can though, in her view, at times mask sham organizations that are mere fronts for groups trying to conceal their true agendas, or trying to add extra weight to an interest already being expressed. Nevertheless, Feitshans views the process as truly important, even the "essence of democracy," for although such freedom of access might clog the process, it is worth it if it affords individual voices a forum through which to be heard.

Is pursuing policy through the judiciary truly unique, in more than a procedural way? Joan Bertin asserted that lobbying in the various venues (legislative, regulatory, judicial) was not as different as one might think. This is due, in her opinion, to the fact that all forums have become adversarial and that they simply represent different mechanisms through which to work out controversy. Lawyers and lobbyists, she says, do essentially the same thing, which is build a case—the style of advocacy is simply more formalized in the judicial setting. So, in a sense, she was confirming the thesis here—advocates will seek change in all venues, and their adversaries will meet them there.

But the formality of litigation is such that it *can* truly serve to constrain debate on issues in two primary ways. First, the nature of litigation and its procedural rules can limit who participates. Procedural rules can preclude certain issues from being raised (for example, issues waived below often cannot be revisited on appeal), circumstances particular to the parties at interest can even render an entire case moot, and, technically, amici must get permission even to file. A group must have standing or wait for someone else with standing to engage in litigation and file an amicus brief to get involved at all, assuming that it is aware of the pending case in the first place.

As was shown in this case, the majority of the amici on the side of the UAW were invited to join the case, while others did so because they were well-established organizations with the resources to monitor pending litigation for issues pertinent to their agendas. The process itself does not necessarily facilitate widespread participation by all interests who might be affected by the outcome, and thus not all relevant information will necessarily be presented to the court. By contrast, significant regulatory proposals are typically published in the Federal Register and public comment is solicited. While the legislative process is not entirely transparent, Congress is structured in such a way so that if an issue has salience for a particular interest, some legislator at some point in the process is likely to consult at least a lobbyist for that interest, and sometimes even his or her own constituents.

But the courts are not supposed to balance all competing interests in a policy issue, only those of the parties in the case before them, which may not represent all who are affected. The American judiciary was not intended to be a political forum, certainly not the "essence of democracy." Federal courts do not render advisory opinions, operating under a mandate to rule only on actual cases or controversies between parties with direct real interests. Modern public interest litigation, however, has grown far from this model. The UAW itself turned this into a major battle on behalf of all workers similarly situated by pursuing it as a class action and persisting through the U.S. Supreme Court, and the legions of amici further rendered the case a large-scale group conflict.

The second way in which moving an issue into court serves to constrain the policy process is in the very nature of litigation. Parties cannot go to court seeking new legislation or implementing regulations—this kind of primary policy making is the purview of the legislative and executive branches. Once a group is in court, it must by definition cast its claims in terms of already-existing law. This imperative serves to render the process of seeking "policy" from a court more conservative—or, to put it another way, it has a moderating influence upon the interests before the court. Organizations cannot go to court simply because they do not like the current state of the law. They must present a cognizable claim, one recognized in either the common law or via a constitutional or statutory grant. One might argue that a congressional statute is unconstitutional, or that a regulatory body exceeded its statutory authority, but not simply that the law is disagreeable to one's interests.

This was borne out by comparing the stated agendas of many of the organizations involved in the Johnson Controls litigation with the arguments that they presented in their briefs. Thus, while the Chamber of Commerce might well want to see all regulations that constrain private businesses disappear, it could not claim that when helping Johnson Controls defend itself in a Title VII claim such as this. The UAW might have preferred a law explicitly banning fetal protection policies, but instead argued that existing law already proscribed them. The ACLU Women's Rights Project might have preferred to argue that the OSHA lead standard—indeed, all workplace regulations—should use the pregnant woman as the standard rather than the average male worker typically envisioned by such regulations. (This was in fact the philosophical position of some of its allies, such as the Women's Legal Defense Fund.)

All of this bears upon the question of genuine interest representation. When cases with the potential to affect public policy are tried in court, there are several layers of interests present: the parties to the case (that is, the distinct plaintiff and respondent), their attorneys, organizations with which those parties or attorneys may be affiliated, and potentially a host of amici, also with attorneys, staff, and members, many of whom may be unaware that their interests are being implicated in a specific case. It seems safe to conclude in this study that the interests of the original plaintiffs provided the impetus for the litigation and were faithfully represented. But unions are unique among organized interests, as they legally represent their members under collective bargaining agreements that bear directly on those members' livelihoods. The same cannot be said for the members of voluntary public interest groups. As Scheppele and Walker (1991) observed, unions have strong reasons to use the courts, and they do use them extensively. But their representational link to their constituents is far stronger than most other groups that engage in similar litigation. The degree of congruence of interest between organizations, attorneys, and mass constituencies thus remains a viable field of exploration, as it may be difficult to extrapolate the findings herein beyond the organized labor context.

Also, cases of unusually high salience such as *UAW v. Johnson Controls* may not provide the best vehicles for discerning general patterns about group litigation, as they may elicit ad hoc participation by groups that do not usually engage in this process. The number of briefs and groups is higher than average, compromising the ability to generalize. What a study like this does reveal, however, are the various dynamics at play in a litigation campaign. In order to further explore how interest representation and policy formation differ between political institutions, it may be fruitful to compare how policy arguments are presented in legal briefs to how they are made in other forums like the legislature. Language is essential in politics, and it would be illuminating to compare how organized interests convey their philosophies and goals to their membership (or potential members), to legislators, and to jurists.

The events in this litigation and the observations about the group litigation process made by many of the attorneys interviewed confirm many of the findings of earlier scholars: groups do indeed look to the courts for sympathetic policy outcomes; they do so for various reasons, not all related directly to the outcome; they do it either directly or via amicus briefs; and more and more of them are learning how to do it. Beyond this, the foregoing account has provided a detailed look at one significant campaign, to demonstrate the intricate dynamics involved in a complex litigation effort, dynamics that emanate from the plaintiffs outward to dozens or even hundreds of other interested parties. At the same time, some new insights emerged into the interconnectedness of the feminist and labor movements in their struggle to combat age-old views of women's roles in the family and the workforce.

Appendix: Interviews

Name	Party Represented	Date/Location
Marsha Berzon	UAW	11/2/95 (in person)
Patricia Shiu	Employment Law Center	11/2/95 (in person)
Prudence K. Poppink	California FEHC	11/5/95 (in person)
Joseph Kinney	National Safe Workplace Institute	12/20/95 (telephone)
James D. Holzhauer	National Safe Workplace Institute	12/27/95 (in person)
Timothy B. Dyk	U.S. Chamber of Commerce	1/29/96 (in person)
Jane Hadro	Concerned Women for America	2/2/96 (in person)
Quentin Riegel	National Association of Manufacturers	2/8/96 (in person)
Joan Bertin	ACLU Women's Rights Project	2/8/96 (telephone)
Stephen Bokat	Chamber of Commerce	2/14/96 (in person)
Mark Chopko	U.S. Catholic Conference	2/15/96 (telephone)

Jordan Lorence	Concerned Women for America	2/15/96 (telephone)
Doug McDowell	Equal Employment Advisory Council	2/19/96 (in person)
Ilise Feitshans	Industrial Hygiene Law Project	2/19/96 (telephone)
Arthur Bryant	Trial Lawyers for Public Justice	2/20/96 (telephone)
Margaret Phillips, Ph.D.	Industrial Hygiene Law Project	3/5/96 (telephone)
Stanley S. Jaspan	Johnson Controls	3/21/96 (telephone)
Anthony T. Caso	Pacific Legal Foundation	3/26/96 (telephone)
Marianne Lado	NAACP LDF	4/2/96 (telephone)
Miriam Horwitz	UAW	4/10/96 (telephone)
Manuel M. Medeiros	State of California	4/10/96 (telephone)
Judith Kurtz	Equal Rights Advocates	4/18/96 (telephone)
Katherine McCarter	APHA	4/23/96 (in person)
Ralph Jones	United Auto Workers (UAW)	6/11/96 (telephone)
Stephen S. Ostrach	New England Legal Foundation	6/12/96 (telephone)
Thomas O. McGarity	NRDC	6/13/96 (telephone)
Susan Deller Ross	Equal Rights Advocates	7/11/96 (in person)

Charles Shanor	EEOC	7/18/96 (telephone)
Beverly Tucker	UAW	7/19/96 (telephone)
Donna Lenhoff	Women's Legal Defense Fund	8/26/96 (telephone)
Marley Weiss	UAW	10/21/96 (telephone)
Carin Clauss	UAW	10/22/96 (telephone)
Nadine Taub	APHA	10/29/96 (telephone)

Notes

Notes to Chapter 1

1. *Oil, Chemical, and Atomic Workers Union v. American Cyanamid,* 741 F2d 444 (D.C. Cir. 1984).
2. *International Union, United Auto Workers v. Johnson Controls,* 680 F. Supp. 309 (E.D. Wis. 1988), *aff'd,* 886 F2d 871 (7th Cir. 1989), *rev'd,* 499 U.S. 187 (1991).
3. 347 U.S. 483 (1954).
4. 410 U.S. 113 (1973).
5. 886 F2d at 920.
6. The disparate impact-business necessity framework was first promulgated in *Griggs v. Duke Power* (1971).

Notes to Chapter 2

1. See generally Foner (1979).
2. 198 U.S. 45 (1905).
3. 208 U.S. 412 (1908).
4. *Radice v. New York,* 264 U.S. 292 (1924).
5. *Goesart v. Cleary,* 335 U.S. 464 (1948).
6. *West Coast Hotel v. Parrish,* 300 U.S. 379 (1937).
7. The U.S. Department of Labor created the Women in Industry Division in 1918, which was intended to ensure the most effective use of working women during the war while maintaining decent working conditions. This division became the permanent Women's Bureau in 1920.
8. 261 U.S. 525 (1923). This decision was a rare instance in which the Court strayed from its prior and subsequent endorsement of legal protections for women in the workforce. The opinion was more a strike against a minimum wage than it was an endorsement of women's equality, which the Court rather facetiously claimed had been attained virtually overnight by virtue of the enactment of women's suffrage three years earlier.
9. Labor Relations Reporter 253–55 (April 25, 1966).

10. The history of the UAW's stance toward women within its ranks will be explored in greater depth in the next chapter.

11. 29 CFR 1604.1(c); 30 *Federal Register* 14927, December 2, 1965.

12. EEOC press release, February 23, 1968.

13. *Federal Register* 13368 (August 19, 1969).

14. 408 F2d 228 (5th Cir. 1969).

15. 444 F2d 1219 (9th Cir. 1971).

16. Initially, the Transportation Communications Employees Union was also named a defendant along with the company, but was not included in the appeal to the 9th Circuit.

17. 400 U.S. 542 (1971).

18. 433 U.S. 321 (1977).

19. Pub.L. 92–261, §2, Mar. 24, 1972, 86 Stat. 103.

20. *Federal Register* 6837 (April 5, 1972).

21. 417 U.S. 484 (1974).

22. 429 U.S. 125 (1976).

23. The labor-feminist alliance also coalesced around advocacy of comparable worth for women's occupations.

24. 462 U.S. 669 (1983).

25. 479 U.S. 272 (1987).

26. "Life or Death for Your Business?" *Nation's Business,* April 1968 (cited in Noble 1986).

27. Politically sophisticated environmental groups emerged just prior to the proliferation of women's rights groups in the 1960s.

28. Occupational Safety and Health Act, P.L. 91–596, sec. 6(b)(5).

29. Some substances that have been regulated include benzene, asbestos, vinyl chloride, and cotton dust.

30. OCAW was the plaintiff in the second major fetal protection suit, *OCAW v. American Cyanamid Company* (1984).

31. All but one standard issued by OSHA have prompted lawsuits challenging their legality. In most instances, the agency's rule is upheld in court.

32. *United Steelworkers v. Marshall,* 647 F2d 1189 (D.C. Cir. 1980).

33. The problem was illustrated as well by an incident the previous year at Allied Chemical Company in Danville, Illinois. Believing that Fluorocarbon 22 caused fetal damage, the company laid off several women workers, two of whom had themselves sterilized in order to be reinstated. It was subsequently discovered that the substance was not indeed teratogenic (harmful to a developing fetus), and that the women's surgery had been needless (Bronson 1979).

34. The General Duty clause states that "each employer shall furnish to each of his employees employment and a place of employment which are free from recognized hazards that are causing or are likely to cause death or serious physical harm to his employees" (29 U.S.C. s. 654 (a)(1)).

35. Interview with Joan Bertin of Columbia University, formerly of the ACLU Women's Rights Project, November 23, 1993.

36. *Wright v. Olin,* 697 F2d 1172 (4th Cir. 1982).

37. *International Union, United Auto Workers v. Johnson Controls,* 680 F. Supp. 309 (E.D. Wis. 1988).

38. *International Union, United Auto Workers v. Johnson Controls,* 886 F2d 871 (7th Cir. 1989).

39. 490 U.S. 642 (1989).

40. The 1991 Civil Rights Act returned the burden of proof scheme to that originally outlined in *Griggs v. Duke Power* 401 U.S. 424 (1971), the case in which the disparate impact standard was promulgated.

41. *Johnson Controls v. California Fair Employment and Housing Commission,* 267 Cal Rptr. 158 (1990).

42. *Grant v. General Motors,* 908 F2d 1303 (6th Cir. 1990).

43. Also in 1990, Representative Pat Williams introduced into Congress the Employee Protection Act of 1990 (HR 4420). The bill would have prohibited employers from discriminating against employees on the basis of their refusal to submit to sterilization or to a fertility test or to refrain from procreation. The measure was not acted upon since it was eventually seen to have been obviated by the Supreme Court's ruling in the *Johnson Controls* case.

Notes to Chapter 3

1. Bureau of Labor Statistics, *Employment and Earnings* (January issues).

2. In another indication of the difference between the UAW and organized labor as a whole, Leonard Woodcock of the UAW sent a good luck telegram to the convention from the union, while the AFL-CIO remained silent and wary (Balser 1987).

3. Interview with Joan Bertin, formerly of the ACLU Women's Rights Project, February 8, 1996.

4. Interview with Miriam Horwitz, April 10, 1996.

5. Interview with Beverly Tucker, July 19, 1996.

6. Interview with Carin Clauss, October 22, 1996.

7. Clauss interview.

8. Ibid.

9. Bertin interview.

10. Interview with Ralph Jones, June 11, 1996.

11. Interview with Susan Deller Ross, July 11, 1996.

12. *Wright v. Olin,* 697 F2d 1172 (4th Cir. 1982); *Zuniga v. Kleberg County Hospital,* 692 F2d 986 (5th Cir. 1982).

13. 726 F2d 1543 (1984).

14. 741 F2d 444 (D.C. Cir. 1984).

15. 908 F2d 1303 (6th Cir. 1990).

16. Interview with Marley Weiss, October 21, 1996.

17. Horwitz interview.

18. Weiss interview.

19. Carin Clauss noted that Weiss was careful to include a male plaintiff in the suit.

20. Interview with Beverly Tucker, July 19, 1996.

21. Interview with Marsha Berzon, November 2, 1995.

22. The AFL-CIO in fact often offers to take over cases from member unions that reach the Supreme Court, as it possesses essential experience at that level that most individual unions lack.

23. Berzon interview.
24. Ross interview.

1. There were in fact several other groups that similarly changed their positions on this issue and joined in support of the UAW, including the American Association of University Women (AAUW) and the National Council of Jewish Women.

2. "The History of the ACLU Women's Rights Project," available at http://www. aclu.org/issues/women/histwo.html.

3. 429 U.S. 190 (1976).

4. 430 U.S. 199 (1977).

5. "The History of the ACLU Women's Rights Project," available at http://www. aclu.org/issues/women/histwo.html.

6. Interview with Joan Bertin, February 8, 1996.

7. Ibid.

8. See Table 6 for a listing of the parties to the certiorari brief. Those that joined different briefs at the merits stage are noted. In addition, the ACLU picked up a number of new organizations when it filed again at the merits stage—see Table 4 for a listing of all the parties to the ACLU brief on the merits.

9. This may occur, for example, when a brief is written by someone who is not a member of the Supreme Court Bar—a member of the Bar may be retained to serve as counsel of record.

10. Bertin, Joan. 1989. "Reproductive Hazards in the Workplace: Proposals for Legislation, Education, and Public Policy Initiatives." In Taub and Cohen, eds. *Reproductive Laws for the 1990s: A Briefing Handbook.*

11. Interview with Nadine Taub, October 29, 1996.

12. Interview with Pat Shiu, November 2, 1995.

13. The ELC had also already signed onto the ACLU's amicus brief supporting certiorari, and the decision to file a separate brief under the auspices of ERA to elucidate the PDA legislative history was made somewhat late in the game, so ELC would have had to in effect abandon the ACLU brief to which it was already committed to move over to join the other women's rights brief.

14. Ibid.

15. At times, a philosophical difference between women's rights activists on the two coasts has become visible, as those on the East Coast have tended to take a more "pure equality" view, while West Coast feminists have embraced a "difference" approach, advocating recognition but not subordination of gender differences—a strategy that the other wing views as potentially leading back to restrictions based on difference.

16. The organization is now the National Partnership for Women and Families.

17. Interview with Donna Lenhoff, August 26, 1996.

18. Equal Rights Advocates, 1989–90 Annual Report.

19. 573 A.2d 1235 (D.C. 1990).

20. 492 U.S. 490 (1989).

21. 506 U.S. 263 (1993).

22. 500 U.S. 173 (1991).

23. The Chamber may in fact be viewed as the ERA coalition's adversarial counterpart in the Johnson Controls litigation in the area of the legislative history of the PDA.

24. 267 Cal Rptr. 158 (1990).

25. Interview with Prudence Poppink, November 5, 1995.

26. Interview with Manuel Medeiros, April 10, 1996.

27. Manuel Medeiros, on the other hand, felt that since the two cases involved the same company and policy California probably would have been preempted by the federal decision.

28. 518 U.S. 515 (1996).

29. 510 U.S. 17 (1993).

30. 476 U.S. 1104 (1986).

31. Finley, Lucinda. "Transcending Equality Theory: A Way Out of the Maternity and the Workplace Debate." 86 *Columbia Law Review* 1118 (1986).

32. Interview with Katherine McCarter, April 23, 1996.

33. Interview with Joan Bertin, November 23, 1993.

34. Paul, Maureen, Cynthia Daniels, and Robert Rosofsky. 1989. "Corporate Response to Reproductive Hazards in the Workplace: Results of the Family, Work, and Health Survey." *American Journal of Industrial Medicine* 16:267.

35. Interview with Marianne Lado, April 2, 1996.

36. 400 U.S. 542 (1971).

37. Lado interview.

38. Interview with Charles Shanor, July 18, 1996.

39. Berzon interview.

40. Shanor interview.

41. 109 S. Ct. 2115 (1989).

42. Berzon interview.

Notes to Chapter 5

1. Dyk was with the firm of Jones, Day, Reavis, and Pogue. He is now a judge on the Federal Circuit.

2. Interview with Stephen Bokat, February 14, 1996. There are of course cases involving Chamber members litigating against one another; in such instances of inter-member conflict, the NCLC will decline to become involved.

3. Interview with Timothy Dyk, January 29, 1996.

4. Bokat interview.

5. The use of the term *unborn children* demonstrates use of language similar to the other parties supporting Johnson Controls who employed more of a fetal rights approach.

6. *The Business Counsel—A Quarterly Update of the Activities of the National Chamber Litigation Center* 17, no. 2 (Winter 1995).

7. For other accounts of the EEAC's litigation activity, see Epstein (1985) and O'Neill (1985).

8. Interview with Quentin Riegel, February 8, 1996.

9. These and subsequent statements taken from interview with Joseph Kinney, December 20, 1995.

10. Interview with James Holzhauer, December 27, 1995.

11. Interviews with Kinney and Holzhauer.

12. Interview with Margaret Phillips, March 5, 1996.

13. The American Public Health Association, by contrast, in its amicus brief supporting the UAW, did use Dr. Bingham as an expert reference.

14. Interview with Ilise Feitshans, February 19, 1996.

15. Interview with Jordan Lorence, February 15, 1996.

16. Interview with Jane Hadro, February 2, 1996.

17. Hadro interview.

18. "Concerned Women for America" newsletter, vol. 13, no. 7 (July 1991): 2.

19. *4th Street, NE* (pamphlet published by the NCCB/USCC), June 1995.

20. Interview with Mark Chopko, February 15, 1996.

21. "Catholic Official Comments on *Johnson Controls* Case," news release from United States Catholic Conference, March 20, 1991.

22. *Associated General Contractors v. City and County of San Francisco* (1987).

23. O'Connor and Epstein (1989), 163.

24. Interview with Stephen Ostrach, June 12, 1996.

25. O'Connor and Epstein 1989, 204.

26. WLF may have thus unwittingly endorsed the view of exclusionary fetal protection policies furthered by opponents of such policies, who often dub them "corporate protection policies" out of a belief that they are indeed intended more to shield companies from suits than they are to shield fetuses from lead or other toxins.

Notes to Chapter 6

1. Interview with Judith Kurtz, April 18, 1996.

2. The amicus briefs for the UAW were all filed between May 23 and June 1, 1990; those for Johnson Controls were filed on either July 17 or July 19.

3. James Holzhauer of Mayer, Brown, and Platt in fact stated that the justices maintain lists of amicus organizations that they feel to be credible, and seek them out when reviewing amicus briefs.

4. These were the appellate courts that had rendered decisions in, respectively, *Wright v. Olin, UAW v. Johnson Controls,* and *Hayes v. Shelby Memorial Hospital,* all fetal protection cases.

Bibliography

Accurso, Allison E. 1985. "Title VII and Exclusionary Practices: Fertile and Pregnant Women Need Not Apply." *Rutgers Law Journal* 17:95–134.

Andrade, Vibiana M. 1981. "The Toxic Workplace: Title VII Protection for the Potentially Pregnant Person." *Harvard Women's Law Journal* 4:71–103.

Ashford, Nicholas A., and Charles C. Caldart. 1983. "The Control of Reproductive Hazards in the Workplace: A Prescription for Prevention." *Industrial Relations Law Journal* 5:523–63.

Auman, Eva M. 1990. "Excluding Women from the Workplace: Employment Discrimination vs. Protecting Fetal Health." *Missouri Law Review* 55:771–802.

Babcock, Barbara Allen, Ann E. Freedman, Eleanor Holmes Norton, and Susan C. Ross. 1975. *Sex Discrimination and the Law: Causes and Remedies.* Boston: Little, Brown and Company.

Baer, Judith A. 1978. *The Chains of Protection: The Judicial Response to Women's Labor Legislation.* Westport, Conn.: Greenwood Press.

———. 1991. "Beyond Rights: Fetal Protection and Sexual Equality." Paper presented at the Midwest Political Science Association meeting.

Baker, Stewart A., and James R. Asperger. 1982. "Forward: Toward a Center for State and Local Legal Advocacy." *Catholic University Law Review* 31:367.

Balser, Diane. 1987. *Sisterhood and Solidarity: Feminism and Labor in Modern Times.* Boston: South End Press.

Barker, Lucius. 1967. "Third Parties in Litigation: A Systematic View of the Judicial Function." *Journal of Politics* 29:41–69.

Bayer, Ronald. 1982a. "Reproductive Hazards in the Workplace: Bearing the Burden of Fetal Risk." *Health and Society* 60:633–56.

———. 1982b. "Women, Work, and Reproductive Hazards." *The Hastings Center Report* (October): 14–19.

Becker, Mary E. 1986. "From Muller v. Oregon to Fetal Vulnerability Policies." *University of Chicago Law Review* 53:1219–73.

Bell, Carolyn. 1979. "Implementing Safety and Health Regulations for Women in the Workplace." *Feminist Studies* 5:286–301.

Bellinger, Leviton, Waternaux, Needleman, and Rabinowitz. 1987. "Longitudinal Analysis of Prenatal and Postnatal Lead Exposure and Early Cognitive Development." *New England Journal of Medicine* 316:1037–43.

Benshoof, Janet. 1989. "Fetal Personhood and the Law." In *Abortion Rights and Fetal "Personhood,"* edited by Edd Doerr and James W. Prescott. Long Beach, Calif.: Centerline Press.

Bentley, Arthur F. 1908. *The Process of Government.* Chicago: University of Chicago Press.

Berch, Bettina. 1982. *The Endless Day: The Political Economy of Women and Work.* New York: Harcourt Brace Jovanovich.

Berger, Margaret. 1980. *Litigation on Behalf of Women: An Assessment.* New York: Ford Foundation.

Bernacki, Edward J. 1980. "The Control of Hazardous Exposures in the Workplace." In *Women, Work, and Health: Challenges to Corporate Policy,* edited by Diana Chapman Walsh and Richard H. Egdahl. New York: Springer-Verlag.

Bertin, Joan. 1989. "Reproductive Hazards in the Workplace: Proposals for Legislation, Education, and Public Policy Initiatives." In *Reproductive Laws for the 1990s: A Briefing Handbook,* edited by Sherrill Cohen and Nadine Taub. Clifton, N.J.: Humana Press.

———. 1993. "Legal and Policy Issues." In *Occupational and Environmental Reproductive Hazards: A Guide for Clinicians,* edited by Maureen Paul. Baltimore, Md.: Williams and Wilkins.

———. 1994. "Reproductive Hazards in the Workplace: Lessons from *UAW v. Johnson Controls.*" In *Prenatal Exposure to Toxicants: Developmental Consequences,* edited by Herbert L. Needleman and David Bellinger. Baltimore, Md.: The Johns Hopkins University Press.

Bickel, Alexander. 1962. *The Least Dangerous Branch: The Supreme Court at the Bar of Politics.* New Haven, Conn.: Yale University Press.

Bird, Caroline. 1968. *Born Female: The High Cost of Keeping Women Down.* New York: David McKay.

Birkby, Robert H., and Walter F. Murphy. 1964. "Interest Group Conflict in the Judicial Arena." *Texas Law Review* 42:1018–48.

Blanco, Alan Carlos. 1985. "Fetal Protection Programs Under Title VII: Rebutting the Procreation Presumption." *University of Pittsburgh Law Review* 46:755–94.

Blank, Robert H. 1991a. "Fetal Protection Policies in the Workplace." Paper presented at the Midwest Political Science Association meeting.

———. 1991b. *Mother and Fetus: Changing Notions of Maternal Responsibility.* Westport, Conn.: Greenwood Press.

———. 1993a. *Fetal Protection in the Workplace—Women's Rights, Business Interests, and the Unborn.* New York: Columbia University Press.

———. 1993b. "Reproductive Technology: Pregnant Women, the Fetus, and the Courts." *Women and Politics* 13:1–17.

Blum, Linda M. 1991. *Between Feminism and Labor: The Significance of the Comparable Worth Movement.* Berkeley: University of California Press.

Bor, Victoria L. 1978. "Exclusionary Employment Practices in Hazardous Industries: Protection or Discrimination?" *Columbia Journal of Environmental Law* 5:97–155.

Boyle, Kevin. 1995. *The UAW and the Heyday of American Liberalism.* Ithaca, N.Y.: Cornell University Press.

Braun, Michelle M. 1991. "The Battle between Mother and Fetus: Fetal Protection in the Context of Employment Discrimination." *Hamline Law Review* 14:403–26.

Brito, Patricia. 1987. "Protective Legislation in Ohio." In *Women, the Law and the*

Constitution, edited by Kermit Hall. New York: Garland Publishing.

Bronson, Gail. "Allied Chemical Compensates Five Women Laid Off to Protect Childbearing Ability," *Wall Street Journal,* January 5, 1979, 1.

Buss, Emily. 1986. "Getting Beyond Discrimination: A Regulatory Solution to the Problem of Fetal Hazards in the Workplace." *Yale Law Journal* 95:577–98.

Caldeira, Gregory A., and John R. Wright. 1988. "Organized Interests and Agenda Setting in the U.S. Supreme Court." *American Political Science Review* 82:1109–27.

———. 1990. "Amici Curiae Before the Supreme Court: Who Participates, When, and How Much?" *Journal of Politics* 52:782–806.

Campanella, Carolyn J. 1987. "Fetal Protection or Employment Discrimination?" *Employment Relations Today* 14:135–42.

Caplan, Lincoln. 1987. *The Tenth Justice: The Solicitor General and the Rule of Law.* New York: Knopf.

Chavkin, Wendy. 1979. "Occupational Hazards to Reproduction: A Review Essay and Annotated Bioliography." *Feminist Studies* 5:310–25.

———, ed. 1984. *Double Exposure: Women's Health Hazards on the Job and at Home.* New York: Monthly Review Press.

Cigler, Allan J., and Burdett A. Loomis, eds. *Interest Group Politics,* 2d ed. Washington, D.C.: Congressional Quarterly Press.

Clayton, Cornell W., ed. 1995. *Government Lawyers: The Federal Legal Bureaucracy and Presidential Politics.* Lawrence: University Press of Kansas.

Clemens, Elisabeth S. 1997. *The People's Lobby: Organizational Innovation and the Rise of Interest Group Politics in the United States, 1980–1925.* Chicago: University of Chicago Press.

Clyne, Robert M. 1980. "Fetotoxicity and Fertile Female Employees." In *Women, Work, and Health: Challenges to Corporate Policy,* edited by Diana Chapman Walsh and Richard H. Egdahl. New York: Springer-Verlag.

Condit, Deirdre M. 1991. "Constructing Fetal 'Personhood': An Examination of Law and Language." Paper presented at the Midwest Political Science Association meeting.

Cortner, Richard C. 1968. "Strategies and Tactics of Litigants in Constitutional Cases." *Journal of Public Law* 17:287–307.

Crenshaw, Carrie. 1995. "The 'Protection' of 'Woman': A History of Legal Attitudes toward Women's Workplace Freedom." *Quarterly Journal of Speech* 81:63–82.

Crowell, Donald R., and David A. Copus. 1978. "Safety and Equality at Odds: OSHA and Title VII Clash Over Health Hazards in the Workplace." *Industrial Relations Law Journal* 2:567–95.

Daniels, Cynthia R. 1993a. "The Pregnant Citizen: Pregnancy, Self-Sovereignty, and Citizenship for Women." Paper presented at the annual meeting of the American Political Science Association.

———. 1993b. *At Women's Expense: State Power and the Politics of Fetal Rights.* Cambridge, Mass.: Harvard University Press.

Darcy, Lynne. 1979. "Birth Defects Caused by Parental Exposure to Workplace Hazards: The Interface of Title VII with OSHA and Tort Law." *University of Michigan Journal of Law Reform* 12:237–60.

Doerr, Edd, and James W. Prescott, eds. 1989. *Abortion Rights and Fetal 'Personhood.'* Long Beach, Calif.: Centerline Press.

Doudera, A. Edward. 1982. "Fetal Rights? It Depends." *Trial* 39–44.

Duden, Barbara. 1993. *Disembodying Women—Perspectives on Pregnancy and the Unborn.* Cambridge, Mass.: Harvard University Press.

Duncan, Allyson K. 1989. "Fetal Protection and the Exclusion of Women from the Toxic Workplace." *North Carolina Central Law Journal* 18:67–86.

Epstein, Lee. 1985. *Conservatives in Court.* Knoxville: University of Tennessee Press.

———. 1993. Interest Group Litigation during the Rehnquist Court Era. 9 J.L. & Pol. 639.

Epstein, Lee, and Joseph F. Kobylka. 1992. *The Supreme Court and Legal Change: Abortion and the Death Penalty.* Chapel Hill: University of North Carolina Press.

Epstein, Lee, and C. K. Rowland. 1986. "Interest Groups in the Courts: Do Groups Fare Better?" In *Interest Group Politics,* 2d ed., edited by Allan J. Cigler and Burdett A. Loomis. Washington, D.C.: Congressional Quarterly Press.

———. 1991. "Debunking the Myth of Interest Group Invincibility in the Courts." *American Political Science Review* 85:205–17.

Evans-Stanton, Sherri. 1987. "Gender Specific Regulations in the Chemical Workplace." *Santa Clara Law Review* 27:353–76.

Faludi, Susan. 1991. *Backlash: The Undeclared War against American Women.* New York: Crown Publishers.

Finley, Lucinda. 1986. "Transcending Equality Theory: A Way Out of the Maternity and the Workplace Debate." *Columbia Law Review* 86:1118.

Finneran, Hugh M. 1980. "Title VII and Restrictions on Employment of Fertile Women." *Labor Law Journal* 31:223–31.

Fintel, Edward J. 1983. "The Legality of Fetal Protection Policies under Title VII: Wright v. Olin Corp." *Syracuse Law Review* 34:1131–54.

Foner, Philip S. 1979. *Women and the American Labor Movement.* New York: The Free Press.

Freeman, Jo. 1975. *The Politics of Women's Liberation.* New York: Longman.

Furnish, Hannah A. 1980. "Prenatal Exposure to Fetally Toxic Work Environments: The Dilemma of the 1978 Pregnancy Amendment to Title VII of the Civil Rights Act of 1964." *Iowa Law Review* 66:63–129.

Gabin, Nancy F. 1990. *Feminism in the Labor Movement.* Ithaca, N.Y.: Cornell University Press.

Galanter, Mark. 1974. "Why the 'Haves' Come Out Ahead: Speculations on the Limits of Legal Change." *Law & Society Review* 9:95.

Gallagher, Janet. 1985. "Fetal Personhood and Women's Policy." In *Women, Biology, and Public Policy,* edited by Virginia Sapiro. Beverly Hills, Calif.: Sage.

Gelb, Joyce. 1989. *Feminism and Politics.* Berkeley: University of California Press.

Gonen, Julianna S. 2001. "Removing Informed Consent from HIV Testing of Pregnant Women: A Return to the Maternal-Fetal Conflict." *Georgetown Journal of Gender and the Law* 2:765.

Graham, Tolle, Nancy Lessin, and Franklin Mirer. 1993. "A Labor Perspective on Workplace Reproductive Hazards: Past History, Current Concerns, and Positive Directions." *Environmental Health Perspectives Supplements* 101:199–204.

Grossman, Alison E. 1991. "Striking Down Fetal Protection Policies: A Feminist Victory?" *Virginia Law Review* 77:1607–36.

Hakman, Nathan. 1966. "Lobbying the Supreme Court: An Appraisal of Political Science Folklore." *Fordham Law Review* 35:15–50.

———. 1969. "The Supreme Court's Political Environment." In *Frontiers of Judicial*

Research. edited by Joel B. Grossman and Joseph Tanenhaus. New York: J. Wiley.

Hatch, Maureen. 1984. "Mother, Father, Worker: Men and Women and the Reproduction Risks of Work." In *Double Exposure: Women's Health Hazards on the Job and at Home,* edited by Wendy Chavkin. New York: Monthly Review Press.

Hembacher, Brian. 1989. "Fetal Protection Policies: Reasonable Protection or Unreasonable Limitation on Female Employees?" *Industrial Relations Law Journal* 11:32–44.

Hill, Ann Corinne. 1979. "Protection of Women Workers and the Courts: A Legal Case History." *Feminist Studies* 5:247–73.

Hirschmann, Albert O. 1970. *Exit, Voice and Loyalty.* Cambridge, Mass.: Harvard University Press.

Hoff-Wilson, Joan. 1987. "The Unfinished Revolution: Changing Legal Status of U.S. Women." *Signs* 13:7–36.

Howard, Linda G. 1981. "Hazardous Substances in the Workplace: Implications for the Employment Rights of Women." *University of Pennsylvania Law Review* 129:798–855.

Hubbard, Ruth, Mary Sue Henifin, and Barbara Fried, eds. *Biological Woman: The Convenient Myth.* Cambridge: Schenkman

Huckle, Patricia. 1988. "The Womb Factor: Policy on Pregnancy and the Employment of Women." In *Women, Power and Policy: Toward the Year 2000,* 2d ed., edited by Ellen Boneparth and Emily Stoper. New York: Pergamon Press.

Hunt, Vilma R. 1979. "A Brief History of Women Workers and Hazards in the Workplace." *Feminist Studies* 5:274–85.

Ivers, Gregg. 1995. *To Build a Wall: American Jews and the Separation of Church and State.* Charlottesville: University Press of Virginia.

Ivers, Gregg, and Karen O'Connor. 1987. "Friends as Foes: The Amicus Curiae Participation and Effectiveness of the American Civil Liberties Union and Americans for Effective Law Enforcement in Criminal Cases, 1969–1982." *Law and Policy* 9:161–78.

Jacob, Herbert. 1978. *Justice in America,* 3d ed. Boston: Little, Brown and Company.

Jason, Meredith L. 1990. "International Union v. Johnson Controls, Inc.: Controlling Women's Equal Employment Opportunities through Fetal Protection Policies." *American University Law Review* 40:453–502.

Jasso, Sonia, and Maria Mazorra. 1984. "Following the Harvest: The Health Hazards of Migrant and Seasonal Farmworking Women." In *Double Exposure: Women's Health Hazards on the Job and at Home,* edited by Wendy Chavkin. New York: Monthly Review Press.

Johnsen, Dawn E. 1986. "The Creation of Fetal Rights: Conflicts with Women's Constitutional Rights to Liberty, Privacy, and Equal Protection." *Yale Law Journal* 95:599–625.

Katz, Joni F. 1989. "Hazardous Working Conditions and Fetal Protection Policies: Women Are Going Back to the Future." *Boston College Environmenal Affairs Law Review* 17:201–30.

Kearney, Joseph D., and Thomas W. Merrill. 2000. The Influence of Amicus Curiae Briefs on the Supreme Court. *University of Pennsylvania Law Review* 148:743

Kelman, Steven. 1980. "Occupational Safety and Health Administration." In *The Politics of Regulation,* edited by James Q. Wilson. New York: Basic Books.

Kenen, Regina. 1993. *Reproductive Hazards in the Workplace: Mending Jobs, Managing Pregnancies.* New York: Haworth Press.

Kenneally, James J. 1978. *Women and American Trade Unions.* St. Albans, Vt.: Eden Press.

Kenney, Sally J. 1992. *For Whose Protection? Reproductive Hazards and Exclusionary Policies in the United States and Britain.* Ann Arbor: University of Michigan Press.

———. 1993. "Who Is Protected? What's Wrong with Exclusionary Policies." *Women and Politics* 13:153–73.

Kessler-Harris, Alice. 1984. "Protection for Women: Trade Unions and Labor Laws." In *Double Exposure: Women's Health Hazards on the Job and at Home,* edited by Wendy Chavkin. New York: Monthly Review Press.

Kirp, David L. 1991. "The Pitfalls of 'Fetal Protection.'" *Society* 28:70–76.

Kobylka, Joseph F. 1987. "A Court-Created Context for Group Litigation." *Journal of Politics* 49:1061–78.

———. 1991. *The Politics of Obscenity: Group Litigation in a Time of Legal Change.* Westport, Conn.: Greenwood Press.

Koshner, Andrew Jay. 1998. *Solving the Puzzle of Interest Group Litigation.* Westport, Conn.: Greenwood Press.

Krislov, Samuel. 1963. "The Amicus Curiae Brief: From Friendship to Advocacy." *Yale Law Journal* 72:694–721.

Legator, Marvin S., Michael J. Rosenberg, and Harold Zenick. 1984. *Environmental Influences on Fertility, Pregnancy, and Development.* New York: Alan R. Liss.

Lehrer, Susan. 1987. *Origins of Protective Labor Legislation for Women, 1905–1925.* Albany: SUNY Press.

Lindgren, J. Ralph and Nadine Taub. 1988. *The Law of Sex Discrimination.* St. Paul: West Publishing Company.

Losco, Joseph. 1991. "Fetal Rights: An Examination of Feminist Viewpoints." Paper presented at the American Political Science Association annual meeting.

Manwaring, David. 1962. *Render unto Caesar: The Flag Salute Controversy.* Chicago: University of Chicago Press.

Maschke, Karen J. 1991. "The Ideology and Practice of Fetal Protection." Paper presented at the Midwest Political Science Association meeting.

Mattson, Lynn Paul. 1981. "The Pregnancy Amendment: Fetal Rights and the Workplace." *Case and Comment* 86:33–41.

McCaffrey, David. 1982. *OSHA and the Politics of Health Regulation.* New York: Plenum Press.

McGill, Linda D. 1990. "Reproductive Hazards and Sex Discrimination: A Delicate Balance." *Employment Relations Today* 17:15–20.

McGlen, Nancy E., and Karen O'Connor. 1983. *Women's Rights: The Struggle for Equality in the Nineteenth and Twentieth Centuries.* New York: Praeger.

Mendeloff, John. 1979. *Regulating Safety: An Economic and Political Analysis of Occupational Safety and Health Policy.* Cambridge, Mass.: MIT Press.

Mezey, Susan G. 1992. *In Pursuit of Equality: Women, Public Policy, and the Federal Courts.* New York: St. Martin's.

Moelis, Laurence S. 1985. "Fetal Protection and Potential Liability: Judicial Application of the Pregnancy Discrimination Act and the Disparate Impact Theory." *American Journal of Law and Medicine* 11:369–90.

Needleman, Herbert L., and David Bellinger. 1988. "Recent Developments." *Environmental Research* 46:190–91.

————, eds. 1994. *Prenatal Exposure to Toxicants: Developmental Consequences.* Baltimore, Md.: The Johns Hopkins University Press.

Neier, Aryeh. 1982. *Only Judgment: The Limits of Litigation in Social Change.* Middletown, Conn.: Wesleyan University Press.

Noble, Charles. 1986. *Liberalism at Work: The Rise and Fall of OSHA.* Philadelphia: Temple University Press.

Note. 1983. "Life with Mother: The Fourth Circuit Reconciles Title VII and Fetal Vulnerability in Wright v. Olin Corp." *Alabama Law Review* 34:327–38.

O'Connor, Karen. 1980. *Women's Organizations Use of the Courts.* Lexington, Mass.: Lexington Books.

————. 1983. "The Amicus Curiae Role of the U.S. Solicitor General in Supreme Court Litigation." *Judicature* 66:256–64.

O'Connor, Karen, and Lee Epstein. 1981–82. "Amicus Curiae Participation in U.S. Supreme Court Litigation: An Appraisal of Hakman's Folklore." *Law and Society Review* 16:701–11.

————. 1983a. "Beyond Legislative Lobbying: Women's Rights Groups and the Supreme Court." *Judicature* 67:134–43.

————. 1983b. "The Rise of Conservative Interest Group Litigation." *Journal of Politics* 45:479–89.

————. 1983c. "Sex and the Supreme Court: An Analysis of Judicial Support for Gender-Based Claims." *Social Science Quarterly* 64:327–31.

————. 1983d. Court Rules and Workload. *Justice System Journal* 8:35.

————. 1984. "A Legal Voice for the Chicano Community: The Activities of the Mexican American Legal Defense and Educational Fund, 1968–1982." *Social Science Quarterly* 65:245–56.

————. 1989. *Public Interest Law Groups: Institutional Profiles.* New York: Greenwood.

O'Connor, Karen, and Bryan Scott McFall. 1992. "Conservative Interest Group Litigation in the Reagan Era and Beyond." In *The Politics of Interests: Interest Groups Transformed.* Mark P. Petracca, ed. . Boulder, Colo.: Westview Press.

Olson, Susan M. 1981. "The Political Evolution of Interest Group Litigation." In *Governing Through Courts.* R. Gabritta, L. May, J. C. Foster, eds. Beverly Hills, Calif.: Sage.

O'Neill, Timothy J. 1985. *Bakke and the Politics of Equality: Friends and Foes in the Classroom of Litigation.* Middletown, Conn.: Wesleyan University Press.

Orren, Karen. 1976. "Standing to Sue: Interest Group Conflict in the Federal Courts." *American Political Science Review* 70:723.

Paskal, Steven S. 1988. "Dilemma: Save the Fetus or Sue the Employer?" *Labor Law Journal* 39:323–41.

Paul, Maureen, ed. 1993. *Occupational and Environmental Reproductive Hazards: A Guide for Clinicians.* Baltimore, Md.: Williams and Wilkins.

Paul, Maureen, Cynthia Daniels, and Robert Rosofsky. 1989. "Corporate Response to Reproductive Hazards in the Workplace: Results of the Family, Work, and Health Survey." *American Journal of Industrial Medicine* 16:267–80.

Petchesky, Rosalind. 1979. "Workers, Reproductive Hazards, and the Politics of Protection: An Introduction." *Feminist Studies* 5:233–46.

Phillips, Jimmie W. 1983. "Employment Discrimination: Fetal Vulnerability and the 1978 Pregnancy Amendments—Wright v. Olin Corp." *Wake Forest Law Review* 19:905–29.

Presser, Arlynn Leiber. 1990. "Women at Work: Should "Fetal Protection" Policies be Upheld? Yes: For Risky Business." *ABA Journal* (June): 38.

Puro, Stephen. 1971. "The Role of Amicus Curiae in the United States Supreme Court, 1920–1966." Ph.D. diss., SUNY Buffalo.

Randall, Donna M., and James F. Short Jr. 1983. "Women in Toxic Work Environments: A Case Study of Social Problem Development." *Social Problems* 30 (April): 410–24.

Riffaud, Marcelo L. 1990. "Fetal Protection and *UAW v. Johnson Controls, Inc.*: Job Openings for Barren Women Only." *Fordham Law Review* 58:843–63.

Rosen, Judith C. 1989. "A Legal Perspective on the Status of the Fetus: Who Will Guard the Guardians?" In *Abortion Rights and Fetal "Personhood,"* edited by Edd Doerr and James W. Prescott. Long Beach, Calif.: Centerline Press.

Rosenberg, Gerald. 1991. *The Hollow Hope: Can Courts Bring About Social Change?* Chicago: University of Chicago Press.

Roth, Rachel. 1993. "At Women's Expense: The Cost of Fetal Rights." *Women and Politics* 13:117–35.

Rothenberg, Lawrence. 1988. "Organizational Maintenance and the Retention Decision in Groups." *American Political Science Review* 82:1129–52.

Rothstein, Mark A. 1983–84. "Reproductive Hazards and Sex Discrimination in the Workplace: New Legal Concerns in Industry and on Campus." *The Journal of College and University Law* 10:495–514.

———. 1985. "Substantive and Procedural Obstacles to OSHA Rulemaking: Reproductive Hazards as an Example." *Boston College Environmental Affairs Law Review* 12:627–700.

Salisbury, Robert. 1969. "An Exchange Theory of Interest Groups." *Midwest Journal of Political Science* 13:1–32.

Salokar, Rebecca Mae. 1992. *The Solicitor General: The Politics of Law.* Philadelphia: Temple University Press.

———. 1995. "Politics, Law, and the Office of the Solicitor General." In *Government Lawyers: The Federal Legal Bureaucracy and Presidential Politics,* edited by Cornell W. Clayton. Lawrence: University Press of Kansas.

Samuels, Suzanne Uttaro. 1992. "Interest Group Participation in the Courts: An Examination of the Use of Amicus Curiae Briefs in *UAW v. Johnson Controls.*" Paper presented at the annual meeting of the American Political Science Association.

———. 1993. "Analyzing Employer Motives: Evaluating the 'Scientific Evidence' Upon Which Fetal Protection Policies Were Based." *Women and Politics* 13:137–52.

———. 1994. "The Fetal Protection Debate Revisited: The Impact of *UAW v. Johnson Controls* on the Federal and State Courts." Paper presented at the annual meeting of the American Political Science Association.

———. 1995. *Fetal Rights, Women's Rights: Gender Equality in the Workplace.* Madison: University of Wisconsin Press.

Samuelson, Joan I. 1977. "Employment Rights of Women in the Toxic Workplace." *California Law Review* 65:1113–42.

Schattschneider, E. E. 1960. *The Semi-Sovereign People.* New York: Holt, Rinehart, and Winston.

Scheppele, Kim Lane, and Jack L. Walker. 1991. "The Litigation Strategies of Interest Groups." In *Mobilizing Interest Groups in America,* edited by Jack L. Walker. Ann Arbor: University of Michigan Press.

Schlozman, Kay Lehman, and John T. Tierney. 1986. *Organized Interests and American Democracy.* New York: Harper and Row.

Schroedel, Jean R., and Paul Peretz. 1994. "A Gender Analysis of Policy Formation: The Case of Fetal Abuse." *Journal of Health Politics, Policy and Law* 19:335–60.

Scott, Judith. 1984. "Keeping Women in Their Place: Exclusionary Policies and Reproduction." In *Double Exposure: Women's Health Hazards on the Job and at Home,* edited by Wendy Chavkin. New York: Monthly Review Press.

Shabecoff, Philip. "Job Threats to Workers' Fertility Emerging as Civil Liberties Issue." *New York Times,* January 15, 1979, A1, D8.

Shaiko, Ronald G. 1990. "Citizen Motivations to Participate in Public Interest Organizations." Presented at the annual meeting of the International Society of Political Psychology.

Simon, Howard A. 1990. "Fetal Protection Policies after Johnson Controls: No Easy Answers." *Employee Relations Law Journal* 15:491–514.

Singer, James W. 1980. "Should Equal Opportunity for Women Apply to Toxic Chemical Exposure?" *National Journal,* October 18, 1980, 1753–55.

Sorauf, Frank. 1976. *The Wall of Separation: Constitutional Politics of Church and State.* Princeton, N.J.: Princeton University Press.

Spalter-Roth, Roberta M., Claudia Withers, and Sheila R. Gibbs. 1990. "Improving Employment Opportunities for Women Workers: An Assessment of the Ten Year Economic and Legal Impact of the Pregnancy Discrimination Act of 1978." Washington, D.C.: Institute for Women's Policy Research.

Stellman, Jeanne M., and Mary Sue Henifin. 1982. "No Fertile Women Need Apply: Employment Discrimination and Reproductive Hazards in the Workplace." In *Biological Woman: The Convenient Myth,* edited by Ruth Hubbard, Mary Sue Henifin, and Barbara Fried. Cambridge: Schenkman.

Stevens, Gina M. 1990. "*UAW v. Johnson Controls, Inc.:* Sex-based Employment Discrimination under Title VII of the 1964 Civil Rights Act." Congressional Research Service Report for Congress.

Stillman, Nina G. 1979. "The Law in Conflict: Accommodating Equal Employment and Occupational Health Obligations." *Journal of Occupational Medicine* 21:599.

———. 1980. "A Legal Perspective on Workplace Reproductive Hazards." In *Women, Work, and Health: Challenges to Corporate Policy,* edited by Diana Chapman Walsh and Richard H. Egdahl. New York: Springer-Verlag.

Timko, Patricia A. 1986. "Exploring the Limits of Legal Duty: A Union's Responsibilities with Respect to Fetal Protection Policies." *Harvard Journal on Legislation* 23:159–210.

Truman, David B. 1951. *The Governmental Process.* New York: Alfred A. Knopf.

Tushnet, Mark V. 1987. *The NAACP's Legal Strategy against Segregated Education, 1925–1950.* Chapel Hill: University of North Carolina Press.

Vanderwaerdt, Lois. 1983. "Resolving the Conflict between Hazardous Substances in the Workplace and Equal Employment Opportunity." *American Business Law Journal* 21:157–84.

Vogel, Lise. 1993. *Mothers on the Job: Maternity Policy in the U.S. Workplace.* New Brunswick, N.J.: Rutgers University Press.

Vose, Clement E. 1958. "Litigation as a Form of Pressure Group Activity." *The Annals of the American Academy of Political Science* 319:20–31.

———. 1959. *Caucasians Only: The Supreme Court, the NAACP, and the Restrictive*

Covenant Cases. Berkeley: University of California Press.

———. 1972. *Constitutional Change: Amendment Politics and Supreme Court Litigation Since 1900.* Lanham, Md.: Lexington Books.

Walker, Jack L. 1983. "The Origins and Maintenance of Interest Groups in America." *American Political Science Review* 77:390–406.

———, ed. 1991. *Mobilizing Interest Groups in America.* Ann Arbor: University of Michigan Press.

Walsh, Diana Chapman. 1980. "Challenges to Corporate Policy." In *Women, Work, and Health: Challenges to Corporate Policy,* edited by Diana Chapman Walsh and Richard H. Egdahl. New York: Springer-Verlag.

Walsh, Diana Chapman, and Richard H. Egdahl, eds. 1980. *Women, Work, and Health: Challenges to Corporate Policy.* New York: Springer-Verlag.

Wasby, Stephen L. 1984. "How Planned is 'Planned Litigation'?" *American Bar Foundation Research Journal* 1:83–138.

———. 1995. *Race Relations Litigation in an Age of Complexity.* Charlottesville: University Press of Virginia.

Williams, Louise A. 1988. "Toxic Exposure in the Workplace: Balancing Job Opportunity with Reproductive Health." In *Women, Power and Policy: Toward the Year 2000,* 2d ed., edited by Ellen Boneparth and Emily Stoper. New York: Pergamon Press.

Williams, Wendy W. 1981. "Firing the Woman to Protect the Fetus: The Reconciliation of Fetal Protection with Employment Opportunity Goals under Title VII." *Georgetown Law Journal* 69:641–704.

Wilson, Graham K., and Virginia Sapiro. 1985. "Occupational Safety and Health as a Women's Policy Issue." In *Women, Biology, and Public Policy.* Virginia Sapiro, ed. Beverly Hills, Calif.: Sage.

Wilson, James Q. 1973. *Political Organizations.* New York: Basic.

———, ed. 1980. *The Politics of Regulation.* New York: Basic Books.

Wright, Michael J. 1979. "Reproductive Hazards and 'Protective' Discrimination." *Feminist Studies* 5:302–9.

Index

abortion, 9, 12, 28–29, 89, 96–97, 101,
128–29, 134–35. *See also* Committee for
Abortion Rights and Against
Sterilization Abuse (CARASA);
National Abortion Rights Action
League (NARAL); Religious Coalition
for Abortion Rights; *Roe v. Wade*
Adkins v. Children's Hospital, 18
affirmative action, 12
African Americans: discrimination against,
108 (*see also* racial discrimination);
rights of, 21; women, 101, 102; workers,
102
Air Products and Chemicals Inc., 38
Alan Guttmacher Institute, 36
Amalgamated Clothing and Textile
Workers Union, 19, 36, 46, 47, 66
Amalgamated Meat Cutters Union, 46, 47
American Association of University
Women (AAUW), 22, 29, 85, 170n. 1
American Citizens Concerned for Life
(ACCL), 28–29
American Civil Liberties Union (ACLU),
20, 22, 25–28, 36, 38–39, 42, 53–54, 56,
59, 64–67, 75, 79–80, 82–88, 90, 92, 93,
96, 98, 99, 102, 107, 116, 119, 120, 122,
131, 136, 139, 145, 147, 148, 152,
153–54, 156, 157, 170n. 8, 170n. 13;
Reproductive Freedom Project, 80;
Women's Rights Project, 28, 30, 36, 53,
58, 76–85, 87, 107, 123, 160
American Cyanamid Company, 35, 36, 38,
43, 49, 64. *See also Oil, Chemical, and*

Atomic Workers Union v. American
Cyanamid Company
American Federation of Labor (AFL), 16,
18, 19. *See also* American Federation of
Labor–Congress of Industrial
Organizations (AFL-CIO)
American Federation of Labor–Congress
of Industrial Organizations (AFL-CIO),
20, 22, 25, 27–29, 41, 42, 44, 46–48, 54,
56, 63–64, 66, 77, 107, 123, 143–44,
147, 169n. 2, 169n. 22
American Federation of State, County, and
Municipal Employees (AFSCME), 38,
66
American Federation of Teachers (AFT),
47
American Friends Service Committee, 85
American Industrial Hygiene Association,
38
American Iron and Steel Institute, 34
American Nurses Association (ANA), 22,
37
American Petroleum Institute, 38
American Public Health Association
(APHA), 39, 59, 60, 65, 67, 69, 75,
79–80, 92, 95–99, 100, 102, 107, 121,
135, 151, 152, 154–56, 171n. 13
American Retail Federation, 28
Americans for Democratic Action, 45
Americans with Disabilities Act, 116
animal studies, 67–70, 75, 79, 95, 103, 106,
147–48, 156
Ashford, Nicholas, 99

Association of Black Women Attorneys, 93
Association for Voluntary Sterilization, 36
Americans for Democratic Action, 45
Ashford, Nicholas, 99
AT&T, 37

Battery Council, 37
Bellinger, David, 99
Bertin, Joan, 36, 51, 53–54, 56, 58, 59,
    62–63, 64, 66, 75–77, 79, 80, 82–84,
    86–88, 93, 96, 97, 99, 102, 107, 119, 145,
    147, 151–52, 158
Berzon, Marsha, 29, 50, 51, 56, 59–61,
    62–63, 65–67, 71, 72, 82–83, 87, 94,
    104, 106, 107, 126–27, 145, 152, 155
Bieber, Owen, 41
Bingham, Eula, 33, 98, 126
birth defects, 114, 115
Blackmun, Harry (Justice), 41, 126, 153
Bokat, Stephen, 112–13, 117, 131
bona fide occupational qualification
    (BFOQ), 22–25, 39, 40–41, 46–47, 61,
    69–72, 79, 83, 90, 95, 100–102, 105,
    114, 116, 120, 122, 127, 130, 134–35,
    137–39, 145, 149, 154–56
Borg & Warner Chemicals, 38
Boston Women's Health Book Collective, 85
Bray v. Alexandria Women's Health Clinic, 89
Brown v. Board of Education, 2, 4
Bryant, Arthur, 93
Bunker Hill Company, 35
Bush administration, 106, 156

Califano v. Goldfarb, 77
California, state of, 24, 27, 60, 65, 98, 103,
    115; Fair Employment and Housing
    Commission, 67, 90
*California Federal Savings & Loan v.
    Guerra,* 29, 30, 79, 85, 86, 88
California Teachers Association, 30
Campaign to End Discrimination Against
    Pregnant Workers (CEDAPW), 28, 86,
    87, 107
Carter administration, 28, 37, 59
Carter, Jimmy, 33
Casella, Gilbert, 119
Caso, Anthony, 136–37
Center for Constitutional Rights, 85

Center for Law and Social Policy, 26, 36;
    Women's Rights Project, 86
Central New York Council on
    Occupational Safety and Health, 128
Chemical Manufacturers Association, 37, 38
Chemical Workers Union, 66
Chopko, Mark, 132–34
Citizens Advisory Council on the Status of
    Women, 27
civil liberties, 35, 139. *See also* American
    Civil Liberties Union (ACLU)
civil rights, 28, 35, 36, 45, 84, 85, 86, 99,
    101, 119
Civil Rights Act of 1964, 21, 23, 25, 29, 101,
    130. *See also* Title VII
Civil Rights Act of 1991, 169n. 40
Clauss, Carin, 50–52, 53, 56, 58, 59, 62, 82,
    98
Coal Employment Project, 38
Coalition of Labor Union Women
    (CLUW), 24–25, 36, 47, 48, 49, 66, 107
Coalition for Medical Rights of Women, 38
Coalition for the Reproductive Rights of
    Workers (CRROW), 36–38, 48, 50, 52,
    53, 56, 77, 86, 107, 139
collective bargaining, 18, 45, 46, 56, 57, 62,
    63, 132, 160
Commission on the Status of Women, 20, 21
Committee for Abortion Rights and Against
    Sterilization Abuse (CARASA), 38
Communications Workers of America
    (CWA), 27, 47, 66
Concerned Women for America (CWA),
    65, 109, 110, 128–33, 148
Congress of Industrial Organizations
    (CIO), 19, 45. *See also* American
    Federation of Labor–Congress of
    Industrial Organizations (AFL-CIO)
Copus, David, 115
Corn, Morton, 126
Council of Economic Advisors, 34
Council on Wage and Price Stability, 34
Craig v. Boren, 77

Davis, Nancy, 88, 107
Democratic Party, 19, 31, 45
Depression, 46
Dothard v. Rawlinson, 25

Dow Chemical Company, 36, 37
DuPont, 37
Dyk, Timothy, 112–13, 117, 171n. 1

Easterbrook, Frank (Judge), 7, 8, 40, 61
Edelsberg, Herman, 21
Employee Protection Act of 1990, 169n. 43
employment discrimination, 9, 21, 35, 57,
    77, 90, 130, 133, 140, 154
Employment Law Center (ELC), 38, 39, 75,
    83–85, 90, 146, 149, 170n. 13
Equal Employment Advisory Council
    (EEAC), 29, 38, 65, 109–11, 116, 117,
    118–21, 147
equal employment opportunity, 11, 91, 95,
    116, 121, 125, 133–34, 140, 147, 155
Equal Employment Opportunity Act, 25, 26
Equal Employment Opportunity
    Commission (EEOC), 9, 21–28, 35,
    37–38, 40, 42, 46–48, 50, 52, 54, 56, 59,
    61, 63, 65, 68–69, 72, 79, 86, 87, 90, 93,
    100, 102–7, 118–22, 127, 135–36, 138,
    147, 150, 152, 154–56; "Policy Guidance
    on Reproductive and Fetal Hazards," 39
equal pay, 20
Equal Pay Act of 1963, 20, 21, 26, 111, 147
Equal Rights Advocates (ERA), 26, 30, 36,
    38, 60, 65–66, 69, 76, 83–84, 85, 88–89,
    98, 107, 115, 120, 132, 135, 147,
    149–150, 154, 156–57
Equal Rights Amendment (ERA), 18, 19,
    25, 46, 47, 55, 66, 77
Ethyl Corporation, 38

Fair Labor Standards Act of 1938, 20
Feitshans, Ilise, 124–27, 157, 158
fertility, male, 48
fetal rights, 2, 8, 9, 109–10, 113, 128–35,
    147, 148, 170n. 5, 171n. 5
fetal safety, 91–92, 145, 147
fetal vulnerability rule, 38
Finley, Lucinda, 94
Fourteenth Amendment, 77
Friedan, Betty, 21

Geduldig v. Aiello, 27, 28, 136, 147
gender discrimination, 9, 21–23, 25, 26, 34,
    35, 38, 42, 44–55, 58, 63, 66, 77, 79, 80,

87–88, 91, 93–94, 97, 100–101, 104–5,
    113, 139, 143, 147, 153, 155–56
General Electric (GE), 27, 28, 66
General Electric Co. v. Gilbert, 27–29, 62,
    86, 87, 104, 147
General Motors, 37, 58, 59. See also *Grant
    v. General Motors*
Georgia, State Labor Commission Rule 59,
    23–24
Ginsburg, Ruth Bader, 77
Gold, Laurence, 56, 59, 90
Gompers, Samuel, 16, 17
Grant v. General Motors, 40, 53, 56, 70, 153
grassroots efforts, 3, 13, 126, 158
Griggs v. Duke Power, 169n. 40

Hadro, Jane, 129–31
Harris v. Forklift Systems, 94
Hayes v. Shelby Memorial Hospital, 56, 77,
    172n. 4
Health Insurance Association of America
    (HIAA), 28
Health Research Group, 34
Holzhauer, James, 123–24, 157, 172n. 3
Horwitz, Miriam, 49, 51, 58, 59

In Re A.C., 89
Industrial Hygiene Law Project (IHLP), 65,
    109, 110, 116, 121, 124–27, 148, 151,
    157, 158
International Chemical Workers Union, 36,
    38, 66
International Ladies Garment Workers
    Union (ILGWU), 19, 22, 46
International Union of Electrical, Radio, and
    Machine Workers (IUE), 22, 27, 28, 46

Jaspan, Stanley, 71, 90, 120, 152
Johnson, Lyndon B., 21, 31
Johnson Controls, 7, 8, 29, 34, 36, 39–40,
    43–44, 48, 51, 53–57, 58–59, 61, 64–65,
    67, 68–72, 73, 75–76, 83–84, 90–91, 93,
    94, 96–99, 101, 105, 107–11, 113–15,
    119–20, 122, 124–27, 129, 132, 138–41,
    145, 150–52, 153–54
*Johnson Controls v. California Fair
    Employment and Housing Commission,*
    68, 83, 90, 153

Jones, Ralph, 50, 51, 52, 54, 58, 62, 145

Kennedy, Anthony (Justice), 41, 155, 156
Kennedy, John F., 20
Kennedy, John P., 115
Kinney, Joseph, 121–24, 127, 157
Krekel, Sylvia, 49
Kurtz, Judith, 62, 84, 86, 89, 145, 149

labor law reform, 33
labor laws, protective, 14, 15, 16, 18, 19, 22, 24, 46, 77, 82
labor movement, 16–41, 44, 45, 48, 146, 161
lead exposure, 35, 40–41, 48, 57–58, 69, 79, 101, 114, 130, 140, 154. *See also* Occupational Safety and Health Administration, lead standard
Lead Industries Association (LIA), 34, 37, 38, 98, 147
Leadership Conference on Civil Rights, 45
Legal Aid Society of San Francisco, 83. *See also* Employment Law Center (ELC)
Legator, Marvin, 99
LaHaye, Beverly, 129
Lenhoff, Donna, 52, 86, 87, 88, 146
Lewis, John L., 19
Lichtman, Judy, 88
Lochner v. New York, 16–17
Lorence, Jordan, 128–31, 151

Madar, Olga, 25, 47–48
Marshall, Thurgood (Justice), 153
Massachusetts, 37, 60, 65, 67, 96, 100, 103, 140, 154, 156; Department of Health, 99
Massachusetts Coalition for Occupational Safety and Health, 128
Mattison, Donald R., 99
maximum hours law, 16–17
McCarter, Katherine, 96–97
McDowell, Doug, 116–21
McGarity, Thomas, 103
Meany, George, 31
Mechanical Contractors Association of America, 38
Mexican-American Legal Defense and Education Fund (MALDEF), 30, 85
Meyerhoff, Al, 103
minimum wage law, 17, 18

Monsanto, 38
Muller v. Oregon, 15, 17, 18, 24, 93

NALCO Chemical, 38
National Abortion Rights Action League (NARAL), 29, 74, 85, 89
National Association for the Advancement of Colored People (NAACP), 5, 21, 45, 53, 64, 101, 108, 140; Legal Defense and Education Fund (LDF), 60, 65, 74, 75, 96, 101, 102, 139, 145, 156
National Association of Manufacturers (NAM), 27, 28, 31, 41, 109, 110, 111, 116–21, 132, 136
National Black Women's Health Project, 101, 140
National Chamber Litigation Center (NCLC), 111–16, 127, 148, 171n. 2; Constitutional and Administrative Law Advisory Committee, 115
National Conference of Catholic Bishops, 132
National Council of Jewish Women, 85, 170n. 1
National Employment Law Project, 36
National Institute for Occupational Safety and Health (NIOSH), 48
National Organization for Women (NOW), 21–23, 25–26, 28, 36, 47–48, 55, 85, 120; Legal Defense and Education Fund (LDEF), 26, 28, 30, 84, 85, 88–89, 120, 145
National Retail Merchants Association, 28
National Right to Life Committee, 128
National Safe Workplace Institute (NSWI), 65, 109–10, 121–24, 126, 127, 157
National Trades' Union, Committee on Female Labor of, 15
National Union of Hospital and Health Care Employees, 66
National Woman's Party (NWP), 19, 22
National Women's Health Network, 85, 94
National Women's Law Center (NWLC), 26, 30, 84–86, 88
National Women's Political Caucus (NWPC), 28, 48, 85
National Women's Trade Union League (NWTUL), 18

Natural Resources Defense Council (NRDC), 65, 67, 95, 96, 102–3, 106, 148, 156

Needleman, Herbert L., 99

New England Legal Foundation (NELF), 109, 110, 136–39

New York City Bar Association, 60, 65, 92–93, 102, 155

New York City Commission on Human Rights, 93

New York Council on Occupational Safety and Health, 128

New York County Lawyers' Association, Committee on Women's Rights, 93

Newport News Shipbuilding & Dry Dock v. EEOC, 29, 56, 60, 86, 147

9 to 5 National Association of Working Women, 85

Nixon, Richard, 32

Nontraditional Employment for Women, 85

North Carolina Occupational Safety and Health Project, 128

Northwest Women's Law Center, 30, 85

Norton, Eleanor Holmes, 38

Occupational and Environmental Reproductive Hazards Clinic and Education Center, 128

Occupational Safety and Health Act of 1970, 31, 32, 33, 49, 114, 143, 147

Occupational Safety and Health Administration (OSHA), 9, 31–32, 35, 36, 37, 48, 86, 115, 121, 125–26, 128, 139, 155; General Duty clause, 57, 72; lead standard, 33–34, 39, 48, 50, 57, 59, 69, 98, 105, 147, 160

Occupational Safety and Health Review Commission (OSHRC), 35, 36

O'Connor, Sandra Day (Justice), 153

Ohio v. Akron Center for Reproductive Health, 97

Oil, Chemical, and Atomic Workers Union (OCAW), 34, 35, 36, 38, 43, 49, 52, 64, 66, 168n. 30

Oil, Chemical, and Atomic Workers Union v. American Cyanamid, 2, 35, 41, 54, 56, 79, 82, 88, 126, 139, 168n. 30

Olin Corporation, 38, 43. *See also Wright v. Olin*

Ostrach, Stephen, 136–37

Pacific Legal Foundation (PLF), 27, 65, 109, 110, 111, 136–39

Paul, Alice, 19

Paul, Maureen, 99

Pennzoil, 38

Peterson, Esther, 20

Pharmaceutical Manufacturers Association, 37

Philadelphia Area Project on Occupational Safety and Health, 128

Phillips, Margaret, 124–27, 157, 158

Phillips v. Martin Marietta, 25, 26, 87, 101

Physicians' Forum, 27

Planned Parenthood, 36, 38, 85

Planned Parenthood v. Casey, 97

Poppink, Prudence, 90, 91, 92

Posner, Richard (Judge), 8, 40

poverty, 71, 100, 102

pregnancy, 10, 20, 25–30, 33, 38, 39, 41, 71, 79, 86–89, 104, 115, 117, 128, 136, 147, 153, 155

pregnancy discrimination, 25, 26, 27, 30, 77, 88, 146. *See also* Pregnancy Discrimination Act (PDA)

Pregnancy Discrimination Act (PDA), 8, 25, 26–30, 35, 36, 38, 39, 41, 52–53, 56, 59, 60–63, 66, 69, 71, 72, 76, 79, 80, 84–91, 93, 100, 102, 103, 107, 111, 114, 115, 128, 132, 135, 141, 144–45, 147, 149, 150, 153–57, 170n. 13, 170n. 23

Price Waterhouse v. Hopkins, 77, 93, 97

protective labor laws, women's, 14, 16, 18, 18, 19, 22, 24, 77

Queen Foster/Employment Law Center, 59, 60, 83, 84, 92

racial discrimination, 10, 21, 77, 101, 102

Reagan, Ronald, 106; administration, 38

Reed v. Reed, 26, 77

Rehnquist, William (Justice), 28, 41, 155, 156

Religious Coalition for Abortion Rights, 28

Reproductive Rights National Network, 36, 38

Republican Party, 31, 32

Reuther, Walter, 45

Riegel, Quentin, 116–19

Rochester Council on Occupational Safety and Health, 128

Roe v. Wade, 2, 4, 96, 129

Rosenfeld v. Southern Pacific Co., 24, 61

Ross, Susan Deller, 25, 26, 28, 54, 64, 66, 86–88, 92, 125, 145, 146, 154, 157

Rossen, Jordan, 49, 50, 58–59

Rust v. Sullivan, 89, 97

San Francisco Women Lawyers Alliance, 30

Sangiacomo, Laura, 1

Santa Clara Center on Occupational Safety and Health, 128

Scalia, Antonin (Justice), 41, 155–56

segregation: gender, 16, 17, 20, 45; racial, 53

Service Employees International Union, 66

sex discrimination. *See* gender discrimination

Shanor, Charles, 104, 105

Shell Oil, 37

Shiu, Pat, 83, 84–85, 90, 119, 146, 149

Silicon Valley Toxics Coalition, 128

Silkwood v. Kerr McGee, 94

Smith, Howard, 21

Souter, David, 153

Stellman, Jeanne, 99

sterility, 7, 41, 154

sterilization, 1, 2, 7, 35–36, 39, 97, 126, 167n. 33, 169n. 43

Stevens, John Paul (Justice), 153

suffrage, women's, 18, 166n. 8

Synthetic Organic Chemical Manufacturers Association, 38

Taub, Nadine, 80, 82, 92, 97

television dramas, 1, 7

Title VII, 8, 10, 13, 21–26, 28–29, 35, 38–47, 49, 52–54, 60, 61, 67, 68–72, 73, 75, 77–79, 80, 83, 85, 86, 90–92, 95, 97–98, 100, 101, 103, 105, 106, 111, 114–16, 119, 125, 130, 134, 137, 139, 144–45, 147, 153–57, 160

Toxics Use Reduction Institute, 128

toxins, 1, 8, 10, 15, 33, 36, 37, 68, 71, 95, 99, 102–3, 114–15, 127, 132, 140, 147, 171n. 26

trade unions, 16, 17, 18, 33, 36, 45, 47, 62, 66. *See also* National Women's Trade Union League (NWTUL)

Transportation Communications Employees Union, 168n. 16

Trial Lawyers for Public Justice (TLPJ), 60, 65, 67, 92, 93–94, 108, 140, 148, 150, 154, 155

Tucker, Beverly, 49–50, 51, 52, 57, 58, 65

unborn, rights of. *See* fetal rights

UAW v. Johnson Controls, 2, 7–11, 13, 14, 27, 38, 42, 43, 49, 52, 54, 56, 60, 62, 64–66, 71, 73, 77–79, 82, 84, 86, 89, 91, 94, 97, 100, 101, 104–6, 111–12, 116, 122–24, 126, 128, 129, 132, 136, 142, 143–46, 147, 152, 157, 160, 172n. 4

Union Carbide, 37

United Auto Workers (UAW), 8, 13, 19, 22–25, 28, 29, 34, 36, 38, 39, 42–62, 64–72, 73, 75–77, 83, 93, 97, 103–6, 109–10, 115, 118, 121–23, 126, 128, 132, 135, 138–41, 143–47, 149–50, 154–56, 159, 160, 168n. 10, 169n. 2, 170n. 1; Women's Committee, 21–22; Women's Department, 45

United Mine Workers of America, 66, 74, 81

United Rubber Workers, 36, 38

United States v. Virginia, 94

United Steelworkers Union, 29, 34, 36, 37, 47, 52, 121

U.S. Catholic Conference, 42, 65, 109, 110, 128, 132–36

U.S. Chamber of Commerce, 27, 28, 29, 31, 37, 42, 65, 69, 109–17, 120, 127, 132, 136, 147, 150, 154, 160, 170n. 23, 171n. 2. *See also* National Chamber Litigation Center (NCLC)

U.S. Department of Health, Education, and Welfare (HEW), 30

U.S. Department of Labor, 31, 32, 53; Office of Federal Contract Compliance Programs (OFCCP), 37; Women in Industry Division, 167

Van Horn, Edith, 47
violence, occupational, 78, 124
Virginia Military Institute, 94

Wards Cove Packing Co. v. Atonio, 40, 77, 105, 118, 153
Washington Legal Foundation (WLF), 36, 65, 109, 110, 111, 139–40, 151, 172n. 26
Webster v. Reproductive Health Services, 89, 97
Weeks v. Southern Bell, 23, 24
Weiss, Marley, 51, 52, 53, 56, 57, 58, 145
welfare, 31, 100
West Coast Hotel v. Parrish, 45
Western New York Council on Occupational Safety and Health, 128
Weyand, Ruth, 28
White, Byron (Justice), 41, 155, 156
Williams, Wendy, 88

Women Employed, 38, 85
Women's Equity Action League (WEAL), 24, 26, 27, 28, 48
Women's Law Project, 26, 27, 30
Women's Legal Defense Fund (WLDF), 26, 30, 36, 38, 84–86, 88, 92, 107, 125, 146, 154, 157, 160
Women's Rights Litigation Clinic (Rutgers), 26, 80
women's rights movement, 5, 9, 16, 18, 23, 26, 28, 29, 37, 41, 45, 48, 61, 76–85, 97, 107, 126, 144, 146, 168n. 27, 170n. 15
World War I, 18
World War II, 18–19, 46
Wright, Theresa, 38
Wright v. Olin, 38–40, 53, 56, 66, 77, 116, 172n. 4

Zuniga v. Kleberg County Hospital, 56, 77

.

www.ingramcontent.com/pod-product-compliance
Lightning Source LLC
Chambersburg PA
CBHW020704270326

41928CB00005B/254